W9-AEH-892

The Cycle of Violence

Suzanne K. Steinmetz

The Praeger Special Studies program—utilizing the most modern and efficient book production techniques and a selective worldwide distribution network—makes available to the academic, government, and business communities significant, timely research in U.S. and international economic, social, and political development.

The Cycle of Violence

Assertive, Aggressive, and Abusive Family Interaction

PRAEGER SPECIAL STUDIES IN U.S. ECONOMIC, SOCIAL, AND POLITICAL ISSUES

Praeger Publishers   New York   London

Library of Congress Cataloging in Publication Data

Steinmetz, Suzanne K
    Cycle of violence.

    (Praeger special studies in U.S. economic, social,
and political issues)
    Bibliography: p.
    Includes indexes.
    1. Conjugal violence—Delaware—New Castle Co. —Case
studies.   2. Problem family—Delaware—New Castle Co. —
Case studies.   3. Violence—Delaware—New Castle Co. —
Case studies.   I. Title.
HQ555.D3S73   1977   301.42'7   77-24411
ISBN 0-03-022876-X

PRAEGER SPECIAL STUDIES
200 Park Avenue, New York, N.Y., 10017, U.S.A.

Published in the United States of America in 1977
by Praeger Publishers,
A Division of Holt, Rinehart and Winston, CBS, Inc.

789   038   987654321

I wish to dedicate this book to two colleagues, Barbara H. Settles and Jacqueline P. Wiseman—friends as well as exemplary role models. They have provided much encouragement and support throughout my academic career.

Surveys of the methods used to resolve marital conflict reveal that about 60 percent of the couples studied resorted to physical violence at least once during their marriage. Severe physical brutality is experienced by approximately 7 percent of the wives and over 0.5 percent of the husbands. There are over 300,000 reports of suspected child abuse or maltreatment every year. Serious child abuse, incidents which have required protective services, are estimated to be around 40,000 per year. Furthermore, two thousand children died of abuse during 1975.

Witnessing violence between one's parents and being the recipient of abuse from one's parents are found to be common factors in the background of those who commit political assassination, murder, assault and battery, rape, and suicide. Unfortunately, those who have witnessed or experienced family violence during their childhood tend to approve of the use of violence and use violence themselves to resolve family conflicts in adulthood.

This study of 57 intact families is representative of both urban and suburban areas, a wide range of economic status and ethnic groups, and, because of the high degree of U.S. residential mobility, a wide range of geographic areas. Thus the findings have more general applicability than do most existing studies that focus on limited samples identified as having been involved in child abuse or wife beating. The data suggest several generalizations. First, all families experience conflict. Second, family conflicts and the methods families use to resolve them are linked to stages in the family life cycle. A third, and most important finding, is that consistent patterns exist for resolving conflicts within each family. Specifically, methods that spouses use to resolve marital conflicts are similar to the methods they use to discipline their children. Their children use methods similar to those they have experienced as well as those they have witnessed. Finally, these patterns were found to persist over three generations.

The significance of these findings lies not only in the degree of violence that families use to resolve conflicts, but in the consistency with which these methods are transmitted, from generation to generation.

Although evidence that abusive parents were often abused as children has existed for some time, this study provides evidence that all patterns of conflict resolution, not just severely abusive ones, are passed on. This means that parents who utilize physical force, although not to a degree that could be labeled as severe battering, are preparing another generation to use physically violent forms of family interaction. They are passing on the message that physical force is a socially acceptable method for resolving conflict, thus continuing the "cycle of violence." The question then becomes, What conditions escalate this use of physical force and at what point is the use defined as undesirable?

It is hoped that this study will provide not only base-line data on patterns of intrafamily conflict resolution, but also insight on how typical American families deal with the stresses of marriage and family life and survive.

ACKNOWLEDGMENTS

There are many individuals to whom I owe my sincere thanks for help with this study. First, I wish to acknowledge the cooperation of the 57 families who participated in the research. Secondly, I would like to express my thanks to my husband, Thomas Pickett, who wore a path from his office to the university library retrieving books, photocopying articles, and proofreading numerous drafts. I also wish to express my thanks to my children, George, Gregg, and Singrid Steinmetz, and two of their friends, Mark and Wayne Tisdel, who performed many time-consuming and important tasks such as coding, numbering, and sorting questionnaires. I also owe a debt of gratitude to my interviewers: Helene Lightel, Pat Wagner, Jackie Rossi, Nancy Lightel, and Sally Vernon.

I am grateful to several individuals for their help in the preparation of my dissertation, which formed the nucleus of this book. My sister, Cyndi L. Kurland, provided editorial assistance on earlier drafts. Lucille Smith gave up her vacation, her lunch hours, and her sleep for several weeks in order to complete the typing of the dissertation. John Jones, dean of Parallel Program (North Campus), provided me with numerous valuable services. Professor Marvin B. Sussman, my thesis chair, and Professors Mark Lefton, Jetse Sprey, and Pauline Vincent provided advice and encouragement. And, Wilmington Trust Company, Stanton branch, provided financial support for the study.

This book represents a complete transformation of the original manuscript, including the addition of data analysis, an expanded literature review, and new insights on the interface between family violence and societal violence. Three colleagues were tremendously important in helping me to revise this manuscript, Barbara H. Sandin and Elaine Lunger were responsible for considerable library research, and Dorothy Windish worked beyond the call of duty typing and editing the manuscript.

Support for preparation of this manuscript was provided by National Institute of Mental Health Grant 27557, and a University of Delaware research grant.

CREDITS

CONTENTS

LIST OF TABLES AND FIGURES

The Cycle of Violence

IS THERE VIOLENCE IN THE FAMILY?

As American society becomes more complex and industrialized, the major concern of its people is not to obtain basic survival needs—food, clothing, or shelter—but rather to define and provide a quality life for all citizens. It is apparently difficult for a population that bases its levels of advancement on such indicators as number of bathrooms, televisions, and cars per family—frosting on the cake of life—to acknowledge the existence of families in which essential ingredients such as adequate physical and emotional care are lacking.

Similarly, as American society becomes increasingly industrialized and bureaucratic, schools, churches, clubs, and associations expand their facilities and responsibilities, absorbing functions that were previously the responsibilities of the family. The family's major role then becomes one of providing affection, companionship, and emotional support for its members. This, however, places the isolated nuclear family in a position of severe stress because it must assume the total responsibility for absorbing the frustration and emotional tension resulting from external situations as well as internally generated family stresses.

Although data suggest that in fact the nuclear family in contemporary society is not isolated and that extended kin provide many resources, in the form of caretaking, gifts, money, and so on (see Sussman, 1959; Shanas, 1968; Shanas and Streib, 1965), the frequent practice of relatives living some distance from one another (due to the geographic mobility of American society) results in their being unavailable to witness or perhaps prevent violent family outbursts or to provide temporary relief for distressed kin.

Diaries, court records, and newspaper articles suggest that families have always experienced conflict and frequently resorted to physically violent forms of interaction to resolve this conflict. We tend to assume, however, that if we have the technology to send men to the moon, surely we have the ability to prevent or at least control violence between family members. Unfortunately, as the data below suggest, family violence is an unresolved social problem of considerable extent.

Aggression between Family Members

The National Commission on the Causes and Prevention of Crime and Violence, in a large representative sample, found that between one-fourth and one-fifth of the adults questioned felt that it was acceptable for spouses to hit each other under certain circumstances (Stark and McEvoy, 1970). Straus (1973), using a sample of college students, found that 16 percent reported that their parents used physical force to resolve marital conflicts during a one year period. Gelles (1974), in an in-depth interview of 80 families, reported that about 60 percent of the husbands and wives had used physical aggression on each other during a conflict. In a study of divorce applicants (O'Brien, 1971), the wife complained of the use of overt physical force by her husband in 36.8 percent of the cases and verbal abuse in 23.8 percent. Only 3.3 percent of the husbands complained of being physically hurt and just 7.5 percent mentioned verbal abuse. Respondents in this study also reported three suicide attempts, two cases of infant child beating, two cases of father-teenager physical aggression, two cases where the husband purportedly threatened his wife and family at gunpoint, and one case of intolerable sadomasochistic sex relationships. Levinger (1966), in another study of divorce applicants, found that 37 percent of the wives listed physical abuse as one of their complaints.

There is also a considerable amount of physical force being used in normal families as a means of disciplining children. The national commission on the Causes and Prevention of Violence reported that 94 percent of the respondents had been spanked as a child (Stark and McEvoy, 1970). Other studies (Straus, 1971; Steinmetz, 1971, 1974a) found that over half the respondents, as late as their senior year in high school, experienced physical punishment or threats of physical punishment as a means of discipline— and these respondents were college-bound students, not high school dropouts or troublemakers. In 1975, 2,000 children died as a result of abuse (Besharov, 1975).

A small exploratory study (Steinmetz, 1977a) found that nearly all respondents (students at a large urban university) reported the use of verbal aggression—screaming, yelling, and threatening—and a considerable number (about 70 percent in cases of parent-child and sibling conflicts and 30 percent in marital conflicts) reported the use of physical aggression to resolve intrafamily conflicts.

REINFORCING THE MYTH OF
FAMILY NONVIOLENCE

It is interesting to note the influence of social sanctions on the percentage of families reported to have used physical force to resolve intrafamilial conflict. It appears that fighting between children is considered inconsequential and, therefore, in the United States, does not have strong social sanctions against it. Similarly, social sanctions discouraging the use of physical force to resolve parent-child conflicts are also weak, and nearly 70 percent of the respondents in this study reported the use of physical force for disciplining children. Social sanctions against the use of physical force to resolve marital conflicts are apparently strong. Thus, only 30 percent of spouses were reported to have used physical modes for resolving marital conflicts. Since students were reporting the incidents of aggression between their parents and since the norms of working- and middle-class society preclude the open display of husband-wife aggression in front of children, it is possible that this 30 percent is an underestimate of the true extent of physical force between spouses.

These realities, however, are incongruous with the view of the family as an institution surrounded by an atomosphere of love, affection, and gentleness. Sennett (1973: 86) suggests that this results in the "guilt over conflict syndrome":

> To most people it appears that good families, upright families, ought to be tranquil, internally in harmony. . . . For many people, the emergence of conflict in their family lives seems to indicate some kind of moral failure: the family, and by reflection, the individual must be tarnished and no good.

Therefore, it is understandable that given the level of knowledge and resources available in this country, it is painful for most citizens to acknowledge basic family failings. It is indeed more comfortable to view the family as an institution capable not only of providing for its members the basic resources needed for existence in today's modern society, but providing these necessities in a milieu of love and supportiveness.

When extreme instances of aggression, such as child abuse or spouse beating, take place in an attempt to resolve family conflict, the family is usually labeled pathological, and undesirable characteristics, such as mental instability, immaturity, drug or alcohol abuse, are seen as causal. Unfortunately this myth is reinforced and perpetuated by law, social scientists, and historians.

The Law

The premise that the family is a sacred, private institution in which outsiders have no right to interfere can be supported by examing the legal attitudes toward violence. There were laws enacted to protect animals before there were laws to protect children. In fact, the first child-abuse case was actually handled by the Society for the Prevention of Cruelty to Animals (Fontana, 1964: 8). As a result, it requires extreme evidence, such as a severely battered child, to gain the attention of the public. Even then, the legal system is reluctant to interfere with the family's rights (DeCourcy and DeCourcy, 1973). Although spouse beating is regarded as assault and battery, considerably more physical damage is required in assault and battery between spouses than between non-spouses before police will file a report (Gelles, 1976). Furthermore, judges assign marital assault-and-battery cases to family court, resulting in extremely lenient punishments, while assault-and-battery cases between nonspouses are assigned to superior (criminal) courts.

Social scientists

By focusing on particular issues, social scientists are able to direct attention to these areas. Likewise, by systematically ignoring an issue, researchers lend credence to the assumption that only isolated incidents exist, not a social problem.

Until the late 1950s, studies of child abuse were virtually nonexistent. Currently there is a proliferation of child-abuse studies and the topic is addressed in most family books. In preparation for the book *Violence in the Family* in the early 1970's, few empirical studies on spouse beating were found. (Steinmetz and Straus, 1974). A recent computer library research has found few studies concerned with physical force between siblings. In fact, O'Brien (1971) found in a survey of the issues of *Journal of Marriage and the Family* from 1939 to 1969 that the term "violence" had not been used in a single title.

Social Historians

DeMause (1974: 1) postulates that the further back in history one goes, the lower the level of child care, and the more likely children are to be killed, abandoned, beaten, terrorized, and sexually abused. DeMause suggests that the social historians have defended the family and helped to perpetuate the myth of nonviolence in the family. In support of his thesis (which is contrary to that presented by Aries in *Centuries of Childhood* [1965], which portrays the child of earlier times in traditional society as happy and carefree), DeMause offers the following pieces of evidence (1974: 4-5):

1. Seltman (1956: 72) notes the widespread practice of infanticide and declares it "admirable and humane."

2. Miller and Swanson (1958: 10) describe mothers who regularly beat their infants with sticks and, without citing evidence, suggests that "if her discipline was stern, it was even and just and leavened with kindness."

3. Bayne-Powell (1939: 6), reporting the practice of mothers who dunk their infants into ice water to strengthen them, states, "They were not intentionally cruel," and attributes this practice to the mothers' reading of Rousseau and Locke.

4. Valentine, in an examination of 600 letters from fathers to sons, was unable to find one father who wasn't insensitive, moralistic, or self-centered. In an effort to preserve family integrity, Valentine (1963: xx) concludes:

> Doubtless an infinite number of fathers have written to their sons letters that would warm and lift our hearts, if we only could find them. The happiest fathers leave no history, and it is men who are not at their best with their children who are likely to write the heartrending letters that survive.

Evidence suggests that lawmakers, historians, and social scientists, as well as the general population, tend to deny the existence of family violence or to assume violence only occurs in sick families, families living in inner-city ghettos, or families characterized by some other pathology such as drugs, alcohol, gambling, or mental aberrations. By this means it is possible to resolve the dissidence between the socially desirable view of the family and the unpleasantness of reality. It has been suggested that rather than view child abusers and spouse beaters as sociopathologically ill individuals—social deviants—they may be seen as practicing at times the same forms of aggressive behaviors used by and approved by a large number of normal American families. The major difference is that those individuals labeled as abusive have overstepped the normally imposed limitations. (See Steinmetz and Straus, 1974; Pittman, 1964; Pokorney, 1956.)

There is also evidence to suggest that a major difference, especially in the less severe cases of battered spouses or child abuse, exists in the detection and labeling of the perpetrator as abusive. This is similar to the difference between being a homosexual and being labeled as one. The sexual act is the same; it is when a society discovers this behavior, and labels the individual as a deviant, that there is a major difference.

PROBLEMS WITH RESEARCH
ON FAMILY VIOLENCE

Although there has been a recent surge of literature on family violence and conflict, many of these studies have serious shortcomings. As in any topic only sparsely developed, the initial attempts can only hope to scratch the surface. However, even at this early stage, there are several apparent gaps in the research. The first problem is that these data tend to focus on a general frequency of behavior over a broadly specified time, for example, "during the last year." Although this provides information regarding trends in interaction, there are several limitations. What one family defines as "frequently" another family might consider "almost always." Furthermore, one needs to consider just how much of a behavior constitutes "sometimes." This mode of measurement does provide some indication of the individual's perceptions of frequency of a behavior, but an objective measure of how much of this behavior occurs is not possible by this means. It is important to know objectively how much of a behavior occurs as well as how frequently a family perceives the behavior to occur on a general, subjective level.

A second and closely related problem is that most of this research depends on retrospective data. Families were asked how much aggression or what kinds of problems they encountered in the past (Straus, 1971, 1973; Steinmetz, 1971, 1974a, 1977a; Gelles, 1974).

The third problem focuses on who is interviewed. Many social scientists have been concerned with a body of family research that is almost entirely from the viewpoint of the wife (see Safilios-Rothschild, 1969; Steinmetz, 1974b, for a discussion of sex bias in research). Therefore, there is a need to gather data from father-husbands as well as mother-wives.

A fourth problem, closely related to the above, is the limitation placed on the data if they are obtained from only one member of the family. In a discussion of response validity, Niemi (1974: 1) notes that "information is most often obtained from the respondent who forms the basic unit of analysis without any attempt to verify independently their reports." Family members may bias their responses to make themselves and their family appear more socially acceptable, or to make the other family members seem more similar in attitudes and actions to the respondent. By obtaining data from several family members, a more rounded picture of family interaction, although not necessarily a more accurate one, may be obtained. This also provides a measure of concurrent validity (Campbell and Fiske, 1959).

A fifth concern is the need to extend the current research on problem solving or conflict resolution, which focuses on a particular dyadic combination. For example, the child-abuse research has examined parent-child interaction with almost no mention of the presence (or absence) of violence between husbands and wives in these families. Likewise, the literature on families who have experienced spouse beating has been confined, almost exclusively, to husband-wife interaction, ignoring the possibility of violence between other members of these families. Case studies of adolescents and adults who commit violent acts suggest, however, that there might be a relationship between husband-and-wife violence and child abuse. Furthermore, individuals who have experienced physically violent interaction within the family setting have been found to commit physically violent acts outside the family unit. Satten, Menninger, and Mayman (1960) and Duncan, et al. (1958), Easson and Steinhilber (1961), and Duncan and Duncan (1971), in studies of the family environment of murderers, noted evidence of extreme parental abuse toward children as well as physical violence between parents.

Silver, Dublin, and Lourie (1969), in a three-generational study, found considerable support for the premise that abusive parents had usually been abused as children. Furthermore, they found that many abusive parents were simultaneously engaged in spouse beating, and their children were rapidly accumulating criminal records for committing physically violent acts. This suggests that understanding the causes of family-related violence might have ramification for understanding violence in the society at large.

A sixth problem involves the sample used. Many studies dealing with negative aspects of family interaction, such as child abuse, utilize a sample composed almost entirely of families identified and labeled as deviant. There is need to examine the interactions of families not labeled as deviant, and to investigate similarities and differences that result in differential labeling of families.

A final concern revolves around the type of data collected. Questionnaires have the advantage of obtaining standardized, easily comparable data, but lack the ability to gain in-depth insights and relate first-person experiences. While in-depth interviews, especially semistructured and unstructured ones, do provide an opportunity for in-depth data, these data are not standardized. Thus, you are often examining apples and oranges, which is theoretically valuable and exciting but lacking in the ability to predict specifics such as frequency and degree. A research design that combines the advantages of semistructured interviews with questionnaires would provide a better method of collecting data on family interaction.

GOALS OF THE RESEARCH

The major goal of this study is to obtain a more accurate view of how family members in normal American families interact—assertively, aggressively, and abusively—in an attempt to resolve intrafamilial conflicts. The research design used in this study has attempted to close some of the gaps listed above by including the following:

1. Selecting a stratified quota sample of normal American families composed of husband, wife, and two or more children between three and eighteen years of age. This criterion allows the researcher to measure husband-wife, parent-child, and sib-sib interaction in each family.

2. Obtaining quantitative data on the modes of conflict resolution between husband and wife, parent and child, and sib and sib, through questionnaires. These data, obtained from parents and children, is used to develop a typology of conflict-resolution patterns. Furthermore, the collection of data from at least two family members provides a more rounded view of the family interaction process.

3. Obtaining qualitative data on intrafamilial conflict resolution from these same families through semistructured interviews. These interviews will focus on causes of conflicts within the family; modes utilized by different members for resolving conflict; and life-cycle changes in causes and resolution of conflicts. By utilizing in-depth semistructured interviews and questionnaires completed by both parent and child, theoretical insights are gained as well as standardized data for statistical analysis.

4. Systematic recording of all family conflicts, the source of conflict, methods used for resolving it, and the perceived success of each interaction over a period of one week. The daily recording of intrafamily conflicts helps to eliminate the effect of recall, a problem in retrospective data collection.

Respondents as Researchers

Throughout the project the families who participated in this research were encouraged to act as researchers and to contribute in any way that they could. It was very important that they take an active part in the research process since the recording of conflicts during the one-week period required that they be interested in the research and made to feel a valuable and necessary part of the research process.

A measure of this cooperation can be found in the number of families that noted the time and effort expended in carefully explaining the purpose of the research in order to gain cooperation from all members of the family. One family recorded the following on their conflict-recording sheet:

> Conflict: J was asked to fill out questionnaire. He justifiably objected on the ground he hadn't been consulted in the matter but finally agreed to cooperate.
> How the conflict was resolved: I sat with (not on) him and explained what he was to do; then he decided what answer to give for the questions.
> Outcome: Success (requiring inordinate amount of patience on mom's part).

There is also evidence that respondents shared with the interviewer information that they considered much too private to share with friends or neighbors. A very frequent response was, "I don't know what my neighbors do," or, "We don't discuss those things, you find out things you really don't want to know." Yet these same respondents shared their moments of deepest sorrow and shame, as well as happiness, with the interviewer.

There is some evidence of the Hawthorn effect of the research on family interaction, especially in the amount of conflicts during the weeklong recording period. Being a participant in this research appears to have made older children and adults more aware of all interaction between family members, keeping them on guard and reducing to a minimum overt family conflict.

In one family, categorized as a teenage family, the specter of the recording of conflicts seems to have changed the usual conflicts to a joke and kept them to a minimum. This family noted: "Everytime something comes up someone would say 'there's a conflict, quick, write it down.'"

In another family, with children covering a broad age span, the following was noted:

Conflict: N was angry because she was noted for so many conflicts.
How resolved: Told her to think of this when she argues with others.
Outcome: Failure—she was still angry and felt she was not responsible for so many.

Among small children, participation in the research project gave them a legitimate excuse to tattle on sibs. One mother of small children noted on her conflict sheet: "Children arguing continually—who started it? Both accused the other of starting it."

Although this is one of the pitfalls of research that not only explains the entire project to the participants but also requests them to act as researchers, it is felt the value of this approach in stimulating interest and cooperation outweighs the liability.

Research Questions

There are several research questions that acted as a guide in developing this study. First, evidence suggests that aggressive and abusive adults were frequently the recipients of aggressive and abusive interaction as children (Wasserman, 1967; Steel and Pollack, 1968; Fontana, 1964; Wolfgang, 1958). The data also indicate that physical punishment or aggression on the part of the parent increases rather than decreases aggressive behavior in children (Sears, Maccoby, and Levin, 1957; Hoffman, 1960; 1963; Bellak and Antell, 1974; Eron, Walder, and Lefkowitz, 1971). Bellak and Antell (1974) also note that "nearly all of the Nazi criminals had suffered some sort of serious mistreatment or cruelty in childhoods." It might well be that "man's inhumanity to man is his revenge for the indignities he suffered in his childhood" (Bellak, 1970).

Another body of evidence, based on social-learning theory, would suggest that husbands and wives who develop a successful method of resolving conflicts are likely to transfer this method to other areas such as child rearing (Steinmetz, 1974c, 1977a). Furthermore, since children are likely to emulate the child-rearing techniques they experience, it is possible that they will practice these methods to resolve conflicts between themselves and other children, for example, between peers and sibs (Steinmetz, 1974b, 1977a; Bellak and Antell, 1974).

A final body of data indicates that a society's attitude toward the use of physical force to control others as reflected in the rate of violent crimes is often an indicator of the use of physical force in a familial setting (Steinmetz, 1974c; Bellak and Antell, 1974; Sidel, 1972; Goode, 1971).

From the above findings two general questions evolve, which this study will attempt to answer:

1. Is there a similarity between the methods husband and wife use to resolve marital conflicts, the methods they use in disciplining their children, and the methods their children use to resolve sibling conflicts?
2. Does the use of violence to resolve conflicts mirror the general societal attitude toward the use of verbal and physically aggressive and abusive modes?

2

THE FAMILY AS A
BATTLEGROUND: DIMENSIONS OF
ASSERTIVE, AGGRESSIVE, AND
ABUSIVE INTERACTION

This study deals with 57 families, their sources of intrafamilial conflict, and the various methods they utilized to resolve these conflicts. Although there are many patterns of behavior observable in this research, it should be emphasized that each family unit is a distinct entity with members possessing individual characteristics. Thus, while the focus is on unifying aspects—similarities in patterns of behavior—it must be recognized that this study is composed of 57 unique families.

CONFLICT RESOLUTION VERSUS
PROBLEM SOLVING

There was no objective measure utilized in the research to define a conflict within a particular family. The responsibility of labeling an act a source of conflict and defining appropriate modes of resolution rested with individual family members, based on their perception or definition of the situation.

Although conflict resolution and problem solving will be used interchangeably throughout this study, there are inherent differences. A conflict can be defined as a situation where two or more individuals with different goals (or rivals for the same goal) are attempting to impose their will on each other in order to achieve their goal.

For example, in one family the pet dog appeared to be a source of conflict. "Who last walked the dog" and "who last fed the dog" was a source of conflicts between the children. Keeping the dog in the garage, not the house, was seen as a conflict between "mother vs. all." As she noted, there was "too much cleaning involved, no compromise to save mother's sanity; mother hates housework!"

Problem solving, in the family context, may not necessarily indicate a difference of opinions or desires, but rather some obstacle to efficient family functioning. For example, a family crisis such as death, illness, or a member having a physical or emotional handicap constitutes a problem that, in order to be resolved, requires certain decision-making processes. It does not, however, necessarily connote a difference of opinions in the resolution of the problem or the establishment of a winner or loser.

One family lost a loved pet during the week they were recording conflicts; Snow White, a guinea pig, had been with the family for three years and his death resulted in much sadness and crying at bedtime by the children. Obviously, there is no winner in this situation or even a difference of opinions, and although this problem did result in much unhappiness, it is not a conflict. It is important to note, however, that this family did define the incident as a conflict.

For the purposes of this research, problem solving refers to the conscious attempt to resolve a conflict between two or more family members, the focus being on conflicts as defined by Rosenzweig (1974): "rivalry between contenders who fight for short supplies or for favored social positions . . . behavior to establish a dominance hierarchy." A conscious attempt to resolve a conflict may be carried out by one or several participants by adhering to a stance of neutrality, by avoidance, or by ignoring the situation. He notes that behaviors used to resolve conflict consist of destructive resolutions, an adversary contest in which one opponent attempts to kill, injure, or at least demean the other; and constructive resolution, when the situation is treated as a shared problem that can be solved with mutual benefits.

GENERAL METHODOLOGY

This research combined in-depth interviews of parents with questionnaires completed by both a parent and the eldest child residing at home. After the initial phone call setting up an appointment, an in-depth, semistructured interview was conducted with one or both parents in the family (see Appendix A for a list of topics covered during the interview). The interviewers, five women, had had extensive experience dealing with parents and children—three as teachers, one as a nurse, and one as a counselor and therapist for handicapped children. Four of the interviewers were in graduate school, allowing them maximum flexibility for scheduling interviews.

At the completion of the interview, each family was given a kit of materials. This package contained:

1. A long form of the questionnaire to be filled out by the mother or father. This provided information about the grandparent as well as the parent generation and methods used by each generation to resolve marital, filial, and sibling conflicts.

2. A short form of the questionnaire to be filled in by the eldest child residing at home. This provided data on the child's perspective of how the parents resolve marital conflicts, how they discipline him (her), and how he (she) resolves sibling conflicts. The interviewers made special arrangements, when necessary, such as providing an additional envelope for the child's questionnaire to assure privacy.

3. Daily conflict-recording sheets. Parents were requested to record all conflicts occurring between all members of the family for a period of one week. Information was recorded on the "conflict," the "members involved," the "method used to resolve the conflict," and the "perceived success" of the method (see Appendix A for examples of the questionnaire and conflict-recording sheet).

The interviewer arranged with each family a schedule, convenient for telephone interviews, to remind the participants of the goals of the research and to check on the accuracy of their data recording. In most cases this phone call acted as a probe to obtain more information. But in some cases the interviewer recorded most of the data as a double check. These phone calls also allowed the interviewer to obtain further insights regarding the family's interaction, since many respondents recalled information they had previously forgotten.

After the weeklong period of recording was completed, the interviewer retrieved the kit and presented each family with a box of candy and a thank-you note as a token of appreciation. At the completion of the research, each participating family received a copy of the general findings presented in a nontechnical manner.

Respondents were again given the opportunity to add anything the interviewer might have overlooked. Because of the frequent contact maintained with these families (two home visits and at least five or six phone interviews), this study is able to present a fairly accurate evaluation of the families' interaction as it pertains to the resolution of marital, filial, and sibling conflict.

SELECTING A SAMPLE

The sample frame consisted of a panel of families selected by Gauge Corporation, a public-opinion polling and market-research company located in Wilmington, Delaware. Utilizing an adaptation of a method developed by National Family Opinion (Toledo, Ohio), the state of Delaware was divided into three-digit telephone districts that approximate geographic districts. A quota, representative of the proportion of the population, was set for each district and homes were selected randomly until the quota was reached. This method resulted in a panel fitting the criteria of a stratified quota sample. Although homes were randomly selected from within each district, two biases limit the representativeness of the sample: only those families with listed phone numbers and only those families who agreed to participate were included in the panel.

For the panel, all those families that met the following criteria were selected for this study:

1. The families were to be residents of New Castle County. This was mainly a transportation-and-telephone-cost factor. See Appendix B for a demographic profile of New Castle County.

2. The families were to be intact.

3. There were to be two or more children residing in the home between the ages of three and 18. One family had a grandparent living with them. Another family had eight ex-mental-patient boarders. These additional household members probably affected the family interaction; however, they were not included in the questionnaire or conflict-recording diaries. Foster children were included.

The above criteria are necessary in order to measure the various combinations of interaction: husband and wife, mother and child, father and child, and sib and sib. Because families are dynamic units, we were not able to completely satisfy the above criteria. In one family, the husband and wife had separated just prior to being interviewed. Since this was a recent occurrence, and the father was interacting frequently with the family, they were not eliminated from the sample. As the final draft of this study was being prepared, another couple separated. In two other families, only one child was currently residing at home. A daughter in one family had died, after a long illness, a few months prior to the interview. In another, a child graduated from high school and moved to her own apartment during the summer. Although both these families were part of the sample, they did not participate in the recording of sibling conflicts for the one-week period. They apparently had not fully adjusted to the new family unit and tended to think in terms of the previous composition. The actual current composition of the family did not become evident until after the interview began.

Sample

There were 217 families that fit the above parameters. Out of 217 families, 125 were contacted, 57 were interviewed, 25 refused to participate. Thirty-nine families were contacted but for a variety of reasons were not interviewed. In most of these cases a phone call revealed that the family did not fit the criteria required: parents had separated, deaths had occurred, or children had left home. Some of these families who were unable to participate because of illness or vacations wished to be contacted later. (We were unable because of time limitation to recontact most of the families in this category.) In four other instances,

TABLE 2.1

Comparison of Husbands' and Wives'
Socioeconomic Status
(in percent)

Socioeconomic Class	Husbands	Wives
1	30 (17)	2 (1)
2	21 (12)	26 (15)
3	23 (13)	19 (11)
4	19 (11)	2 (1)
5	7 (4)	4 (2)
Homemaker	0	47 (27)

the family agreed to participate but was not at home when the interviewer arrived. These families were recontacted but declined to participate.

There was no attempt to obtain children within certain age ranges other than the broad criteria of 3-18. The sample does represent the complete age range of young, adolescent, and teenage families, as well as multistage families.

No attempt was made to select families on the basis of socioeconomic status or racial background. Unfortunately, there were no black families in the study; however, there was a broad range of socioeconomic status represented.

Using the Hollingshead and Redlich (1958) two-factor index of social status, the percent of families in each class is presented in Table 2.1. The indices are computed for the wife based on her current or previous occupation. Those wives with no previous or current gainful employment are categorized as home-makers.

To obtain a more rounded picture of family interaction, it was considered desirable to interview fathers-husbands as well as mothers-wives. An attempt was made to actively encourage the husband to participate in the research. In some respects this attempt was quite successful in obtaining male participation. This was in respect to the self-administered questionnaire part of the data. Seventeen questionnaires were completed by the father-husband. In three families, both parents, using a system of different-color pens, filled out the form. It was the families' decision for both spouses to participate and is an indication of the tremendous cooperation of most families. For this part of the study 35 percent of the husband-fathers participated. Furthermore, in exactly one-third of the families, we obtained data from both parents in addition to the data from one of the children.

The study was not too successful, however, in obtaining interviews with husbands. Of the 57 interviews, four were joint husband-and-wife interviews, and one was husband only. Therefore, on only approximately 9 percent of the interviews was there male participation. There appear to be several explanations for this. Often the time was not convenient for husbands since many of them worked overtime, had second jobs, or were active in volunteer and social organizations. Even when the husband was at home he did not appear, in some instances, to want to participate. There seemed to be the idea that this was the wife's area of expertise and, therefore, participation in the research was seen as her obligation.

The information provided by the interviews, however, suggests that husbands do take very active roles in many home-management and child-rearing decisions. Perhaps this is defined as their backstage behavior rather than the onstage view they wish to present to the public.

THEORETICAL APPROACHES FOR STUDYING INTRAFAMILIAL CONFLICT RESOLUTION

There are several methods for delineation of a theoretical approach appropriate for the study of a given topic. For the study of family-conflict resolution methods, for example, one could utilize two distinct, but related, sources: focus on family theory, especially as it deals with interpersonal relationships, and adapt it to the specific case of family-conflict resolution; or discuss the various theories dealing with aggression and violence and adapt them to the specific case of family conflict and violence (see Christensen, 1964, for a discussion of various family theories; see Straus, Gelles, and Steinmetz, for a discussion of theories of violence that can be applied to the family).

Rather than a specific, particularistic theoretical approach, this research has borrowed from several major theoretical approaches those aspects considered most relevant to the study of intrafamilial conflict resolution.

Conflict Theory

A major assumption, derived from a conflict-theory perspective, is that this research does not view violence, tension, social change, or struggles between subordinate or superordinate individuals as deviant or abnormal. This viewpoint sees tension, struggles, and aggression between individuals or groups as a condition of social change and as such an integral, vitally necessary part of the individual growth as well as societal development process. It is certainly very much a part of family life. As one respondent noted: "I don't think that you can live with someone twenty-four hours a day without having an occasional problem, or just getting on each other's nerves. I think that is a normal thing to happen with people who live together."

Coser (1963, 1966) suggests that often group members tend to regard conflict as so harmful that the emotions resulting from it are stifled. The greater the importance attributed to the group's maintenance, for example the family, the more likely the perceived wrongdoings of others within the group will be suffered in silence. Respondents who suffer in silence often desire another way to resolve this conflict, but are afraid of the possible consequences. One wife suggested: "We have never really yelled and screamed at each other because I just keep quiet because if I would say things sometimes that I would like to say it would hurt his feelings. . .I think we would be better off if we did."

Resource Theory

Additional concepts, related to a conflict-theory approach, are borrowed from Weber. Weber (1947a: 152) defines authority as "the probability that a command with a given specific content will be obeyed by a given group of persons." Power, according to Weber (1947, as cited by Dahrendorf, 1959: 166), is defined as "the probability that one actor within a social relationship will be in a position to carry out his own will despite resistance, regardless of the basis on which this probability rests." As Dahrendorf (1959: 166) notes, the important difference between the concepts of power and authority is that power is tied to the personality of the individual, while authority is associated with social positions or roles. These two concepts are extremely valuable tools for analyzing intrafamily relations, especially within a resource-theory framework. Authority conveys the idea of subordinate and superordinate positions or roles, that is, husband-wife, parent-child, and so on. The power relationship, that is, personality factors, or additional nonnormative resources or debits, frequently are utilized in order to question the traditional authority vested in a particular role.

For example, the traditional parent-child relationship where the parent has the authority to be in the superordinate position, may be upset by a gifted, knowledgeable child or a severely ill child. Both circumstances may result in the parent relinquishing power.

A similar situation exists in contemporary society where the male as the traditional, authority-vested power holder may relinquish some power to his spouse (or have it usurped) because of her educational level, income, or kinship support. (See Blood and Wolfe, 1960, for a discussion of the resource theory. This theory attempts to account for the effect of the wives having differential amounts of resources, that is, education, income, children, on the relative amounts of marital power within a family).

It would appear from the participants studied in this research, that the most conflict-ridden families are those where authority is being questioned. As one respondent noted, "There is no conflict, my husband makes *all* the decisions." In this family all members "bow to authority," unlike the numerous families who complained that conflicts started when their relatively obedient children reached adolescence and became transformed into "mouthy teenagers."

Social-Learning Theory

Also seminal to the investigation of intrafamily conflict, specifically the learning of conflict-resolution modes, is social-learning theory. Bandura (1973: 43) suggests that man, in a social-learning approach, "is neither driven by inner forces (drive theorist view), nor buffeted helplessly by environmental influences (behaviorist view). Rather psychological functioning is best understood in terms of continuous reciprocal interaction between behavior and its controlling conditions."

Since the family is a dynamic unit, the social-learning approach is useful in explaining the reciprocal-socialization process among family members, both inter- and intragenerationally. This approach is also helpful in delineating the theoretical linkages between the larger macrostructure and the family in utilizing various modes of conflict resolution.

Symbolic Interaction Theory

There is no attempt made (and it is probably questionable that one could do so) to reduce these various theoretical approaches to a single all-encompassing theory. However, the interactional aspects of each of these theoretical approaches, with a major emphasis on the phenomenological aspects, that is, the individual's perception and definition of the situation, does provide this study with a unifying framework for explaining the findings. This research will examine the individual family members' definition of the home environment and compare their views with those held by other families. The behaviors these families label as a conflict and how they attempt to resolve it are perhaps more important to the understanding of family aggression and violence than how the researcher categorizes and labels the act. It is believed that the former, rather than the latter, provides insights into the motivation for their behavior.

THE THREE A'S OF CONFLICT RESOLUTION: ASSERTION, AGGRESSION, AND ABUSE

There are numerous tactics used by the respondents in their attempts to resolve family conflict. These methods include avoidance, ignoring the situation, or withdrawal of one of the participants; discussion, which includes an exchange of ideas as well as arbitration and mediation; verbal aggression such as yelling, screaming, threats, sarcasm, ridicule; and physical aggression such as hitting, slapping, throwing objects, pushing. These modes can be generally categorized into the three A's: assertion, aggression, and abuse.

Assertion will be defined in this study as the attempt of one family member to impose his will on the other. Assertion can take place through discussion, threats, or physical interaction such as restraining, or confining to a room.

Aggression will be defined as the intentional use of physical or verbal force to obtain one's goal during a conflict.

Abuse will be defined as the intentional, illegitimate, or unsanctioned use of verbal or physical control. The point at which an act becomes labeled as illegitimate, however, may be differentially defined by each respondent.

Avoidance

While many of the modes used to resolve conflict may have a desirable effect (see Coser, 1966 for a discussion of the positive values of conflict and violence), in other environments the same methods may be counterproductive. The difference lies in the perception of the individual and the norms operating within each segment of society. In certain cultures, for example, Amish, avoidance is a most powerful, last-resort form of punishment. The shunning places the errant individual in a situation whereby he has lost all social contact with significant others. This produces desirable results for the group as it helps to insure social control and to illustrate to the errant one the social expectation of the group.

Avoidance, however, appears to be one of the least productive modes of resolving marital conflict in contemporary American families. In a joint interview, one couple expressed the destructiveness of avoidance as a conflict-resolution technique. The husband reported: "My wife goes into one room, I go into the other" His wife responded:

> Very frankly, if we're really angry with each other, he won't argue. If he'd argue with me once in a while, get it all out, it would be over and done with. But he'll clam up. When we're really angry, he clams up and I have gone so far as to throw dishes across the room—not at him—and break 'em. I remember one time I slammed the cabinet door, and I broke the hinges off because he wouldn't argue with me or wouldn't even reply.

Another respondent actually resorted to talking to the wall:

> He does a lot that irritates me. . . . Try to get his attention while he's reading or watching TV or whatever he's doing and try to hold a conversation, it's terrible. . . . I just sit there and stare at him till he dicides to finish the answer. Or I'll turn to the wall and start talking to the wall; then I get a reaction out of him. It works out very well, I get his attention very fast.

Closely related to the use of avoidance in resolving a conflict is withdrawal of one or more of the partners. It appears, in this research, that withdrawal is frequently a tactic employed by the more introverted partner: "If I don't watch myself I very easily get into a shell. I know it is a fault. I guess he [my husband] is right. I try to be more outgoing and pay more attention to him."

One respondent saw avoidance or withdrawal as a contributing factor in her divorce:

I used to be that way, I kept everything to myself and I just catered to the other person all the time. I went with their wishes whatever they wished. Well, it just started to get on my nerves so bad that I couldn't cope with it, so now, since I am married to my [2nd] husband I am going to start off on the right foot with him, because I was never like that with my first husband, and I think that is why my husband and I were divorced. We never discussed anything.

Although the consequences are seen as powerful, avoidance or withdrawal, unlike shunning, does not foster the change of one's behavior to conform to the social expectation of the group.

Discussion

Most respondents felt that discussion was the ideal way to resolve conflicts, although many had not yet reached this ideal. One respondent expressed her feelings as follows: "We feel that it is extremely important to talk about things. How we feel about everything. We are not completely there, but we are doing pretty well in communicating.

Another wife, however, had difficulty communicating verbally with her husband and resorted to letter writing. "He'll say, 'let's have a talk.' Then he sits down and he talks and he doesn't listen. So, if I want to say something and get the whole message across without being interrupted, I write him a note."

Verbal and Physical Aggression

It was found that many families had used the full range of conflict-resolution methods—not just the quieter modes but the yelling, throwing, and hitting as well. This does not mean that this was the usual way that they resolved a family conflict, but rather the extreme to which they would go in an attempt to resolve a problem. Yelling was a common method employed by parents and children alike. One mother described her children as "noisy children. . . . They are more likely to have five minutes of hysterics. . . they get all excited. Blow off. Two minutes later they're finished." Another parent described herself as follows: "I am not always nice! Oh, I am a yeller. We never have physical fights, but I slam the doors and scream and yell."

Anger is also expressed by throwing things, not only against the wall, but also at the individuals involved in the conflict. One wife suggested that her husband was testing her, "to see how far I'd go, and that's how far I went. I threw a picture and shattered the glass."

In a joint interview, one husband recalled his wife "throwing pots and pans" but did not remember her actually "hitting me with her hands." And another respondent, noting that her throwing is currently confined to pillows, suggested that although she surprised her husband by throwing a few things at him, she "was not daring enough to throw a bowl at him or something, and . . . had never thrown anything hard at him."

Although no incidents of self-abuse, for example, pounding the wall or throwing oneself on the floor to gain attention and sympathy, were reported, this method should also be considered. Physical aggressions, whether directed toward oneself or toward another, are more distructive and are generally undertaken with great trepidation. They seem to indicate to both partners the seriousness of the action. When asked if she and her husband were ever physical with each other for example, by pushing or shoving or hitting, one wife reported:

> Me, not him. In fact, just before the separation period, I had kept it in for so long. He had gone to bed this one night and I forgot just why it was, but I went up and hit him on the back. It wasn't the best thing in the world and I couldn't get away with it a second time.

Another wife noted: We really had one good argument before we separated. . . . He pushed on me a couple times and I hit him. He busted a chair over my arm.

UNDERSTANDING ASSERTIVE, AGGRESSIVE, AND ABUSIVE INTERACTION

Although the modes of conflict resolution have been grouped into three major categories (assertion, aggression, and abuse), the movement from one category to another has not been objectively defined by the researcher according to some external criteria, for example, hitting with hand, or hitting with something hard. Instead it is defined by the family members according to their perception of the situation. Therefore, what might be considered aggressive behavior by one family might simply be viewed as assertive behavior by another. Similarly, behavior labeled as aggressive, that is, the sanctioned use of verbal or physical force, by one family might be considered unsanctioned, outright abuse by another. In this section, the term "aggression" will be used simply because it falls in the middle of the assertive-aggressive-abusive continuum, with the understanding that this label might vary with each individual.

As a concept, aggression is rich in dimensions. Aggression can connote positive attributes such as an aggressive (ambitious) young man. It can also connote negativeness, and frequently the difference lies in the appropriateness of the person's aggressive behavior. Thus, the aggressive female (she "doesn't know her place") or aggressive child (he "doesn't know his limits") is seen by a large segment of the population as a negative personality.

Intent

In any form of verbal or physical interaction, one must consider the intent of the action. For example, the parent who slaps a misbehaving child intended to "hurt" the child. However, if the child, in order to avoid the slap, steps back, trips, and suffers a severe blow on the head, this act was not intended. Likewise, a parent who yells at or degrades a child does so with the intent to inflict verbal pain. This differs from a situation where a parent, while discussing a child's shortcomings, is unintentionally overheard by the child.

Because the evidence of physical aggression is visible, while that of verbal aggression must be imputed (usually after the fact, as an emotional, psychological, or mental problem), there is more concern, by the public as well as the professional population, with the elimination of physical aggression. The evidence is lacking, however, as to the relative harm each mode produces and it is possible that verbal modes, such as degradation or insults, might be more detrimental for some individuals, for example, shy, self-conscious people, than would a more physically painful, but possibly less emotionally damaging slap.

In all the instances cited, the child experienced pain either physically or through humiliation or embarrassment. In this study, however, the focus will be confined to the intentional use of assertive, aggressive, or abusive modes of interaction between family members to resolve conflicts.

Success-Failure of the Act

Another important dimension of aggressive behavior is the relative success or failure of the behavior to achieve one's goals, and how this success (or failure) is perceived by the individuals participating. Bandura (1973: 2) suggests, "Behavior that is punishing for the victim, can at least on a short-term basis, be rewarding for the aggressor."

For many family members the goal is to relieve tension; thus, spanking the child, or yelling at one's spouse may produce short-term success. However, this success is short-lived if the conflict-producing behavior is only stalled and not corrected. This problem was expressed by one mother who found that spanking, not yelling, solved the problem: "There are times when you cannot get through unless you spank. Yelling does not make you feel better."

The perceived success, or, put another way, the perceived lack of a conflict, is perhaps as important as is the objective success, that is, the behavior no longer occuring. One mother recorded only two conflicts, one involving sibs, during the entire week of recording. With each phone call she related that "they had been so quiet." When questioned by the interviewer as to why that week was so quiet, she said "The children were very good. They have been attending Bible school in the morning and just didn't fight with each other."

The interviewer noted, however, that the children were "fighting" when she went to pick up the kit, and that the mother appeared to be oblivious to conflict and rationalized that this is the way a certain person is. This mother defined her home as a conflict-free one and thus did not define the "fighting" that occurred as a conflict needing a resolution.

Instrumental-Expressive Dimension

A third dimension of aggressive interaction focuses on whether the aggressive act is used to obtain a particular goal—instrumental aggression; or the aggression is the goal itself—expressive aggression. An example of instrumental aggression might be the yelling at or slapping of a child for a particular disobedient act. Some parents feel that spanking a disobedient child is necessary for proper child rearing. One parent noted: "For discipline, I think hitting is important, for the Bible says, 'Spare the rod and spoil the child.' Now it's according to whether or not it is appropriate for what has been done."

Support for the acceptance of and need for hitting or slapping one's spouse, under certain circumstances, was found in this study. During one interview the following was recorded:

> Respondent: I think he has probably hit me once in eight years. . . .
> It was a shock. It was totally unexpected.
> Interviewer: Did he seem to feel it was justified?
> Respondent: Yes. He was sorry he did it, but he thought it was the right thing to do. I guess it is the same case as when a parent says it hurts me worse than it does you. He felt the same way. . . . It was just like a slap in the face to turn it off and calm me down. It did work.
> Interviewer: Did you feel it was justified?
> Respondent: I don't know—it served its purpose. It ended my emotional upset, it served its purpose.

Spanking a child, as a last resort when patience is worn thin, or the child taking out his anger by kicking the dog are examples of expressive aggression. In these instances it is the act itself that is the goal. There is also a widespread belief that it is better to spank a child than to hold back one's anger; to let siblings "fight it out"; and to engage in marital screaming bouts, provided things are held within socially sanctioned limits. The belief that the expression of normal aggression between family members is best released rather than allowing to be bottled up, increasing the friction and contributing to possible severe violence, has been identified as the "catharsis myth" (Steinmetz and Straus, 1973, 1974). This myth is widespread in both popular thinking and among certain social scientists. Bettelheim (1967) suggests that the excessive training in self-control, typical of American middle-class families, denies the child outlets for the instinct of human violence and thereby fails to teach children how to deal with violent feelings.

This idea of "letting it out," which is seen as beneficial for parents and children, is a commonly expressed theme. This idea was expressed in reference to parent-child conflicts, marital conflicts, and sibling fights. Regarding parental use of physical punishment, one father suggested that "it lets out the parent's frustration." Several respondents felt that expressing aggression improved their marriage. One respondent noted: "I used to sulk, not sulk, but be very quiet. Now we get into loud discussions where I just get things out. It doesn't solve anything, but I do feel much better." Another said: "We were not allowed to cry or to get angry when we were growing up. I mean my life was one of keep cool, you know, don't show your emotions, which is bad. My husband taught me how to really say what I thought."

This approach was also frequently used to allow children to settle their own disagreements:

> I let them settle it themselves. If they start hitting or fighting with sticks and things like that, I don't care for that at all, and I'll go in and stop it. Otherwise, if they're just yelling back and forth, I just let them yell back and holler, get it out of their system.

One respondent explained her feelings toward the use of physical punishment as follows: "My basic attitude is that I am only teaching my children to hit if I hit. That if it is alright for me to hit, then they are going to feel that it is alright for them to hit." This respondent noted, however, that "I am very human and I have a temper too; and, I have three small children, and I'm up over my head with it; I use my hand, too, but I would rather not."

The evidence suggests that the use of physical punishment to decrease aggression in children produces the opposite effect—often increasing their aggressiveness (Sears, Maccoby, and Levin, 1957; Eron, Walden, and Lefkowitz, 1971). Although a particular child's aggressive acts might have increased, it is difficult to prove that without physical punishment, aggression, for this particular child, would have decreased, since very few families operate on the basis of controlled experimental conditions. Therefore, for any specific child, the use of physical punishment could have inhibited the child's use of aggression. Similarly, rather than getting rid of anger by screaming, spouses who use this mode of conflict resolution tend also to use physical means (Straus, 1973).

This is illustrated by the following discussion of a fight between one husband and wife:

> Respondent: We would get into a big argument and I would just keep needling and pushing until he would slap me to shut me up.
> Interviewer: Did you shut up?
> Respondent: No, I would hit him back. It just ended up in a bigger argument. . . .
> Interviewer: Did he seem to feel that he was justified in doing it?
> Respondent: I think he felt relieved in doing it because he really did want to do that at the time. . . . I think he did it because he really wanted to do it.

Therefore, the question becomes, Did this husband slap his wife to punish her for needling and pushing, much as one smacks an annoying child—an instrumental act—or was he striking out in frustration and anger—an expressive act?

Legitimate—Illegitimate Acts

A fourth dimension of aggressive behavior refers to the social sanctioning of certain acts as legitimate behavior, and to other acts as unsanctioned, illegitimate. While it is considered legitimate to defend oneself with a knife, gun, or fist against an attacker, it is not considered legitimate to perform the same act on a nonprovoking individual. It is important to recognize that except for the more dramatic example, such as severe child abuse and murder, the process of labeling an act as illegitimate is done in accordance with the norms regarding socially accepted behavior. The boundary separating the continuum of legitimate-illegitimate acts is not a universal one and reflects the influences of the parents' own childhood, social class, education, religion, as well as emotional, psychological, and personality factors. Thus, behavior that is accepted or at least tolerated in one family may be considered totally unacceptable in another group. For example, Parnas (1964) reports that the police respond to complaints of "family disturbances" according to these presumed norms of different groups. He illustrates this with the case of a Puerto Rican woman who, when asked by a judge, "Should I give him 30 days" [for beating you?] replied, "No, he is my husband. He is supposed to beat me." Parnas also found that the police have, in some instances, come to accept (and, therefore, treat lightly or ignore) black slum women "cutting" their husbands or lovers. Therefore, some families might tolerate higher levels of aggression while other families consider all physical force to be illegitimate.

For example, while a majority of the parents felt that spanking, especially when dealing with a young child, was justified, others defined spanking and even screaming as illegitimate. As one mother stated: "I think it is always wrong. . . .

I think it is wrong to scream and yell. That's the wrong approach. I think that if the children are doing something wrong, you should tell them it's wrong."

Another mother labeled as unsanctionable physical fighting between her boys. When asked about her reactions if she saw them physically fighting, she noted: "I would be upset. I don't know what I would do. I would show them I was upset. . . . It's important if you can direct their anger, and get rid of it other ways. I sometimes send them out to throw stones against the tree or something like that."

Many women also expressed the belief that their husbands had the right to use physical force on them if they deserved it. As one wife remarked, "I think if the wife starts in, he [the husband] has every right to go back at her." Another respondent suggested that not only was her husband's behavior justified, but it was necessary. When asked if she had ever been slapped, she responded: "Yes, once. . . . I lost my temper. I think I asked for it, really. I threw something."

Most women, however, shared the viewpoint that physical force between spouses, although it might occur, was never legitimate. When asked if their husbands had ever slapped them, they noted that this form of interaction was intolerable and completely unacceptable. One woman noted, "If he ever did slap me I'd walk right out the door. That's one thing I wouldn't take from him." Another said, "I think I made it clear that he would only do it (slap me) once."

Based on the data provided by the respondents, it appears that the conflict-resolution methods most likely to be repeated would be those deliberate acts that are considered to be legitimate behavior by society (or at least perceived as such by the respondents); are aimed at changing another's behavior (instrumental); and are perceived to be successful by the individuals participating. These relationships, presented in the Figure 2.1, are illustrated by the following quote:

FIGURE 2.1

Variables Influencing the Choice of Methods of Conflict Resolution

Variable	Likelihood of Act Becoming a Part of One's Conflict-Resolution Repertory	
	+	−
Intent	Deliberate	Accidental
Societal view of act	Legitimate	Illegitimate
Perceived goal of act	Instrumental	Expressive
Perceived outcome of act	Success	Failure

I've heard that you shouldn't spank when you're angry, but I can't agree with that, because I think that's the time you should spank; before you have a chance to completely cool off, too. I think that the spanking helps the mother or dad as well as impresses the child that they did something wrong, and when they do something bad, they are going to be physically punished for it. You don't hit them with a stick or a belt, or a hairbrush, but a good back of the hand . . . they remember it.

This quote richly illustrates the dimension of aggressive interaction noted in Figure 2.1. First, the respondent suggests an expressive dimension ("spanking helps the mother or dad" [get rid of frustration]). Secondly, the instrumental dimension ("impresses the child that he did something wrong") is mentioned. A third point is the respondent's differentiation between what she considers legitimate ("a good back of the hand") and illegitimate (" you don't hit them with a stick or a belt or a hairbursh"). Furthermore, her action is deliberate ("I think that's the time you should spank; before you have a chance to completely cool off, too") and perceived to be successful ("they remember it"). While this respondent was more articulate in defining the various dimensions influencing her selection and retention of conflict-resolution techniques, the data suggest that all family members are influenced in their development of conflict-resolution techniques by these dimensions.

Before investigating the specific findings related to assertive, aggressive, and abusive interaction between family members, it is helpful to examine the conditions under which the more extreme acts occur. Are there differences in the conditions that foster the use of physical violence between family members and the conditions that foster other acts of interpersonal physical violence, such as police and military brutality? Or, are the facts of physical violence between family members a similar phenomenon with different actors filling the role of perpetrator and victim? The data presented in the following chapter supports the latter. It appears that similar conditions are found on the societal, community, and family levels that foster the use of physical violence by the societal-supported power holder to control the behavior of those under its control.

SOCIETAL ACCEPTANCE OF
PHYSICAL FORCE: PARENTS,
POLICE, AND THE MILITARY

Lt. Calley and a member of his platoon opened up with automatic rifle fire on a large group of Vietnamese women, children, babies and a few old men they had gathered and were guarding. Calley ordered his men to shove another group of men, women and children into an irrigation ditch where they were executed. Someone yelled, "A child is getting away, a child is getting away." Calley picked up the child, threw him in the ditch, shot and killed him.

New York *Times*, February 1, 1970, p. 3.

Joshie Johnson was sitting on the fender of his car and squinting thru the autumn dusk at a parking ticket when a fist in a black leather glove smashed his nose.
Two policemen with drawn guns watched Patrolman Antonio Francis pound Johnson's face with his black gloved fist until Johnson fell unconscious in a Chicago alley.
When Johnson regained consciousness, he had a fractured jaw, broken nose, two black eyes, and cuts on his face . . . and faced charges of assaulting a police officer, resisting arrest, and disorderly conduct.

Chicago *Tribune*, November 4, 1973, p. 40C.

Police have charged Mrs. Mary John, 28, with murder, voluntary manslaughter, and endangering the life of a child after she allegedly beat her 4-month old daughter to death.

Police said Mrs. John had repeatedly beaten the infant following a quarrel with her husband, Joseph. They said Mrs. John was apparently angered by his leaving their apartment.

Wilmington (Delaware) *Evening Journal*, June 24, 1974, p. 23.

THE RELATIONSHIP OF SOCIETAL VIOLENCE AND INTRAFAMILY AGGRESSION

To the casual reader of the above news items, the question that immediately comes to mind is, What is the possible connection between reported acts of violence that were perpetrated by child abusers, the police, and the military, and how is this related to family violence in general? As American society is faced with increasing rates of violent crimes, there is an almost desperate demand by its members to find the solution to this problem. As this problem unfolds, the family becomes an integral variable in the dilemma.

First, the family is the primary socialization agent and, therefore, has the responsibility for developing in the child the appropriate attitudes and behaviors considered important by society. The importance of the family in providing this socialization can be noted by the voluminous research correlating inadequate socialization (frequently defined in terms of family structure and supportiveness) with a wide variety of criminal behavior (cf. Cohen, 1955; Glueck and Glueck, 1956; Bieber et al., 1962).

Secondly, the family is a setting in which much violence occurs. Gil (1971) estimates that approximately two million incidents of child abuse occur each year. Furthermore, family members make up the single largest category of homicide victims (Wolfgang and Ferracuti, 1967), and marital conflicts are considered to be the most dangerous police calls to answer (Parnas, 1964). Thus the child's first contact with how to resolve conflicts is usually learned in the family setting. The magnitude of family-related violence in the United States is illustrated by the finding that as many people were murdered by their relatives in one six-month period in New York City as had been killed in all the disturbances in Northern Ireland in three and one-half years (Straus, Gelles, Steinmetz, 1973).

A third factor is the apparent relationship between rates of violent crime on a societal level, as measured by homicide, assault and battery, and rape, and violent acts between family members. In a comparison of a U.S. and a Canadian college sample, the level of husband-and-wife aggression was found to be related to the level of parent-child and sibling aggression for both samples. It was found, however, that Canada, with considerably lower levels of a wide variety of criminal behavior such as assault and battery, homicide, and rape, also tended to have lower levels of intrafamilial aggression (Steinmetz, 1974b).

In a study of playground behavior, Bellak and Antell (1974) found that the aggressive treatment of a child by his parents was correlated with the aggressiveness displayed by the child. The authors found that levels of both parent and child aggression were considerably higher in Frankfurt than in Florence or Copenhagen. The rates for suicide and homicide, considered by the authors to be additional indications of personal aggression, were also much higher in Germany. Other studies support the above findings, suggesting the frequent use of severe physical punishment of children in Germany. Havernick (1964) found that 80 percent of German parents admitted to beating their children and 35 percent did so with canes (as cited by deMause, 1974:42), and a German poll showed that up to 60 percent of parents interviewed believed in beating (not slapping or spanking) their children (Torgeson, 1973, as cited by Bellak and Antell, 1974).

Although tentative, it appears that the level of societal aggression as reflected in violent crime rates may be an indicator of the level of intrafamilial aggression. This may be because the level of societal aggression, in a small but important way, reflects the societal attitude toward the appropriateness of using physical force to resolve interpersonal conflicts.

There are two possible linkages that could account for this relationship. First, it is possible, as suggested in the following diagram, that certain societal conditions result in both high crime rates and high levels of family aggression:

Macrolevel conditions ⟷ high crime rates
  poverty
  inadequate housing
  unemployment
  glorification of violence   high levels of family
  acceptance of violence   aggression

A second possible linkage suggests that societal conditions that result in high crime rates foster a tolerance of acceptance of aggression, and this detrimentally affects family functioning and results in family aggression. This linkage is presented as follows:

Macrolevel conditions ⟶ high crime rates ⟶ family aggression
  poverty   and an acceptance
  inadequate housing   or tolerance
  unemployment   of violence
  glorification of violence
  acceptance of violence

In order to test the above linkages, one would need to identify societies with a similar quality of life but possessing either high crime rates or high levels of family aggression, but not both. This would suggest that macrolevel conditions are causes of two separate phenomena—high crime rates and high levels of family aggression. If societies could not be identified filling the above conditions, this would argue for the second set of linkages, that is, macrolevel conditions, resulting in high crime rates and an acceptance or tolerance of aggression and violence. This societal acceptance of aggression and violence on a macrolevel provides a model for the use of aggression and violence in a microlevel (family) interaction. The data are complex, but an examination of police, parental, and military abuse suggests that in the United States, the second linkage appears to have more explanatory power.

A final reason for comparing the acts of police and military brutality with child abuse is that although these three groups might seem like dissimilar entities, they are very much alike in one important dimension; they all have societal sanction as well as legal authority to use physical force to control their charges. There is a point, however, beyond which this use of physical force is no longer considered by society to be a sanctioned use, and is instead considered an unsanctioned act and labeled as brutality or abuse.

ACCEPTABLE AND UNACCEPTABLE
LEVELS OF AGGRESSION

In order to gain conceptual clarity, it is necessary to define the terms "force" and "violence," and the way these concepts are being utilized in this study. Goode's (1971) definition of force and violence is helpful. Goode suggests that force is the legitimate use of physical control to effect a positive goal. This usage was supported empirically. Blumenthal et. al., (1972: 77-79) note that "American men in general did not differentiate among burglary, draft card burning, looting, and sit-ins in applying the label of violence or non-violence. These items tend to be defined alike by an individual, although his definition may differ from his neighbor; . . . it seems possible that people use the word violence as a term meaning illegitimacy." Examples of such sanctioned force are a parent spanking a child, a police officer using physical force to apprehend a criminal, or a soldier fighting to protect our country from aggressors.

Violence, however, is the unsanctioned use of physical force. It is the use of force that does not have normative legitimization. Therefore, the key focus of this chapter will be to examine the point at which society no longer defines an act as legitimate force and instead labels it as violence, an illegitimate or nonsanctioned act.

This labeling, however, is not universally applied and varies in different segments of society. For example, while a majority of youth and the liberal population recoiled at the horrors of the Kent State incident, in which the National Guard gunned down four college students, there were elements of the population who strongly supported the Guard's actions (Michener, 1971). There were also vehement expressions of anger and disgust against the youth who participated in, or were identified with, the antiwar demonstrations. This support for the guard was even expressed by parents who had children attending Kent State (Michener, 1971). While the individual soldier's action may be excused and the blame directed toward the social system that created these conditions, the fact that considerable support was offered for this action suggests the degree of importance society places on the use of force for socially desirable ends. Unfortunately the sanctioned use of killing during a war was found to have a residual effect on the level of homicide in the society during peacetime, suggesting a legitimation model (Archer and Gartner, 1976). This relationship held for both large and small wars; for both defeated as well as victorious societies; in societies with improved as well as worsened economic conditions as a result of the war.

The societal view of the use of physical control is couched in a dual message. On one hand the message is "turn the other cheek"; on the other hand, however, the message is "an eye for an eye." We are essentially told that violence is destructive, immoral, and should be controlled, and yet we glorify legitimized force in our folk heroes and in the media as exemplified by the success of police and private-eye shows on TV and in the movies. It appears that when the strong, the good, and the powerful use violence, it is a noble deed.

Legitimizing Violence

One mechanism for reconciling these conflicting norms is to legitimize certain degrees of physical force that fall within this realm. It is realized, however, that in order for the act to be labeled as unsanctioned, it must first be made visible to a large number of people. Thus, it was only after years of collecting hospital-admission data that doctors and researchers identified and began reporting on the battered-child syndrome. Similarly, it took the testimony of the Wickersham report (1931) or the recent Chicago *Tribune* report of police brutality (1973) to stir the public awareness and concern over those unacceptable acts, to the point of limiting the police's authority to use physical force. Although reacting negatively to the unsanctioned use of physical force, American society not only sanctions or allows, but it actually demands that a certain degree of physical force be used to control or modify the behavior of its citizens.

Parents, for example, are not only sanctioned in their use of physical force but this is expected of them. The quote "spare the rod and spoil the child" warns parents of the problems that might arise if they do not use physical force to control their children. In colonial America, a 1646 law gave parents the right to put to death unruly children (Brenner, 1970: 37). The Great Law enacted in Chester, Pennsylvania, in 1682 and modified in 1700, stated that anyone who attacked or menaced "his or her" parents was to suffer six months' imprisonment at difficult work and to be publicly whipped with 31 lashes on his or her back, well laid on (Frost, 1973: 136).

Although attitudes and laws regarding the appropriate degree of physical chastisement have changed, the practice of using corporal punishment as a disciplinary measure is still very much in evidence today. Stark and McEvoy (1970) reported that about 94 percent of respondents surveyed reported being spanked as a child. There is much concern over child abuse, with approximately 300,000 reports of suspected incidents of child abuse each year (Besharov, 1975), and numerous programs and agencies have been developed within the last few years to aid both children and parents. Concurrently, however, there is an equally strong concern over the results of permissive child-rearing practices and a growing movement, especially in large metropolitan school systems, to reintroduce corporal punishment. For example, the Delaware legislature in 1976 passed a law to allow teachers the right to use corporal punishment. That same year, a law passed in New Jersey gave school-bus drivers a similar right. A recent supreme court decision (Ingraham vs. Wright, 1977) upheld teachers' right to use corporal punishment to discipline students.

While parents' authority to use physical force extends only to their children, the police have legitimate authority over whole communities. Again, society not only sanctions the use of force by police "in the line of duty" but demands that police use this authority. In their book *Justifying Violence: Attitudes of American Men*, Blumental et. al. (1972: 79) note: "The state alone can exercise major force within the law. This is legitimate violence and legitimate violence is not really violence. The police are agents of the state; therefore their acts are legitimate and therefore not violent."

In many cities, the police are trained to shoot a fleeing criminal, and not just to shoot to maim, but to shoot to kill. Thus, police have only a split second to act as apprehender, judge, and jury (in defining the individual's criminality) and to take the necessary action. One must remember that this action on the part of the police is contrary to the body of law that states that one is innocent until proven guilty.

In Chicago, a 14-year-old boy was bashed in the eye, resulting in its loss, because he refused to stop when so ordered; he was being chased as a robbery suspect who had been described as a Puerto Rican male, in his 20s, with long black hair and a goatee. The unfortunate youth, a blond child, makes the case of mistaken identity extremely improbable (New York *Times*, November 4, 1973: 10). This is not an isolated event. Stark (1972: 98) estimates that there are perhaps three million instances of the use of unnecessary physical abuse, or 7.5 incidents per officer. Black and Reiss (1967), using trained observers who accompanied police in patrol cars in Boston, Chicago, and Washington, D.C., recorded 37 incidents involving 54 policemen during a seven-week period. They found that 3.2 percent of the suspects were unnecessarily beaten.

Wherever a strong belief in law and order exists, the police are awarded total discretion in their use of physical force, and given strong support for their actions. This authority has a long tradition. During the Tompkin Square riot of 1873, an attempted peaceful demonstration by unemployed workers was routed by mounted police who charged and clubbed them indiscriminately. The police commissioner remarked that it was a glorious sight as the men charged with their clubs uplifted. The press, also supporting the police action, stated that should the communistic spirit arise, the city should "club it to death at the hands of the militia" (Hofstaater and Wallace, 1970: 345).

The same attitude prevails today in a large sector of the population. In a survey undertaken by Michener after the shooting at Kent State, a large number of parents felt that the Guard members had been entirely justified in shooting (to kill) the disobedient students. In fact, one parent, when told by the interviewer that her child was en route to class and passed the area only a few moments before the shooting, replied, that it would have been her child's fault if she had been shot—she shouldn't have been there (Michener, 1971: 266).

These findings are not presented to indicate a nationwide picture of the degree of police brutality, but rather to support and illuminate the fact that police brutality is not an isolated occurrence. When police are given staunch public support for the use of physical force to control undesirables, it is but one short step to redefine and relabel a wide variety of acts as undesirable which require the use of extreme physical force to eliminate them.

This abuse is not just a police problem. It is found in other institutional settings such as mental institutions, prisons, and schools, the commonality being that the authority is vested in a few individuals allowing the use of physical force to control the community members.

One of the major causes of the Attica Prison revolt was guard brutality (New York *Times*, October 10, 1971: 20), and the brutality of prison guards has frequently been a factor in other prison disorders (*Senior Scholastic*, 1969; *New Statesman*, 1972).

An editorial concerned with the use of corporal punishment in schools (Philadelphia *Sunday Bulletin*, February 1, 1975) noted that the mounting violence in suburban as well as city schools was being reflected in the reintroduction of corporal punishment in those schools that previously had prohibited or limited its use. This is seen as a popular panacea. In one recent poll, only 300 out of 7,600 parents questioned objected to the use of corporal punishment in one upper-middle-class school district.

This same editorial related an incident reported by a Delaware state official in which a school administrator, "in a fit of anger over a 'minor infraction,' swung at a child with a paddle and hit the child's spine instead of his buttocks." Previously, only administrators were permitted to use corporal punishment in Delaware. However, the recently passed Senate Bill 27 now extends that privilege to teachers.

In contrast to the authority of parents and police, the military has been empowered to protect the nation. As the authority to use physical force expands to encompass whole societies, it becomes increasingly more difficult for society to exercise control over the exploitation of this power. And, because of the military's importance in protecting the nation, society is even more reluctant to interfere in the administering of physical force, even when it appears to be of the unsanctioned genre.

For the military to be effective, complete and unquestioned obedience is expected from its members, and cowardly or questioning behavior cannot be tolerated. The soldier is not trained or expected to make individual decisions and certainly not those countermanding a decision of a superior. Those unable to follow orders, to indiscriminately "waste" the enemy are labeled as traitors or cowards, and likely to face on-the-spot sentencing. The whole training program of the military is geared to have the men think of the enemy not as humans, but as faceless gooks, or enemy devoid of gender or age or any human likeness (Lifton, 1971; Bourne, 1971). Sanford and Comstock (1971) suggest that denying people the status of peers or even of human beings serves as an important rationalization for acts of violence. An example of this process occurred during the House of Krupp's brutal treatment of slave labor when the laborers ceased to be referred to as workers or people but were termed *stucke* (cattle) (Manchester, 1970: 540).

Although it is easy to understand the army's desire to overlook evidence of military brutality, even in the face of incidents such as the My Lai or Song My massacres, there exists tremendous support (from nonmilitary as well as military sources) to clear the participants of the blame. This feeling of support for the military exists among liberal as well as conservative groups, although for different reasons. The law-and-order segment of society, which adhered to an ideology of "better dead than red" or "might makes right," saw this military abuse as simply the following of necessary orders. The liberal faction questioned the rationality of training men to kill; rewarding them with medals and awards for the highest body counts; and then condemning them for killing in another setting while still under orders. A Harris poll, conducted shortly after the My Lai incident became public, reported that only 15 percent of the respondents thought that soldiers who killed civilians at Song My under orders should be court-martialed and a majority believed that it is acceptable to kill civilians suspected of assisting the enemy (New York *Times*, February 1, 1970, Section 4:3).

The picture that emerges is one of a society in which parental, police, and military brutality is an unfortunately frequent occurrence. Furthermore, much of this brutality, while labeled as an unsanctioned act, receives silent support by a large majority of the population.

Because of cultural as well as legal authority given to parents, police, and the military to use physical force, society is reluctant to interfere. Law-enforcement agencies define the excessive use of brutality (especially in apprehending and questioning suspects) as necessary for the protection of society, and develop normatively supported codes for covering up or rationalizing their behavior. A soldier is charged with the cold-blooded murder of over 100 Vietnamese, yet the President intercedes on his behalf. And, because of parental rights, doctors and social agencies are reluctant to report child-abuse cases, and remove the child (or parent) only as a last resort (see DeCourcy and DeCourcy, 1973). There is the fear that if society were to impose restrictions on their use of power, they would no longer be able to effectively discharge their duties.

THE PEOPLE WHO COMMIT ACTS
OF BRUTALITY

What kinds of people commit acts of brutality? Are these sick, mentally disturbed, emotionally troubled individuals? What are the conditions that foster acts of brutality? Are they socially produced or individual, personality characteristics? Are these individuals mentally deficient, insane, abnormal?

The evidence would seem to suggest that this is not the case. Just as it is easy to say that any individual who assassinates or attempts to assassinate our president must be mentally ill, in-depth studies of their backgrounds would suggest that had they not committed the act of assassination, they would not for the most part be labeled as mentally ill (Steinmetz, 1973). It appears that the act of assassination was the major impetus for labeling these individuals as sick, mentally ill people.

This appears to be the stance taken by the public regarding parents who abuse their children; police who brutally (and without obvious cause) beat up suspected offenders; and military men who, without the need, murder unarmed, civilian enemies. After all, normal people wouldn't do such things.

Unfortunately, the evidence indicates otherwise. Although any individual might have a mental or personality problem, and his or her actions might be the result of excessive use of alcohol or drugs, as perpetrators of physical abuse these groups are no more or less normal than nonabusing individuals. We need only to refer to the Milgram experiments (1974) in which volunteers willingly administered high-voltage electric shocks to "pupils" as part of a learning experiment to realize the violence potential in "normal American citizens." Studies of child abuse and police brutality also support this view. Research suggests that most abusive parents are not mentally ill and that they function as normal adults in all other situations (Gil, 1971; Gelles, 1973). In his classic study of the police, Skolnick (1969) found them to be inclined toward masculine activities such as physical skills and hunting, but there was no evidence of their having abnormally aggressive or rebellious tendencies. Niederhoffer (1967) suggests that police recruits, as a group, are not especially sadistic or authoritarian. Furthermore, it was shown (MacNamara and Sagarin, 1971) that rookies in the New York City Police Department scored considerably lower on a measure of punitiveness than a sample of community leaders. It appears that it is not so much what the man was before joining the force but what kind of man he becomes on the force as the result of the occupational demands of the job.

Kohn and Schooler (1973) suggest that a man's job affects his perceptions, values, and thinking processes primarily because it confronts him with demands he must try to meet. These demands, in turn, are to a great extent determined by the individual's job and its location in the larger economic and social structure. Therefore, the occupational setting has considerable effect on the psychological functioning of individuals. Stark (1972) suggests that we should view police brutality as the product of a sick system, not sick men.

A poignant example of the effect of the occupational setting is that of a soldier who was accused and convicted of killing over 100 Vietnamese, mostly old men, women, and young children. During a pretrial interview, he was asked about the deerskin in his room. He remarked that he could never kill an animal (Hammer, 1971: 358). Thus under nonmilitary conditions this individual could not bear to harm an animal, yet he stood accused and later convicted of cold-blooded murder during a military conflict in which he had been given the military-oriented sanction to "waste" the enemy. Psychiatric examinations of William Calley and other soldiers accused of committing war crimes suggested that they were normal, not mentally ill individuals.

SOCIETAL CONDITIONS THAT PRODUCE VIOLENCE

Evidence suggests that it is socially produced conditions, especially the occupational setting, that affect antisocial behavior, rather than innate mental or personality characteristics. Thus, one can posit the question of which social conditions might cause normal, nonaggressive adults who usually keep within socially sanctioned norms to resort to the unsanctioned use of physical force.

Acceptance of Violence

Several factors appear to be relevant. First, there is a general acceptance and glorification of agents of force (for example, John Wayne, "Mission Impossible," "Mannix") in the name of law, order, and the American way.

Physical force, for the glory of God, has led to crusades and inquisitions, as well as contemporary conflicts in Northern Ireland and in the Middle East. Therefore, the crossing of the boundary from the sanctioned to the unsanctioned use of physical force usually represents an impermissible extension of these basic violent practices present in many contemporary societies, such as the United States.

Frustrated and Trapped

The second factor that appears to be important is the feeling of being trapped or frustrated by the boundaries imposed by society. For example, many parents, police, and military men receive inadequate, or what is perceived to be inadequate, income, respect, or power. Furthermore, they find their jobs to be unrewarding. For example, parenting is not a high-status job in our society as indicated by the salaries received by parent surrogates—nursery attendants, housekeepers, babysitters.

Police are rarely given the respect and admiration they feel they deserve. Often, the only contact the public has with the police is when they are reprimanded for breaking the law. As Westley notes (1970: 100), the police perceive the public as hostile. Therefore, their social and occupational inter-action is limited to other police, which fosters strong ingroup attitudes and controls the conduct of members so that it conforms to the interests of the group. These interests serve to protect the police's authority and reinforce self-esteem and respect from society.

Among the troops, especially those who fought in Vietnam, there was often the feeling that by fighting this dirty, unpopular war they were more likely to be despised than glorified. These men were caught in a war that was not of their making and most were not old enough to use politics to make their wishes known.

The Unknown

Fear of the unknown is a third condition fostering abusive behavior. A major concern in guerrilla-type warfare is the fear and constant frustration of unsuspected attacks. It was not uncommon during the Vietnamese conflict for young children or old women to carry concealed grenades and guns, similar to the situation in Northern Ireland today. Therefore, no one was above suspicion.

Police frequently are provoked into brutal attacks under the same con-ditions. An unexpected motion on the part of an apprehended suspect may be interpreted as dangerous. Body stance or verbal language may express disrespect or a questioning of the officer's authority. Extremely large, loud, or restless crowds may invoke fear and uncertainty in the police causing them to react in a brutal, nonrational way. Being unsure of the crowd's next move, the police feel trapped and resort to an overt, physically violent offensive.

Inexperienced or incompetent parents are often unable to cope with the demands of children and interpret whimpering, crying, or minor acts of dis-pleasure as a show of disrespect and a questioning of parental authority (see Steel and Pollack, 1968; Helfer and Kempe, 1968; Gil, 1970).

Lack of Communication

Inability to communicate with the victim is a fourth variable related to abusive parents, police, and soldiers. The lack of communication between parents and children, especially infants and toddlers, acts to increase parental frustration, which often turns a disciplinary action such as spanking into child abuse. Even with older children, there is a tendency among some parents to avoid verbal communication and rely on physical discipline. Not only does this method restrict interpersonal communication between parent and child but it sets a pattern of disciplinary processes, in which sanctioned limits of physical force are continually extended—a kind of "push comes to shove."

Although the Geneva code provides a guideline for behavior in international warfare, in the field, war, especially guerrilla war, is not likely conducted by these gentlemanly rules and regulations. There is no normative pattern for allowing communications between soldiers of warring nations, and those communications that do occur cannot be trusted since there is no established basis for trust. Unlike animal societies, which rely on body stance and verbal signals to indicate submission and defeat, modern man (and his war) is without trusted and respected interpersonal signals that would indicate defeat and avoid the need to inflict mortal wounds. Thus, force used against a military enemy easily becomes violence against a civilian enemy.

This inability to communicate with a suspected enemy also contributes to police brutality. The police, with their law-and-order morality, do not speak the language of various segments of the society that appear to question the status quo. The inner-city black is distrusted and despised. The hippy college youth frequently degrade the very materialistic, middle-class values that police have worked to achieve.

Questioning of Authority

A final factor contributing to abuse is the questioning of authoriy. The police highly value and demand respect and obedience to authority from the people they serve. These are the two qualities least likely to be offered by a suspect. Just the act of attempting to state one's innocence indicates a questioning of the officer's judgment. Studies indicate that lack of respect and questioning of police authority are the two major conditions contributing to police abuse. Physical abuse to instill respect in a suspect carries normative, although nonlegal, support of the police hierarchy (Chicago *Tribune*, 1973).

Since child abuse is usually an extension of discipline, parents are likely to interpret the child's undesirable actions (a small disobedience, whimpering, or crying) as an indication that the parent has lost control of the situation. Just as normal discipline is an attempt to restore authority, abuse is a more desperate attempt to do so.

Respect for the authority of superiors is crucial to a well-trained military. Soldiers are taught that "all orders are to be presumed legal and all orders are to be obeyed" (*Newsweek*, March 8, 1971: 51-52). Military training prepares the soldier to respond to orders with unquestioned obedience, not individual judgments on the moral or ethical nature of these orders. Likewise, the soldier acts in an authoritarian manner in the field and tolerates no action from the enemy that interferes with his orders.

Applying these findings to intrafamily conflict resolution, one would expect the frequency of assertive, aggressive, and abusive interaction to—

1.   increase as the acceptance of violence to obtain socially desirable goals increases;

2.   increase as frustration and dissatisfaction with one's job, one's role,
      one's family setting increases;
3.   increase with the individual's lack of understanding of, or inability to
      cope with, the increase in family demands;
4.   increase as communication barriers increase;
5.   increase when the traditionally assigned role of authority is questioned by
      the individual(s) in the traditionally assigned subordinate role.

SUMMARY

Parents, police, and the military have as a major commonality the social
sanction to use physical force when performing their duties. A comparison of
the backgrounds of parents, police, and military men who abuse this power
show them to share many similarities, such as lower-class status, inadequate
education, frustrating life circumstances, and lack of prestige in their work.
Furthermore, there are many social structural conditions that tend to increase
the chances of an act of brutality occurring, such as frustration resulting from
society-imposed boundaries, fear of the unknown, inability to communicate
with the victim, the questioning of authority, and lack of respect.

The most salient factor, however, is that these individuals, like a large
segment of society, accept and glorify physical and verbal force under the right
circumstances. The use of physical force is glorified by TV, movies, magazines,
and newspapers. For example, a recent article in *Time* (1977: 58) reported that
women shown as "bound, gagged, beaten, whipped, chained, or as victims of
murder or gang rapes" currently grace record-album covers, advertisements in
fashion magazines, department-store windows, and billboards. Loren Miles,
a creator of "abused women" ads, who notes "I don't think women deserve
to be beaten any more than men," is planning an advertisement campaign to
show women abusing men (*Time*, 1977: 57). Violence is also abundant in literature. Nursery rhymes, and children's stories extol the glory as well as the fear
of violence; for example, "Hansel and Gretel," "There was an old woman,"
"Humpty Dumpty."

In an analysis of children's books from 1850 to 1970, Huggins and Straus
(1975) found a mean of 2.1 violent acts per 15 pages with an increase in the
proportion of women aggressors over the 120-year period. They suggest: "The
implicit message communicated defines and labels physical violence as an appropriate instrumental act and lays out the vocabulary of motive and the script
for violence in a form which can be learned by the next generation."

Today this message is not only learned through television, magazines,
and movies but is also transmitted in a wide variety of other forms such as the
glorification of violence in sports or martial arts. A 1967 Beatles song, "Getting
Better," states, "I used to be cruel to my woman, I beat her and kept her apart

from the things that she loved." Another popular ballad, "Run Joey Run" (Geddes, 1975), relates the tragedy of a teenage girl who runs to her boyfriend with "tear filled eyes and bruises on her face" after being beaten by her father. The song ends with the daughter being shot by the father when she attempts to protect her boyfriend from the enraged father. A recent article describing the newest dance craze had the headlines "Punch, Spin, then Kick: That's the Kung-fu Dance." The article intimated that those who might not have the desire to learn the "fighting" version might find satisfaction in the less violent dance form (Wilmington, *Evening Journal*, January 7, 1975: 3).

The message is clear. As long as we sanction and glorify the use of physical and verbal force to control others, under the proper conditions, and as long as we allow considerable discretionary powers in defining these conditions, then one can expect considerable use of verbal and physical force to control others along with frequent abuse of such power.

An illustration of this is found in a comparison of preliberation and postliberation China. In preliberation China, physical abuse between husband and wife, mother-in-law and daughter, parent and child, and landlord and peasant was common. This abuse, based on oppression of the weak and less powerful, had a long tradition and was perpetuated in the culture. Today these acts are not tolerated. They do not fit an ideology that considers all people as equals (Sidel, 1972).

This suggests that as long as there are legal prescriptions as well as social sanctions to use physical force to control others, then there is a high probability that many individuals will extend this use beyond that which is considered acceptable. It is also expected that many families will be extending this training in the desirability and viability of using verbally and physically aggressive modes of resolving conflict to the next generation, thereby continuing the cycle. Therefore, the first step in reducing the excessive use of violence in all segments of our society might be to replace aggressive and abusive family interactions with more human, effective modes of interaction. Since much criminal behavior is also linked to inadequate socialization, society at large, as well as the immediate family unit, might benefit.

4

BROTHERS AND SISTERS:
WAR AND PEACE

She loves him and he loves her, but they don't like each other
very much.

Mother of three adolescent children

INTRODUCTION

This chapter will focus on the sources of sibling conflict as well as the
modes used to resolve these conflicts. The effect of the ages of the siblings
on both the sources of conflict and the way in which the conflict is resolved
will be examined. The perceived success of different methods of resolving
sibling conflict will also be investigated.

Conflict between siblings, or sibling rivalry as it has often been labeled,
is probably the most generally acknowledged form of family aggression. Perhaps
because of its near universality, this aspect of family interaction has been generally ignored. In a survey of the literature from the earliest editions of available
journals until 1975, this author was unable to locate any empirical research
on physical aggression between noninfant siblings. Using a *Psychological
Abstracts* data base running from January 1967 to December 1976, a computer
search was conducted using the code words: hostility, aggressive behavior,
arguments, aggression, conflict, violence, threat postures, and aggressiveness.
This produced 8,192 articles. Yet when these references were crossed with the
words brother, sister, sibling, and sibling relations, only 67 articles were cited
and only a couple, according to the abstracts, directly related to verbal and

physical aggression between noninfant sibs.* The only available literature focused on the nursery-school-age child's increased aggressiveness toward the newborn infant, and a women's magazine article, on how the author "stopped her children from squabbling."

Evidence that fights between brothers and sisters are not just a contemporary problem is provided by the diary kept by Philip Fithian, a tutor for the Carter children in eighteenth century Virginia. He recorded the following (Fithian, 1945: 66):

> Bob called Nancy a Lyar: Nancy upbraided Bob, on the other hand, with being often flog'd by their pappa; often by the Masters in College; that he had stol'n Rum & had got drunk; & that he used to run away &c. These Reproaches when they were set off with Miss Nancys truely feminine address, so violently exasperated Bob that he struck her in his rage.

About one month later, Fithian recorded the following incident (Fithian, 1945: 85):

> Before Breakfast Nancy and Fanny had a fight about a shoe brush which they both wanted. Fanny pull'd off her shoe and threw it at Nancy, which missed her and broke a pane of glass of our school room. They then enter's upon close scratching &c. which methods seem instinctive in Women.

A considerable number of parents in this study also saw conflicts between brothers and sisters as inevitable. In responding to the question "How do your children get along?" one parent's comments were typical of answers given by most: "Terrible! They fight all the time. Anything can be a problem. . . . Oh, its just constant, but I understand that this is normal. I talk to other people, their kids are the same way." Another parent noted: "The first two absolutely hate each other, . . . they are a year apart, and although we have not made anything of it, there is naturally competition there."

It is important to recognize that a set of behaviors may be labeled a conflict in one family while being ignored in another. It appears, in this particular study, that families define a conflict as a situation where a possible resolution is perceived to be available, but is not being used (or else is not working). For example, if a child does something wrong, is corrected, and the disobedient behavior is halted, this is not seen as a conflict. This is particularly the case with

---

* The researcher's growing interest in aggression and violence is illustrated by comparing entries in *Psychological Abstracts*. From January 1967 to April 1975, 4,041 entries, using the aggression-related code words above, were found. Twenty months later this number had more than doubled.

sibling and parent-child conflict. Perhaps most parents see this interaction as normal—a constant push between sibs and a constant tug-of-war between parents and child. They do not define this behavior as a conflict, but rather as a normal part of interaction between sibs—a problem, an annoyance, perhaps, but not a conflict.*

As a result, the most difficult part of the data gathering was to get parents to identify conflicts between brothers and sisters. Even when examples of conflicts were presented, the typical comment was, "I don't consider that a conflict." Therefore, the conflicts that were recorded are most likely considerable underestimates of the actual frequency, since only those incidents that were witnessed by parents, and were considered too disruptive to overlook were noted. It should be mentioned, however, that while the smaller, less disturbing conflicts are likely to be overlooked, the more verbally and physically aggressive acts are likely to be accurately recorded.

Since the attitude of most parents is to ignore, as much as possible, these aggressive interactions between sibs, the resolution of most minor conflicts probably takes place between the sibs themselves. Therefore, parents are likely to underestimate the frequency of conflict for two major reasons: much aggressive behavior between sibs is considered to be normal interaction rather than a conflict; parents actively attempt to ignore aggressive sibling interaction, and therefore are not likely to witness or record minor conflicts.

Support for this position comes from the conflict-data sheets and interviews. All conflicts occurring in the family were recorded for a period of one week. In almost all families the recording was done by the parents, usually the mother. Therefore, these are conflicts that she witnessed, or that the children related to her for mediation. In some cases parents suspected that conflicts existed, but were lacking concrete evidence regarding the source and sequence. One parent, while discussing the family's younger daughter's practice of irritating the older girl, felt sure that "there is conflict there, but I'm never entirely sure of what she does do because I've never caught her at it."

In conflicts between sibs it appears that parents are often a resource; that is, they are brought into the battle in an attempt to strengthen one's position. This appears to be the predominant pattern for the child who perceives that he is in the weaker position; for example, he is younger, smaller, physically or personalitywise weaker, or less sure that he is right. Many parents saw tattling or the request for parental intervention in sibling conflicts as an attention-getting device, and felt that their children got along better when parents weren't available. One mother, who noted that her children fight all the time when she is home, wondered how her children settled their squabbles when she is at work.

---

* With spouses, however, because of the delicacy of the marital bond, which in contemporary American society is based on equality, trust, love, and so on, rather than unquestioning submission of the wife to the husband, certain words are likely to be defined and recorded as a sign of conflict.

Commenting on this, she remarked, "It's a wonder they're not all bruised and bloody. They must get tired of yelling at each other."

LIMITATIONS IN THE DIARY APPROACH
TO GATHERING DATA

There are several limitations in the data obtained by the recording of intrafamily conflict resolution during the one-week period. While these limitations must be considered when interpreting the data presented in the following two chapters, they are especially relevant to the data on siblings.

The first limitation is the tendency to generalize the conflicts. This results when numerous closely related conflicts occur repeatedly during the day. For example, when children are having a bad day, are out of sorts or argumentative, there is a tendency to record the conflicts by lumping several together and to generalize the causes, modes of resolution utilized, and success of the modes used.

The following entry was made for one family: "Children arguing continually—who started it? Both accuse the other and want me to write the other side down. Went to church where it is air-conditioned."

The mother attributed the children's fussiness to the extreme heat and humidity that prevailed during the recording period. The problem for the researcher is to try to decide if the causes of the conflict, methods of resolution, and its success were similar or if different factors contributed, separately, to each of the conflicts that occurred.

Closely related to the first limitation is the problem of deciding if an incident was one large conflict, or many small ones. Conflicts do not occur in isolation, but are part of the day-to-day interaction between various personalities within the family. Thus, they tend to occur as a sequence of closely related events. Although some parents recorded each interaction as a distinct unit, the tendency was for parents to record the series of events, frequently power struggles between several family members, as one conflict. For example:

> Son would not put on his shoes. Mother warns that she will go to the store alone. Daughter begins to cry and son agrees to put on shoes, but doesn't do it. Mother tells daughter she could go tomorrow. Daughter gets upset, son grabs at this chance to tease daughter. They begin to fight. Mother sent them to their rooms and after ten minutes went up and read them a story. After the story, they began to fight again. [Mother] puts them to bed, hollering and screaming. Daughter cried for 15 minutes then fell to sleep. Son yelled for 45 minutes, was quiet for 15 minutes, resumed his screaming.

A third factor limiting the accuracy of daily conflict-recording sheets revolves around the notations developed by parents to indicate how their children interact. For example, one conflict over toys was noted as follows: "The child who had it first was given the toy. If the slighted child still persisted in fighting over toy she is put in a chair till she can play without fighting. THIS HAPPENS 10 X A DAY EVERY DAY!"

Another family noted: "Car squabbles." "He's touching me. She's hitting me." "Mother yells at them and they stop for a few minutes. (Happens just about every time in car.)" Another mother related that fighting over toys was "daily" conflict.

Although a respondent may note that a particular incident occurs ten times a day or at least once a day, if it is only entered on the conflict sheet once, then it is only counted once. There are, however, valuable insights gained from these notations suggesting that a particular set of interactions have become a pattern in that family.

A fourth and most important consideration is that, in addition to the active schedules of most of the families studies, in many families both parents worked. It would be inconsiderate and probably not feasible to expect these individuals to devote one full week to recording each and every assertive, aggressive, or abusive interaction they saw or had reported to them and to conduct regular third-degree sessions to route out the conflicts they did not observe. It is probable that there were families whose schedules on certain days left very little time for the immediate recording of incidents. This increases the possibility that minor conflicts might be forgotten, even with the prodding of the daily phone call from the interviewer.

Some families noted that they had been too busy to record on a particular day, usually noting that it had been a typical day, that is, one with no dramatic confrontation. Other families recorded no conflict, but the phone call revealed that the parents (or the children) had been gone the entire day, so that no conflicts were observed, which is different from no conflicts occurring.

Special occasions also affect the number of conflicts that do occur. One respondent noted that it was her birthday and everything was delightfully under control; everyone was on their good behavior. "No conflicts—beautiful day" was recorded by another respondent. Another family, after recording only two conflicts in two days followed by a conflict-free day, predicted: "Next week will probably be hell on wheels around here. This can't be a lasting peace—war must be at hand!"

A final limitation of the data is that most methods of conflict resolution in the data presented below are the methods parents used to resolve the problem, rather than those the sibs used. This is because in most families the parents were recording the conflicts, and if the parent did not observe the conflict or was not called in to mediate the dispute, then the chances of the parent reporting the incident were slim. With younger children, this mediation usually took the form of punishment, separation, or threats on the part of the parent. With the older sibs, the mediation was more likely to be in the form of discussion and compromises.

One difficulty with categorizing the modes of conflict resolution is that frequently the cause of the conflict and the mode of resolution are similar, but are attributed to different individuals. For example, the child may be hollering and hitting another child (the conflict), and the parent, in resolving the conflict, may holler or hit the offending child. In categorizing the results, the parents record their act as the method used to resolve the conflict. It is recognized, however, that the hollering and hitting by the child involved in the incident is the child's attempt to resolve the conflict.

Since parents tend to record the children's activity as the conflict, this scheme was used for analyzing the data. Furthermore, if an incident, regardless of how complex and involved, was noted as a single incident, then it was counted as a single conflict for analysis.

METHODS USED TO RESOLVE CONFLICTS
BETWEEN SIBS

During the one-week recording period, 49 participating families recorded 131 conflicts between sibs. The 131 conflicts recorded, however, probably are a considerable underestimate of the actual number that occurred. The methods used to resolve the 131 conflicts are shown in Table 4.1.

Parents were likely to consider their methods to be fairly successful. Of the 131 recorded conflicts, 77.1 percent were considered to be resolved successfully, and 14.5 percent of the resolutions were partially successful or a temporary success. In only 4.6 percent of the cases was the method selected considered to be a failure (3.8 percent of the outcomes were unknown).

Since parents may consider some methods to be more successful than other methods, the data were analyzed by percentaging the perceived success of each method used. The data, presented in Table 4.2, suggest that parents perceive threats, compromises, and restriction (either by removing privileges or removing children to separate rooms or having them sit on chairs) to be the

TABLE 4.1

Methods Used to Resolve
Conflicts between Siblings

Method Used	Percent of Conflicts	
Hollering, screaming, yelling, arguing	23.7	(31)
Discussion	23.7	(31)
Assertion, threat	17.6	(23)
Compromise	13.0	(17)
Ignoring	12.2	(16)
Restriction of privileges	6.1	(8)
Physical force	3.8	(5)

TABLE 4.2

Percent of Sibling Conflicts Resolved by Various Methods, by Perceived Outcome

Method*	Perceived Outcome			
	Success	Partial Success	Failure	Unknown
H	64.5	16.1	12.9	6.5
	(20)	(5)	(4)	(2)
D	80.7	16.1	3.2	0
	(25)	(5)	(1)	
A	91.3	8.7	0	0
	(21)	(2)		
C	88.2	11.8	0	0
	(15)	(2)		
I	56.3	25.0	6.3	12.5
	(9)	(4)	(1)	(2)
R	87.5	12.5	0	0
	(7)	(1)		
P	80.0	0	0	20.0
	(4)			(1)

* H = hollering, yelling, arguing, screaming; D = discussion, talking it over; A = asserting one's will, threat; C = compromise; I = ignoring; R = restriction (withdrawal of privileges, separating, sending to one's room); P = physical punishment.

most successful modes of resolving sibling conflicts. Discussion and physical punishment appear to be the next most successful mode, while yelling and screaming appear to be successful in about two-thirds of the conflicts. The least effective method appears to be that of ignoring the situation. This finding is especially interesting because most parents expressed a belief that ignoring sibling conflicts is the best policy. For example:

> I used to get involved and found that I lost everytime because I never could be fair completely . . . it starts and you're not there. So unless it gets physical, I usually try to go to another part of the house and I don't get involved . . . that is the only way I can get away without two of them saying: "Mom, make her do this" and "make him do that," which is the opposite. And you really can't satisfy them at all.

It may be that parents attempt to ignore the minor conflicts, but there is a tolerance point beyond which they can no longer comfortably do so. To attempt to ignore these conflicts beyond the tolerance point, which probably differs for each parent, is to bring discomfort to the parent witnessing the battle, and thus the incident is recorded as unsuccessful. It is also possible that beyond this tolerance point, other means are used to resolve the conflict. As one mother noted: "I try to avoid their conflicts most of the time, figuring that a third person is not necessarily going to help. But I don't always have the fortitude." Another mother reported: "If it stays at a level I can ignore, then I do just that. But every once-in-a-while, I let go and I say 'Look, let's stop this, if you can't stop then you both go to your rooms.'"

RELATION OF LIFE-CYCLE STAGE
TO SIBLING CONFLICT

The above data are a composite of the sibling conflicts in all families. Since we expect that as children go through different stages, the sources of conflicts as well as the modes used to resolve them may change, it is necessary to examine the data according to the ages of the children in each family.

It should be recognized that in any cross-sectional study you are comparing families living in different historical time spaces. The voluminous number of parent-education books, courses, and articles currently in vogue may have a definite infuence on parents with young children. Thus the methods used to resolve conflict may be reflecting this new expansion of parent-education awareness as much as the ages of the children in the family.

In order to investigate these differences, the sample was divided into young, adolescent, and teenage families. The ages of all children currently residing in the home were averaged. Those families with children whose mean age was eight years or younger were designated as young families. Those families whose children's mean age was between nine and 13 years were categorized as adolescent families. Families with children whose mean age was 14 years or over were considered to be teenage families. In a few cases where there were essentially two sets of children, for example, a family with two teenageers and a four-year-old, the set with the larger number of children was considered for placing the family in a category. Three families were, however, eliminated from this part of the analysis. These families had a large number of children whose ages covered such a wide span that none of the age categories would give an accurate picture of sibling interaction. To average their ages would obliterate those very differences that an analysis by age groupings attempts to produce. One additional family was eliminated from analysis by age group. In this family the conflicts were recorded on grandchildren and the grandparents recorded conflicts focusing on their daughter's lack of control over the children—an atypical case in the study.

The rationale behind this age grouping is that it corresponds to the groups commonly found in the public schools. Younger families would be those with preschool and grade-school (first to fourth grade) children. The adolescent family would have children predominately in the middle school grades (fifth to eighth). The teenage family would have children attending high school, grades nine to 12. This division in schools has become increasingly more popular because it more closely approximates the social-emotional development as well as physiological stages of youth. The interviews, as well as the conflicts recorded on the data sheets, support this categorization as identifying distinct stages in the family life cycle.

For families with younger children there were 63 conflicts reported. This number decreased to 36 for families with adolescents and to 16 for families with teenagers, suggesting that there is a greater frequency of conflicts among young families. As one mother noted: "I had four in five years. When you have them that small, you do have a lot more fighting . . . the hitting, the scratching, the bopping each other on the head with the toys."

Although teenagers may have a lower frequency of sibling conflicts, it is also probable that they solve most of them by themselves witout the parents' awareness and/or intervention.

These findings, from the conflict sheet, are somewhat inconsistent with what most parents reported during the in-depth interviews. During these interviews, parents frequently complained that in adolescence, especially early adolescence, their children got along less well with sibs. One parent noted: "They used to get along real well. Now they are a little older, I think they fight more." Another found that "they didn't fight a lot when they were little because they were close in age. Now they fight over very minor, silly things, kids' stuff, TV programs—'I was sitting on that chair first.'"

The inconsistency between the actual frequency of conflicts and parent's perception of increasing conflicts as children enter adolescence may be a reflection of parent's definition of appropriate behavior. While they expect fighting with younger children, they expect older children to behave more like young adults. It might also be that the mode of conflict resolution adolescents use— the mouthiness parents complained about—is more annoying to parents. One parent suggested that the amount of conflict doesn't change, only the methods used for resoving them:

> I don't think there has been any change. I think there's always been a fair amount of bickering. Now that they're older, they can verbalize more, and say more hateful things. Whereas, when they were tiny they could throw a handful of sand in each other's head or something. The type of fighting may have changed and they have become more sophisticated.

A note of optimism is provided for parents of adolescents who are currently experiencing this high level of sibling and parent-child conflicts as well as the concomitant strain on marital relationships. Parents of teenagers noted that as their children entered the latter teens, they began to get along much better with each other and their parents, and marital relationships also appeared to improve.

The Young Family

Young families have children whose mean age is eight years or younger. There were 18 families in this research categorized as young families. Sixteen families participated in this part of the project and recorded a total of 63 conflicts between sibs during the one-week recording period. The sibling conflicts in the young family can be characterized as the difficulty involved in sharing of possessions. The conflicts centered around the sharing of toys, games, or attention of adults, and frequently included nonprovoked hitting, shoving or screaming, usually as an attention-getting device.

One family noted the following conflicts during the one-week period: "use of the glider," "sharing the truck," "sharing the tricycle," "knocking down one child's blocks and taking them," "taking one child's toy sticks from the play 'fire.'"

Another respondent, the mother of four-year-old twins, simplified the resolution of conflicts by removing the source: "They both want something at the same time and that's what causes the conflicts. That's why I end up buying two of everything so that there isn't an argument over it." However, during the recording period, the twins fought over "what to watch on TV" and "what color cereal bowl to eat out of."

Since parents resort to a wide variety of techniques to resolve sibling conflicts, a major concern is to discover which methods are considered by these parents to be more successful. Table 4.3 presents the perceived success of different methods used to resolve sibling conflict in young families. The data suggest that the most frequently used method for resolving sibling conflict is discussion, which was used about 22 percent of the time. The most successful method, however, appears to be compromise. Threatening or asserting authority, and restricting privileges or separating the children are also fairly successful. Hollering or yelling, discussion, or physical punishment appear to be successful in about three-fourths of the cases.

Because parents were recording the data, it may be that social desirability is a factor coloring their description of events. Since screaming and yelling have negative connotations, parents may select less emotionally-laden words. Several individuals noted that they spoke in "raised" voices or in "elevated" tones and discussed something "loudly." One mother made the following entry on the data sheet:

> Conflict: Sharing a toy that was left for a while and the other child began to play with it.

TABLE 4.3

Percent of Sibling Conflicts Resolved by Various Methods and Perceived Outcome in Young Families

| Method* | Perceived Outcome | | | |
	Success	Partial Success	Failure	Unknown
H	77.8	11.1	11.1	0
	(7)	(1)	(1)	
D	71.4	28.6	0	0
	(10)	(4)		
A	92.3	7.7	0	0
	(12)	(1)		
C	100.0	0	0	0
	(8)			
I	30.0	40.0	10.0	0
	(3)	(4)	(1)	
R	85.7	14.3	0	0
	(6)	(1)		
P	75.0	0	0	25.0
	(3)			(1)

* H = hollering, yelling, arguing, screaming; D = discussion, talking it over; A = asserting one's will, threat; C = compromise; I = ignoring; R = restriction (withdrawal of privileges, separating, sending to one's room); P = physical punishment.

Method of Resolution: I explained (shouted) above the screaming that she had left the toy to play with something else and M could play with it for a while.
Outcome: M was quiet. L said she hates him but did give up the toy.

Out of the 63 recorded conflicts, only 3 percent of the resolutions were acknowledged failures. Overall, 75 percent of the conflicts were considered to be resolved successfully.

The Adolescent Family

The adolescent family is composed of children whose mean age falls between eight and 14 years. These are children who attend the middle school or junior high school grades. There were 18 families characterized as having adolescent children in the sample. Two of these families did not participate in the recording of daily conflicts.

Within the limits of generalization afforded by this sample, it appears that all adolescents "make faces" or "look funny" at each other. They have as a major source of conflict, touching or picking at each other, pulling hair, teasing, or in some way infringing on the other's personal space as defined by the participants in the interaction.

One father suggested that excessive teasing was the basis for most conflicts between his adolescent children. He felt that this was probably normal among most families: "He taps her. Not the vicious hitting. Some of his taps are exaggerated: 'Man he hauled off and whaled the day-lights out of me!' 'Well [the father says] let me see the bruises.' 'Well [the child says] he didn't really hit me that hard.'"

Comments received from parents of adolescents tended to blame the conflicts on the age of the children, and emphasize the hopelessness of the situation. Typical of these comments is one parent's response:

> They fuss. They say, "He's sitting in my seat." Or, "He has got an inch of his pants on the line where I am supposed to be." Or, "He's got his seat moved right in the middle so I can't see the television." Or, "He has a dirty pair of pants on my bed." It is just nonsense and silliness.

Another parent noted:

> At home, if they have to pass each other or something they just yell, "Why do you have to do that to me?" This morning J told me that S made a face at her, while they were eating. I said to her, "Well what do you want me to do about it? I think you should ignore it or ask him to stop it, or whatever, but there is nothing I can do about it."

One father, however, did come up with a solution for some of these conflicts over territory. This family frequently took long trips. The children, who were required to wear seat belts, and were "bumper to bumper" in the back seat, always argued if one of them crossed the property line, that is, invaded the other's portion of the seat. The mother related: "About one week ago, he [the father] went out with a can of red paint and drew boundary lines, so that when we go away the next time, they will know that you can't put your foot across the line."

There were 38 conflicts between adolescents recorded in these families. As with the younger families, these probably represent the more extreme incidents, ones in which parental interference was unavoidable, or in which the children sought parental intervention.

It appears that parents' biggest complaint at this age was the smart-talk mouthiness used by adolescents in sibling as well as parent-child conflicts. However, yelling and screaming and threats on the part of both the child and

TABLE 4.4

Percent of Sibling Conflicts Resolved by Various Methods and Perceived Outcome in Adolescent Families

Method*	Perceived Outcome			
	Success	Partial Success	Failure	Unknown
H	66.7	22.2	0	11.1
	(6)	(2)		(1)
D	90.9	0	0	9.1
	(10)			(1)
A	88.9	11.1	0	0
	(8)	(1)		
C	60.0	40.0	0	0
	(3)	(2)		
I	100.0	0	0	0
	(3)			
R	0	0	0	0
P	100.0	0	0	0
	(1)			

* H = hollering, yelling, arguing, screaming; D = discussion, talking it over; A = asserting one's will, threat; C = compromise; I = ignoring; R = restriction (withdrawal of privileges, separating, sending to one's room); P = physical punishment.

parents accounted for a large proportion of the methods used in an attempt to resolve sibling conflicts. This is similar to the case of parents of younger children, who do not believe in spanking and use it only when their children hit or physically hurt other children. Could the message be "Do as I say, not as I do?"

To investigate the perceived success of the methods used to resolve sibling conflicts in adolescent families, the data were tabulated according to the perceived success of each method (see Table 4.4). With this age group, discussion and arguing appear to be the most prevalent as well as the most successful modes of resolving conflict. Because this age group has been described as "verbally aggressive," it is understandable why hollering, threatening, arguing, and discussion would be the most common methods used. At this stage, parents do not separate children or appear to use physical punishment, but attempt to resolve the conflict using verbal means.

It is interesting that parents perceived compromise to be more successful with the younger group than with the adolescent children. One explanation of this finding might be that among younger children the compromise often takes the form of the parent providing an alternative solution, for example, substituting another toy for the one desired by both children, with the explicit instruction that if this compromise is not satisfactory, a less desirable solution, such as sitting on a chair, will be used.

Among adolescent families compromise appears to be more in the form of a discussion on how to maximize each child's wishes and minimize each child's loss. This compromise usually involves deciding on schedules for sharing chores such as walking the dog, or household tasks. Because of its increased complexity, success is more difficult to judge.

The Teenage Family

Families having children whose mean age is 14 years or older are the last group to be discussed; 17 of the families in the sample were characterized as being teenage families. Of these 17 families, four did not participate in the recording of sibling conflicts.

While conflict in the young families revolved around possessions, and those in the adolescent families focused on the invasion of personal space,

TABLE 4.5

Percent of Sibling Conflicts Resolved by Various Methods and Perceived Outcome in Teenage Families

| Method* | Perceived Outcome | | | |
	Success	Partial Success	Failure	Unknown
H	33.3	16.7	33.3	16.2
	(2)	(1)	(2)	(1)
D	100.0	0	0	0
	(3)			
A	100.0	0	0	0
	(1)			
C	100.0	0	0	0
	(3)			
I	100.0	0	0	0
	(1)			
R	0	0	0	0
P	0	0	0	0

* H = hollering, yelling, arguing, screaming; D = discussion, talking it over; A = asserting one's will, threat; C = compromise; I = ignoring; R = restriction (withdrawal of privileges, separating, sending to one's room); P = physical punishment.

teenage conflicts tended to be related to responsibilities, obligations, and social grace. Only 14 conflicts were recorded between sibs in teenage families. There appear to be several reasons for this. First, as children mature, they develop outside interests, spending less time interacting with sibs. As a result, less contact means less conflict. Secondly, conflicts tend to be viewed more as differences of opinion, requiring a more sophisticated approach to resolution. Thus, the incidents are less likely to be recorded as conflicts. Finally, not only are siblings interacting less with each other, they are not likely to be interacting with each other in a situation that could be witnessed and interpreted as a conflict by the parents.

Although the small number of cases makes analysis problematic, the data were percentaged according to the perceived success of each method (see Table 4.5). This enables comparisons of these data with the data for the young and adolescent subsamples.

The teenage group experienced relatively high success, with all methods but hollering being successful everytime. By young adulthood, siblings have apparently perfected their repertory of conflict-resolution modes so as to insure the greatest success. Perhaps, that is why hollering, one of the most emotional responses used, has the poorest success record.

Comparing the Three Groups

In comparing these three groups, the most obvious difference is in the total number of conflicts recorded. There is a dramatic decrease in conflicts with an increase in the age of the group. For the younger group, with 16 participating families, 63 conflicts were recorded, resulting in a mean of 3.9 conflicts per family. The adolescent group, with 16 participating families, recorded 38 conflicts and had a mean of 2.4. The 13 families categorized as teenage recorded 14 conflicts with a mean of 1.1. This might be a function of visibility as well as age. As children get older they are increasingly absent from both the home setting and parental observation. The resolution methods used also differ in each age group. The data presented in Table 4.6 suggest that with an increase in age, sibling conflicts are less likely to be settled with physical force, restriction, threats, or by ignoring the situation, and are more likely to be settled by yelling and compromises. There is no apparent difference in the use of discussion between these age groups and this method is used about one-fourth of the time to resolve sibling conflicts.

Since the data just presented reflect the parents' perception of how siblings resolve conflict, rather than the children's report of how they resolve conflict between brothers and sisters, another source of data was utilized. These data, obtained from the questionnaire completed by the eldest child residing at home in each family, were analyzed using the same (mean age) groupings

TABLE 4.6

Comparison of the Percent of Sibling Conflicts Resolved by Various Methods in Young, Adolescent, and Teenage Families

| Method* | Age Group | | |
	Young	Adolescent	Teenage
H	14.3	23.7	42.9
	(9)	(9)	(6)
D	22.2	29.0	21.4
	(14)	(11)	(3)
A	17.5	23.7	7.1
	(11)	(9)	(1)
C	12.7	13.2	21.4
	(8)	(5)	(3)
I	15.9	7.9	7.4
	(10)	(3)	(1)
R	11.1	0	0
	(7)		
P	6.4	2.6	0
	(4)	(1)	

* H = hollering, yelling, arguing, screaming; D = discussion, talking it over; A = asserting one's will, threat; C = compromise; I = ignoring; R = restriction (withdrawal of privileges, separating, sending to one's room); P = physical punishment.

as used above. (See the short form of the questionnaire, Appendix A). The mean scores for discussion, verbal aggression, and physical aggression were computed. These scores, presented in Table 4.7, supported the information provided by the parents' interviews and the diary.

Discussion and verbal aggression, as a conflict-resolution method, tend to increase from young to teenage groups, although the adolescent group had slightly higher scores than did the teenage group. This is consistent with the description, provided by parents, of the adolescent group as verbally aggressive, mouthy, and argumentative. There was a consistent decrease in the use of physical force to resolve conflicts as you move from young to adolescent to teenage families, supporting the data provided by the in-depth interviews of parents as well as the data from the diaries.

The validity of these findings is considerably strengthened by the fact that they represent information provided by two observers, parent and child, as well as three distinct methods of data collection: interview, questionnaire, and recording of conflicts for a one-week period.

TABLE 4.7

Mean Scores for Conflict Resolution Methods among Sibs as Reported by Children

Method	Age Group		
	Young (N = 14)	Adolescent (N = 16)	Teenage (N = 14)
Discussion	5.2	7.2	6.5
Verbal aggression	6.6	7.3	7.2
Physical aggression	8.6	7.8	6.7

SUMMARY

The findings appear to indicate that sibling conflicts decrease, or are less likely to be witnessed and mediated by parents, as children move from the young to adolescent to teenage stage in the life cycle.

In addition, the sources of conflicts are different in origin. With younger siblings, the conflicts frequently revolve around possessions, especially toys. With the adolescent group, the conflicts center on personal space—touching or picking at each other or in some way violating personal space boundaries. The teenage group has relatively few conflicts but those occurring appear to center on responsibilities, obligation, and social awareness.

The modes of resolving conflicts also vary. With younger groups there are more varied modes utilized and there is considerably more use of physical means, such as spanking and restricting the child's freedom.

The adolescent group resorts to more verbal modes and shows a considerable decline in physical means. The teenage group also relies on verbal modes and, with the exception of arguing and yelling, found total success in all other methods.

The following chapter will report on the mode of resolution used to resolve parent-child conflict. A major focus will be on the relationship between different age groups; the conflict-resolution methods used and the perceived success of these methods; and mother-father differences in the use of child-rearing techniques.

5

AS THE TWIG IS BENT:
PARENT-CHILD INTERACTION

I found myself more violent with her[the first child]. It's awful to say. I couldn't control my temper as well as I can now. I look back on it and think, Oh, God, it was terrible.

Mother of two young daughters

If the media accurately reflect society's concerns, then many of today's ills are considered to be the result of parents' loss of control over their children. The newspapers constantly berate parents for this increase in juvenile delinquency and the lack of respect youth show for the person and property of others. One factor contributing to this perceived increase in youth-related delinquency might be the lack of close-knit ties present in traditional societies and to some extent still present in small towns. It should also be recognized, however, that mass media has created a new environment. Generations ago, crime might have occurred in about the same dimensions as it occurs today, but the residents within a small area knew only about crime in their area. Today, with the advent of mass media, especially television, we are made aware of wide varieties of incidents occurring nationwide and worldwide that are likely to be affecting, psychologically, nearly 200 million viewers.

Of course, the eyes that watch children in small towns only become an important social-control factor if the norms, values, and attitudes are held in common. Today these norms may no longer represent a consensus viewpoint of people within a given community, thus creating a void. Since we are not a totalitarian society with only one professed belief system and one set of behaviors tolerated, there is no replacement to fill this void.

With increased social and geographic mobility, communities are composed of individuals with varying backgrounds, goals, values, and attitudes. Youth-peer groups, on the other hand, appear to have strong, stable cohesive bonds. These bonds tend to reinforce the values, goals, and attitudes that the group deems important and may not reflect the values held by individual parents.

While this is not seen as an important concern when the children are quite small, after they enter school, and especially during early teens when so many important decisions regarding occupations, marriage and life styles are being formed, parental concerns grow. These concerns, which frequently are the basis of parent-child conflicts, were often expressed during the interviews. As one mother said:

> I guess a mother will look at her own kids different. . . . I don't want to sound like I'm bragging, but I think they [her kids] are better. A lot of kids out here, you can hear their mother holler at them and they will yell back at them, . . . you can hear kids out there cussing, . . . they are always doing something. . . . I couldn't get over how kids were in a neighborhood like this. . . . They don't sound like they respect anybody or care what anybody says.

Another mother noted: "We feel less secure in letting her go places. Not totally because of herself, but because of her associates, and also a very different set of values and ideas."

For these mothers, the neighborhood represents a negative force to be overcome by setting proper examples within the home. Parents are aware of these strong peer-group bonds and realize that children may adopt the peer groups' beliefs rather than those of the parents. Other mothers, however, saw the neighborhood as a source of parental support. As one parent suggested:

> I am not concerned. The group my daughter plays with are basically good kids. They have good parents and everybody feels the same way. They know what they are allowed to do and when they push it they all get punished.

Parents also expressed a concern that they might be left with the authority to control, and the responsibility for their children, but only a rapidly eroding power, that is, actual ability to carry out their demands.

Most power struggles among the 57 families studies tended to revolve around relatively minor concerns—chores, responsibilities, spending money, hours, and so on. However, some parents were unable to assert their authority in order to prevent major conflicts. When this happened, there appeared to be two predominant modes of resolving the struggle. One was reexamining the issue and developing modes to head off power struggles by focusing on the issue, not the personalities, and realizing that compromises rather than a winner-take-all approach was important. The other was redefining the parameters—usually a two-pronged process. First, there is an attempted change in discipline, that is, "I've been too lenient in the past; therefore, I will become stricter." Secondly, there is an attempt to redefine the offending behavior as no longer offending or at least not as offending.

Perhaps this ultimate loss in power comes when the parent recognizes the hopelessness of a situation and also relinquishes authority. One family related the tragedy of their daughter:

> We went from pillar to post and psychiatrist to psychiatrist and she finally wound up with the police and hospital. We have just continued four years of absolute hell. . . . She's a chronic runaway. . . . We had no common ground with this child after a while. She just chose the life she likes to live. . . . To this day I can't understand how she can choose to be with the people and be in situations that are totally foreign to the way she was raised and totally outside of the neighborhood, environment and the friends that she had as a child. She now seeks the lowest level of humanity to associate with and live with. . . . She goes from man to man and boy to boy and she just chooses to live in the streets and has since she was 13. . . . Our relationship, hers and mine, has deteriorated finally to the point where, I will be perfectly honest, I no longer care what happens to her. In fact, I celebrated the day she became 18 which was about three weeks ago. I finally felt that this enormous weight was being lifted from my shoulder. . . . because she has cost us so much in pain and anguish and time that could have been better spent for positive pursuits, not negative things.

While most power struggles between parents and children are not as severe as this one and do not have such a tragic ending, they do appear to be a normal part of family interaction.

SOURCES OF PARENT—CHILD CONFLICT

The major goal of parent-child conflicts appears to be, as in most other conflicts, a desire to maximize one's perceived gains and minimize one's perceived losses. Although the source of conflict as well as the mode parents use for resolving the conflict differs with each age group, the basic principle remains the same.

With the young child, the conflict results from a lack of consensus regarding the child's ability. For example, the child may feel competent to leave the yard or carry a pitcher of tea to the table. However, the parent's definition of the child's ability to do this may differ. Perception of goals and the ability to fulfill these goals may not be congruent between parent and child.

With the adolescent family, the power struggle becomes a verbal one. This age group appears to be expressing their independence in the form of questioning (or verbally insulting) parental authority.

In one joint interview the parents discussed the following problem with their adolescent daughter that had been going on for about one year, "since she turned twelve":

> The most problems I have [with the thirteen-year old] is smart talk. Like snippy. It is not what she says but how she says it. She acts like I am dumb. She makes faces and stuff and it really gets to me after a while. . . .
> If you try to talk to her she sticks her nose up in the air and walks out of the room. I cannot stand that. . . . She gets on my nerves terrible.

Another parent noted that if anyone in their family of five children might need physical discipline it would be their adolescent ones: "The 12 and 14 year old ones are the ones who might need it because they get really rebellious to the point where they defy you completely." When asked if she thought the problem was related to the ages of the children, she felt sure that it was, "because we had trouble with the others at that age and now we don't."

It is interesting that as children enter the latter teenage years, the major sources of conflicts again revolve around limitation of freedom. With the teenager, the conflicts center on late hours, use of cars, and so on. With both the young child and the teenager the source of conflict apparently grows out of a fear for the child's safety. When asked if she used physical punishment, the mother of a young child noted:

> Once in a while if it's necessary. I'm really out to use physical punishment if it's something that's going to hurt them or another kid. Or sticking things in sockets, things like that. If my kids went out on the street they got it but good. I'd much rather have them cry from me hitting them than be dead in the street.

A similar response was obtained from a mother of a teenager who noted, "When they're out driving a car, you're always worried"; and another who noted:

> The only problems we have had is that she is going to these rock concerts. I worry more about what is going to happen in the crowd and in the parking lot, etc. . . . About two weeks ago we expected her around 10:30 and she did not come in until 1:15. . . . I was so upset that I was sure something had really happened because she had never [done this].

IMPROVING PARENTING

A major concern with many of the families was providing a healthy environment for their children, and a part of environment depended on their ability to provide adequate parenting. Of the 57 families participating in this study, 11, or nearly 20 percent, mentioned during the interview that they had sought professional help for improving family interaction. In two of these cases the aid was sought primarily for a parent, but in the other nine cases the counseling was specifically to improve parent-child relationships. In most of these cases the entire family was involved, which is congruent with therapists' and counselors' emphasis on the need to include the whole family for effective counseling. Since family members play roles intended to fulfill family expectations, there is a need to consider all members when attempting to effect change in any one member (see Cohen et al., 1968, for the effect of family expectations on the patient's role playing).

It should be noted that not all of these families sought aid for correcting an already existing problem. In several families, it was an attempt to perfect healthy relationships and to prepare oneself in order to avoid the pitfalls and mistakes common in child rearing. In other families, however, the aid was sought after the family crisis had occurred. One family reported:

> Well, we had what we thought was a real crisis. She was coming in 3:15 a.m. at 17 years old—we were very concerned. I tried to hold her back, assert power: "You may not go out with these undesirable people." She just as vigorously opposed what we wanted. . . .

This family, by adhering to the philosophy of the book *Parent-Effectiveness Training*, and attending a church-related course on "Living with Your Teenager," felt that they had successfully resolved the conflict.

Another family sought counseling, however, only after their 14-year-old boy had run away:

> We have conflicts quite a bit actually. I felt the kids need you to be strict and my husband doesn't like to be mean to them. And, of course, that causes a lot of problems when something big comes up. But we have gone for counseling; and, in fact, we're going now. . . . Since we've been going we've gotten much more in unison because we discuss the things we aren't sure of.

There are a growing number of families involved in parent-education groups. Frequently, they are church related, and many nursery schools and kindergartens are now including parent education as part of the curriculum. With many families, however, the concern with parenting frequently peaks when a family crisis involving one of the children occurs.

Unlike most occupations, parenting has no formal education or practical experience as a prerequisite. Most parents have only on-the-job-training and learn the basic skills through trial and error. Although there is a trend, starting in the junior high schools and continuing in colleges, toward a greater availability of home-care/child-rearing courses for boys and girls, complete with practical child-care experience, it is a relatively new trend. For most parents in this sample, parenting was learned through a trial-and-error method. One parent noted: "I think it's really sad that they don't teach girls more in high school about what most of them are going to end up doing, and that's being a wife and mother."

Although many parents identified child-rearing procedures they found to be successful, others expressed their concern, during the interview, over whether they were using appropriate techniques. As one mother related:

> How do you enforce what you want kids to do? I tried putting my foot down and being a dictator in my own home. "You will do this because I am your mother." That did not work. A friend of mine mentioned that she was involved with PET [parent-effectiveness training] and she thought it was a good idea. My husband and I went. The philosophy behind the parents' education group was that children are people and have just as many rights as you do. It is just that you have to teach them that they also have to be considerate for the rights of parents. It is hard to think of the fact that our children had just as much right to their life as we did. They [PET group] helped a lot. We found out what a power struggle was and how to realize that we were heading into one and cool it.

Another mother learned from experience that the conflict with her eldest child stemmed from her being inconsistent in her disciplining and too lenient:

> I wasn't going to make the same mistakes [with the second one]; . . . the main thing I found is being consistent. If you tell them not to do something once, you have to tell them that all the time. . . . If you threaten them, make sure you make a threat that you are going to keep. . . . If you're going to dilly dally around, that is where the trouble starts.

One father, however, felt that he had been too strict:

> I think probably I was too critical. Since he's been in college, he has a bit of an inferiority complex. And I'm not trying to blame him for his own shortcomings, but I think maybe we were too hard on him, being that he was first and a boy. And I think he felt we always expected a lot of him.

Of course, hindsight is much clearer than foresight! This experience gained from trial and error with the first child often provided parents with valuable insights for rearing their other children. One mother said she used physical punishment with the first one because, she explained:

> Unfortunately, being a young mother I listened to what everyone told me. I read Dr. Spock and what-have-you. If he [the first child] didn't do what I thought was exactly right, I really gave it to him. The best thing in the world is to listen to your own common sense about what to do. When you're a young mother, you're nervous and you're unsure of yourself.

Another mother completely rejected her earlier child-rearing techniques, partly as the result of maturity, partly as the result of career-related college courses she had recently completed;

> I found myself more violent with her [the first child]. It's awful to say. I couldn't control my temper as well as I can now. I look back on it and think, oh, God, it was terrible. But I have changed quite a bit. I can see what I did wrong then compared to now.

Ideal Punishment

Most parents seemed to feel that along with consistency, an important factor in adequate disciplining is making the punishment fit the crime. For the small child most parents felt that a slap on the hands or an occasional spanking was probably necessary, especially when the child was too young to reason with. Based on the questionnaire data, nearly 70 percent of the parents used physical force to resolve disciplinary problems. Over 98 percent, however, used discussion to resolve conflicts and over 96 percent reported using verbal aggression—yelling, hollering, threats. (These data will be fully discussed in Chapter 7.) Furthermore, the 70 percent reflects the use of physical force "in general," as opposed to "having never used" force. During the interviews, only one parent stated that physical punishment had never been used on their children, although several parents noted that they had used it only on rare occasions, and only with small children. Although most parents did include physical punishment in their child-rearing techniques for small children, as the children became older the parents tended to diverge in the modes they felt appropriate. One mother reported that she

> spanked when her children were real little, to teach them "don't touch." They were never children to go over to someone's house and touch things. Now that they are older, the children are required to come home earlier or restricted from using the family car.

In some families, sending children to their rooms was an effective disciplinary technique. One parent noted that the daughter "hates that with a passion. So then she begs me not to; so then I know I've got her. So she goes.

It depends on what kind of mood I'm in, how long she stays there. But that usually does it real well."

This method of discipline was not always successful since many children enjoyed their room, especially when they had a TV, radio, books, and toys there. Many parents sent the children to the bothroom since they were then deprived of playthings.

Many parents found that restricting privileges worked—for a while. In one family the threat of having to drop off the football team seemed to work. As the father told the son, who had constantly found excuses for not cutting the grass:

> I am not raising any star athlete. We are not all going to bow down because you are co-captain in football, that doesn't make you a star here. Either the grass gets cut by Monday night or the football equipment gets turned into the coach.

Although the parents noted that "it is working out fine right now," they admitted that they were not sure what would happen after football season ends. They were confident that they "would find something else."

In another family the father noted that restricting the child's use of the bike worked in the beginning. However, he soon grew accustomed to that punishment. The father noted that "when he did something wrong, I asked him how he thought he should be punished and he said 'don't let me ride my bike.' Of course, that was the easiest one because it didn't bother him so much."

Most parents admitted that they did their share of screaming and yelling. The responsibility and stresses of taking care of several small children, being confined to the home and having no one to really share the day-to-day child-rearing and housekeeping decisions, place a severe burden on young mothers in today's society. This stress is compounded because women are expected to be experts in child care, immaculate, competent housekeepers, talented hostesses, and vivacious companions to their husbands. When these often unrealistic expectations are not met, this increases the frustrations women experience. As one mother noted, "If women are honest, most of them would admit that they've done their share [of screaming]." However, most mothers, when asked about their feelings toward aggression such as yelling, screaming, and spanking, responded that they were not pleased when they resorted to these techniques, and attempted to reduce this type of verbal and physical aggression. One mother reported:

> Well, there are times when I do all of them. There are times when you cannot get through to them unless you spank. Yelling does not do any good. The only thing yelling does is make you feel better. Makes the neighbors think you're crazy. The children turn a deaf ear when you yell. Eventually, they say, "Oh, there she goes again!" Kids turn a deaf ear when you yell.

Another said:

> When I have had a hard day at work I do the bad thing that every-
> body does in coming home and taking it out on whoever is available
> and unfortunately it is the kids. I have tried to control that by
> taking a ride before I get home. Any kind of pressures that I may
> have, I will get them out before I get home.

Spanking, frequently seen as a method of last resort, was considered to
be an unsuccessful method for disciplining children. First, it appears that parents
resent having to go that far (they would like their children to respond to rea-
soning and discussion). As one mother reported:

> I feel it ends up being punishment where I have lost control. I do use
> it, but I am not happy about it. I use it, I guess, when I feel that
> nothing else at this point is going to work, and I'm not really that
> sure that a spanking is going to do it. It's sort of a desperation
> measure that I deplore.

A second problem with using physical punishment, according to several
parents, is that it really doesn't accomplish the task. Another parent suggested
that it is more effective to "punish them verbally, not punish them with your
hand or something. I found out for myself if I make them just sit in a chair
that hurts more than a beating which they cry over for a few minutes and then
forget about it...."
If the use of physical aggression is seen as the method of last resort, when
all else fails, then a parent certainly does not want evidence of this lack of
control to be public knowledge. Marks and welts on the child's face or body
are seen as "advertisements" of the parent's inability to adequately control
their child. This fear was noted by several parents. One parent said:

> Just the other day I hit Susan. I don't hit them in the face. . . .
> I'd like to. . . . I think they need it, but the older girl has braces on
> and . . . it's implanted in my mind, you know, you can't hit her
> braces because then you have to take her to the doctor. And so
> I've just gotten out of the habit.

Another noted:

> He [the father] has got a bad temper, and one time he lost his
> temper because he thought that R had stolen some money, he
> smacked his face and his hand print showed up, and he felt so bad
> about that, you know, because R had the hand print on his face.

In these interviews, which were the first contact with each family, we
discovered what parents perceived to be the sources of conflict, and the methods

they utilized in resolving them. The following question was posed: "How accurately does the in-depth interview reflect day-to-day interaction?" To answer this question, the parent-child conflicts recorded over the one-week period were analyzed.

DIMENSIONS OF PARENT-CHILD CONFLICTS

There were 49 families who participated in the recording of parent-child conflicts. Two families who were not included in the part of the study on sibling conflict, because there were no sibs at home, were included in other analyses. The discipline (or aggressive interaction) in this chapter focused predominantly on the methods parents used. There were very few reported acts of aggression by children toward their parents in this study and these tended to be verbally aggressive acts. There is, however, increasing evidence of a battered-parent syndrome involving direct abuse (physical and verbal) and indirect abuse (neglect and abandonment) by the adult child toward the elderly parent (Philadelphia *Inquirer*, April 18, 1975: 10A).

Frequency

A total of 313 incidents were recorded. The same limitations noted in the previous chapter should be observed in interpreting the data for this chapter. The frequency with which various methods were used to resolve the conflicts is shown in Table 5.1.

Based on these data, it appears that parents are more likely to resort to threats or discussion to resolve parent-child conflicts. They ignore the incident

TABLE 5.1

Frequency of Various Methods Used to Resolve Parent-Child Conflicts

Method	Percent
Hollering, yelling, screaming	15.8
Assertion, threats	29.4
Discussion	25.3
Compromise	10.9
Ignoring the incident	3.5
Restriction of privileges	10.6
Physical punishment	4.5

TABLE 5.2

Percent of Parent-Child Conflicts Considered to be Resolved Successfully by Each Method

| Method* | Outcome | | | |
	Success	Partial Success	Failure	Unknown
H	54.0	18.0	26.0	2.0
(50)				
D	66.3	17.5	18.0	8.0
(80)				
A	65.9	16.5	11.0	6.6
(91)				
C	73.5	23.5	2.9	0
(34)				
I	63.6	36.4	0	0
(11)				
R	63.6	21.2	6.1	9.1
(33)				
P	64.3	14.3	14.3	7.1
(14)				

* H = yelling, hollering, arguing, screaming; D = discussion, talking it over; A = asserting one's will, threat; C = compromise; I = ignoring; R = restriction (withdrawal of privileges, separating, sending to one's room); P = physical punishment.

or use physical punishment in relatively few cases. Caution must be applied, however, when interpreting these findings as some families did not record for the full week. In other families, not all members were present for the full week, which according to the parents, decreased the number of conflicts.

Successful Versus Unsuccessful Methods

It is of interest to investigate which of the methods listed in Table 5.1 are considered by parents to be most successful for resolving parent-child conflict. Table 5.2 presents the percentage of parent-child conflicts perceived to be resolved successfullly by each method utilized.

These data suggest that compromise is considered to be the best method for conflict resolution. Indeed, compromise is successful 73.5 percent of the time and a failure in only about 3 percent of the incidents. Hollering and yelling is considered to be the least successful mode and is successful just over half the time.

The data further indicate that out of a total of 313 parent-child conflicts, about 64.5 percent (202 conflicts) were considered to be successfully resolved. In 59 incidents, 18.9 percent, the method was considered to be a partial success. In 11.8 percent (37 incidents) the methods were considered a failure. In the remaining 4.8 percent (15) of the cases, the outcome was unknown.

There are several questions that need to be addressed. First, are there differences between the modes utilized by mothers and by fathers in disciplining their children? Second, do parents use different techniques according to the age of the child, or the family's stage in the life cycle?

The interview data suggest that parents tend to use physical punishment and restriction of privileges with younger children, and discussion and threats with older children. It should be pointed out, however, that what parents say they do and what they actually do may differ. Furthermore, the reported punishment may reflect the method used for the more memorable incidents and not necessarily those used in day-to-day minor infractions. The data presented in Table 5.3 examine mother-child and father-child conflict-resolution methods for each children's age group.

TABLE 5.3

Percent of Mother-Child and Father-Child Conflict Resolution Methods Used by Young, Adolescent, and Teenage Families

	Young		Adolescent		Teen	
	Mother-Child	Father-Child	Mother-Child	Father-Child	Mother-Child	Father-Child
Method*	(92)	(21)	(61)	(17)	(46)	(11)
H	10.9	9.5	16.4	58.5	10.9	18.2
A	39.1	28.6	24.6	5.9	32.6	27.3
R	6.5	23.8	11.5	11.8	6.5	18.2
D	26.1	14.3	26.2	11.8	34.8	36.4
I	4.4	4.8	1.8	5.9	0	0
P	4.4	9.5	11.5	5.9	0	0
C	8.7	9.5	9.3	0	15.2	0

* H = yelling, hollering, arguing, screaming; D = discussion, talking it over; A = asserting one's will, threat; C = compromise; I = ignoring; R = restriction, (withdrawal of privileges, separating, sending to one's room); P = physical punishment.

Note: Total number of conflicts is given in parentheses. A total of 16 conflicts occurred, in three families, that were not included because the children's ages covered too wide a span for accurately assigning to an age group. There were also 49 conflicts in which both the mother and father were reported to take part; these were not included in the analysis.

TABLE 5.4

Mean Mother-Child and Father-Child Conflict Resolution Scores for Young, Adolescent, and Teenage Families

Conflict	Young (N = 16)	Adolescent (N = 15)	Teen (N = 14)
Mother-child	5.8	4.1	3.3
Father-child	1.3	1.1	.8

Age

There are several interesting observations to be made from the data. First, it appears that for both mother-child and father-child conflicts, there is a consistent decrease in the number of conflicts as children's ages increase. There were 92 mother-child and 21 father-child conflicts in the younger group. In the adolescent group, there were 61 mother-child and 17 father-child conflicts. Among the teenage group the number of conflicts continued to decrease, 46 for mother-child incidents and 11 for father-child. The mean for mother-child and for father-child conflicts within each age group is listed in Table 5.4.

Further, the data would suggest that fathers appear to have considerably less conflict with children than do mothers, and these findings hold for each age group. In the young group, of the total of 133 parent-child conflicts, 69.2 percent involved mothers, 15.8 percent involved fathers, and 15.0 percent, both parents. Similar results were found in the other two age groups. Among adolescent families with a total of 94 recorded incidents, 64.9 percent involved mothers, 18.1 percent, fathers, and 17 percent, both parents. Of the 71 teenage-group conflicts recorded, 64.8 percent were mother-child, 15.5 percent were father-child, and 19.7 involved both parents.

These differences might be a function of mothers being more available and, therefore, being in the position to administer the discipline and resolve the conflict. There is some support for this position in the data. The one family in which the mother worked a second shift (4:00 - 12:00 p.m.) reported that over 80 percent of the parent-child conflicts were father-child incidents.

The data also suggest that parents do select somewhat different approaches to discipline. Mothers are more likely to resort to threats and discussion as a mode of resolving parent-child conflicts with all three groups. Fathers appear to use more varied approaches, according to the age of the children. With younger children, fathers rely on threats and restriction of privileges. With adolescent groups, fathers rely to a considerable extent on yelling and screaming. With teenagers, fathers use discussion, threats, and withdrawal of privileges.

Some of these differences may lie in semantics rather than behaviors. It should be recognized that parents may be describing the same behavior in different terms. For example, the father may bellow, "Get those chores done or no allowance," which is described as yelling, while mother's "If you don't get those chores done, no allowance," in a slightly raised voice, might be written down as a threat. Since mother recorded the data in almost all cases, it may be that mothers see themselves as speaking in slightly raised voices while fathers yell.

Are Mothers or Fathers More Successful in Resolving Filial Conflict?

The next issue to be addressed is whether mothers or fathers perceive themselves to be more successful in resolving parent-child conflict. And do these differences appear to be related to the age of the child?

In the media we are told that fathers are the authority figure—"Father knows best." Data from the interviews suggested that many mothers felt that the fathers were more successful in disciplining the children. However, the reason for father's apparent success may result as much from the limited contact children have with their father (so they are not sure how much they can get away with), as from the father being seen as the authority figure.

Regardless of the reasons, it is clear that the father is seen as more successful in handling conflicts than is the mother, as noted in the following response:

> He is more successful than I am because he is here less. That is definitely true. They hear me constantly. They hear him from 5 o'clock to 8 o'clock at night. . . . What he says goes. They listen to him better than they listen to me.

Another mother suggested that even the same approach—talking in a stern voice—had a different effect depending on who delivered the command:

> Sometimes he will raise his voice, because if he talks in a stern voice they will snap to. They just seem to know that he means business. I can talk all day long and in a stern voice and it seems to go in one ear and out the other. It is just that they hear it from me all day. They are just used to me and when he comes home this is a change in authority.

Of the 199 mother-child and 49 father-child conflicts recorded in the diaries over a one-week period, 67 percent of the mother-child conflicts and 63.3 percent of father-child conflicts were considered to be resolved successfully. This suggests that mothers, contrary to what they reported during the

TABLE 5.5

Percent of Conflicts Resolved Successfully in Young, Adolescent, and Teenage Families

Family and Conflict	Percent Perceived To Be Resolved Successfully
Young	
Mother-child	59.8
Father-child	76.2
Adolescent	
Mother-child	80.3
Father-child	58.8
Teen	
Mother-child	65.2
Father-child	45.5

interview, are slightly more likely to perceive their methods to be successful on a day-to-day basis.

There were also differences among age groups in the perceived success of methods used by fathers or mothers. These findings are presented in Table 5.5.

In the young group, 76.2 percent of parent-child conflicts were considered to be resolved successfully by fathers while only 59.8 percent of those resolved by the mothers were considered to be successful.

While the fathers appear to more successful with the young children, mothers perceived themselves to be more successful with adolescents—80.3 percent as compared to 58.8 percent of the time. It is interesting to note that fathers resorted to yelling and screaming nearly 60 percent of the time with this age group (see Table 5.3) and this method appears to be the least successful (see Table 5.2). One incongruent finding is that 80 percent of mothers perceived themselves to be successful in resolving conflicts with adolescents. This also is contrary to information provided in the interviews. According to the interviews, adolescents are seen as the real test for family stability. Perhaps it is an age where more dramatic and memorable events occur and these situations flavor the material discussed in the interview. As the nursery rhyme suggests, "When they were good, they were very, very good, but when they were bad they were horrid."

For the teenage group, mothers were considered successful 65.2 percent of the time, fathers 45.5 percent of the time. Both fathers and mothers see a decline in success with teenagers; however, mothers, who probably maintain more open communication with children, appear to be more successful in resolving these conflicts.

There appears to be a steady decline in the perceived success of fathers' resolution of parent-child conflicts as the age of the children increases. It may be that fathers are seen by younger children as unequivocal authority figures, but that as they mature they discover the vulnerability of fathers. It may also be a factor of being able to assess clear-cut successes or failures when the behavior is easily defined, for example, if the child stops teasing the dog or banging a toy. This, combined with a situation in which most fathers have less contact with small children than does the mother, with longer periods of contact, knows that "one hour from now," "tomorrow," or "next week" she will have to reissue the command.

SUMMARY

Power struggles between parent and child appear to be the basis for parent-child conflicts. With the younger child and the teenager the struggle is in defining the limits of ability, usually in terms of safety. With the young child, it involves first attempts as an unrestrained individual (that is, without playpen, crib, and so on); with the teenager, the first attempts as an independent young adult. The major concern of parents with adolescent children is the verbal attempt at independence—questioning authority but not necessarily disobeying it.

Forty-nine families recorded a total of 313 incidents: 133 in young families, 94 in adolescent families, 71 in teenage families, and 16 in families not categorized by stage in the life cycle. These conflicts tended to be resolved by threats and discussion, which accounted for 54 percent of the methods used. Based on the total sample, about 64.5 percent of the conflicts were resolved successfully. The most successful method, generally, is compromise, which is considered to be successful 73.5 percent of the time, and a failure only 3 percent of the time. The remaining percent comprised partial or temporary successes or unknown outcomes. Yelling and screaming are the least effective methods and are considered successful just over half of the time, with a failure rate of over one-fourth of the time.

There is a consistent decrease in the number of conflicts occurring as the age of the children increases. There were 133 parent-child conflicts recorded during a one-week period in the young families, with a mean of 8.3 conflicts per family. In the adolescent group there were a total of 94 parent-child conflicts with a mean of 6.27 per family. The teenage group reported only 71 conflicts with a mean of 5.07 per family. One should apply caution when interpreting these data since in some families not all family members were at home during the recording period, and in a few families the recording period was not a full week. Furthermore, not all families had the same number of members.

It appears that mother-child conflicts are more prevalent than father-child conflicts, and this finding held for each group. Mother-child conflicts accounted for 199 incidents or 63.6 percent; father-child conflicts, for 49 or 15.7 percent. The remainder was comprised of conflicts involving both parents (15.7 percent), or families not categorized by age groups (5.1 percent). However, mothers tend to have more contact with children than do fathers, and therefore are more likely to be in a position to resolve the conflict.

It may also be that in those families with a very strong authoritarian father, there were few if any conflicts, so that we may be measuring parent-child conflicts occurring in families with less clearly defined authoritarian roles. As both the husband and wife noted, on separate occasions, in one family, "There are no conflicts, he [the father-husband] makes all the decisions."

Mothers and fathers appear to utilize different techniques when disciplining children. Mothers are more prone to use threats and restriction of privileges with younger children, yelling and screaming with adolescents, and discussion, threats, and withdrawal of privileges with teenagers. Some differences, however, may result from semantics, that is, selecting different words to describe similar phenomena.

Fathers are more likely to be perceived as successful when disciplining younger children, but this perceived success diminishes with each older group. Mothers' perceived success is more variable; although it is lower than that of fathers for younger children, it is extremely high for adolescent groups. The perceived success decreases, but remains higher than fathers' success for the teenage group.

Possibly one of the major sources of marital conflict revolves around the disciplining of children, especially adolescent aged children. As one mother noted: "Before we had any adolescents, we didn't have too many arguments. We disagreed about things, but it wasn't anything we really got uptight about or upset [over] for a period of time."

The source of marital conflicts and the methods used to resolve them will be the focus of the following chapter.

We just argue over little things. We never really argue over the national debt or whether we should go to war.

Husband, married 18 years

The study of marital interaction is an important key to the understanding of family-conflict resolution. First, the methods that spouses develop for resolving conflict become patterned responses, which are then used when they discipline their children. Secondly, marital conflict that cannot be satisfactorily resolved may result in dissolution of the marital bond. This produces a single-parent family facing a whole new range of family situations such as increased economic pressure; change in parent role, which requires combining employment and child rearing; loneliness experienced by the single parent; conditions that can lead to family-related violence. Therefore, understanding marital-conflict resolution provides insights into other current and future interaction patterns within that family.

Of the 57 families in this study, six represented second marriages. Three couples mentioned that they had separated, and two mentioned that during a rocky period in their marriage, they had considered separation. One couple had separated for the fouth (and final) time just prior to the interview. As this chapter was being completed, one interviewer was notified that a couple she had interviewed had recently separated.

SOURCES OF MARITAL CONFLICT

There appear to be two major categories of conflicts between the husbands and wives in this study: picky, everyday, annoying things, and large-scale, serious conflicts. The picky things tend to be individual idiosyncratic behaviors that bother one spouse or the other. The following response is typical of these types of conflict: "Well, if I told you what we really argue over your . . . . professor will get a kick out of this. It's a gallon jug of cold water in the refrigerator in the wintertime. I want it in." Another respondent said: "We don't really have major conflicts. We just argue because he is too neat and I am too sloppy. He is a neatness nut about drawers and closets. He wants everything in a certain place and it never is."

During a joint (husband-wife) interview, the wife noted that her husband "has this terrible habit of rolling up his bathrobe and throwing it in the closet," while she "likes things where they belong." Her husband noted that his wife was "Miss Perfect, just dusting every day. Vacuuming every day. Just little things. I guess if I can't notice it (the dirt), I don't think other people can notice it."

It appears that these minor sources of irritation tend to be idiosyncratic, reflecting individual personality differences. Of course, what is labeled as picky and annoying by the researcher may be causing real pain to the person experiencing it. It seems, however, that conflicts caused by minor problems serve a function because they allow spouses the opportunity to get things off their chest without threatening the marriage.

Major conflicts, on the other hand, tend to be characterized by similarities in the causes of, and reaction to, the conflict in all families. The major categories of conflict mentioned were disciplining children (especially adolescent children); problems with in-laws; the strain of pregnancy; and changes in sex roles that are not mutually shared.

Disciplining Children

A frequent source of conflict between spouses resulted when one parent did not back up the discipline given out by the other parent. Relating a situation existing with relatives, one mother felt that kids should not be allowed to play one parent against the other:

> I had a cousin . . . his father would correct and his mother would love, [and] vice versa. The kid was, like, in a double bind and couldn't get out of it. He was playing the mother and father against each other. I'm not saying my kids haven't tried that. They still do. In fact, it happened the other day. My husband corrected him [her son] for something and he came to me to see if he could get out of it. Unfortunately for him, my husband heard him, that made it worse.

Another mother felt that in the last two or three years she and her husband had talked about disciplining the children a good bit before making any decision so that they presented a united front. She did note that in general "we got along great before they (the children) came. We've been married 25 years; and I notice as the kids are getting older, that things are getting back to the way they were, you know, when we were first married and didn't have children."

In one family, a physical fight between spouses occurred over disciplining children:

> The last disagreement probably involved something I let my daughter do. It was about two years ago. She wanted to spend Saturday night with a friend, who was not Catholic. She wanted to go to church the next day. I said okay. We told my husband what she was going to do but I was devious. I knew he wouldn't let her miss Mass. When he found out he was mad, he picked up a glass and threw it across the room, then we were physically fighting.

Conflicts over In-Laws and Pregnancy

Another source of conflicts was in-laws. Typically the struggle was between the new wife and her husband's mother. One wife suggested:

> His parents were always trying to needle the situation. For instance, she would come over and try to tell me how to raise the kids, tell me what to do for my husband and things like that, when I was really trying to make a loyal attempt to do it on my own. There was quite a bit of disagreement between us, but when they finally realized that I wasn't going to stand for what they wanted me to do, then we got along pretty well.

Most conflicts over in-laws, however, appeared to be resolved over time.

The additional responsibility of pregnancy also appears to be a source of conflicts affecting both spouses (Gelles, 1974). In fact, a high point of conflict in several marriages occurred during pregnancy. In some families the additional responsibilities that a child brings increased the pressures placed on the husband, causing conflict. In these families the husband was unable to deal with the additional responsibility a baby requires. For example, the following two cases:

> He started drinking about three weeks after we were married and I was teaching, putting him through school. Each time he found out that I was pregnant, each time he heard, he would either go away for a weekend or more. When he found out about the youngest child, that is when he had the breakdown.

> I was pregnant with my second one; he [the first husband] left and ran around with another woman. He came back; I told him I was

pregnant; he left again, and the same way with the fourth. I finally realized that he wouldn't make a living and I told him [the first husband] to leave and not come back.

In other families, the wife saw the new baby as restricting her opportunities to find a job or become involved in outside [the home] activities. In discussing her third pregnancy, one mother reported that she "hadn't planned on having another baby, and I was upset about it. During that time it seems I resented him because I was pregnant."

According to this wife the difficulty arose because "I had really been looking forward to my two children going to school. I wanted to get a job."

None of the study families report the type of physical violence that appears rooted in the husband's possessiveness and jealousy—that is, the fear that the baby will usurp the attention the husband desires—and has been referred to as intrauterine child abuse (Gelles, 1976).

THE EFFECT OF CONTEMPORARY SOCIETY ON TRADITIONAL ROLES

The women's liberation movement has had a tremendous impact on these families. Although the movement did not directly change sex roles in all families, there was evidence that the movement had raised the level of consciousness of husbands and wives.

Throughout history, the male has been placed in the superior position with regard to marital rights (see Kanowitz, 1969, and Calvert, 1974, for a discussion of the legal aspects of these marital rights). Today, with increased pressures toward equal opportunities, for both males and females, families are faced with a new set of variables. No longer are traditional role prescriptions the only ones family members are likely to fulfill. Spouses are finding that they must reevaluate the idea that the one partner, the wife-mother, will have the primary responsibility for the home and children while the other partner, the husband-father, will be considered the primary breadwinner. Illness, unemployment, unforeseen expenses, as well as the situation of children no longer requiring so much attention, all may add pressure for the women to seek increased activities outside the home through employment or volunteer work.

Ideally, if husbands and wives were truly liberated from traditional role constraints, they should have the freedom to choose from among a variety of family and occupational roles. However, social constraints as well as personal ones often limit this freedom. While many families recognize the unsuitability of role allocations assigned to husbands and wives according to tradition, very few are totally ignoring these socially sanctioned roles and instead attempt some compromise that provides a measure of flexibility.

Working Wives

Many women in the sample, 33.2 percent, were currently employed. Approximately 44.4 percent of the mothers of young families (those with children whose mean age was 8 years or younger) were employed. Further, 29.4 percent of the mothers of adolescent families (mean age 9-13) were employed; and 26.3 percent of mothers of teenage families (mean age, over 14), worked outside the home. One mother among the three families not categorized by age was also employed.

It appears that the greater number of mothers in young families who are employed may reflect the expense of starting a family as well as the increased social acceptability of dual-career wives. There is a trend, however, among the families to discontinue employment until the children are grown. Thus, the sample contained many highly educated mothers, for example, market-research analysts, teachers, analytical chemists, nurses, who were currently not employed, but preparing to return to their career in the near future.

There are many reasons for wanting to be employed outside the home. Employment provides for both men and women a sense of independence, self-assuredness, and individuality. As Gove (1972) noted, men have two major roles—family and work, providing them with two areas in which to find fulfillment. If a man is not satisfied with his home life he has his work. Women, however, traditionally have had only one major role option for finding fulfillment—the family. Many women do find a source of satisfaction in this role: "I am a graduate home economist. I decided that keeping my home and taking care of my husband and children was my occupation. I find it a full-time one because as the children get older it really gets hard."

Or, as one woman, who gave up a glamorous career for a family, and was asked by friends if she is happy staying at home, noted:

> They say, "Gosh, it must get dull." I think that any woman that stays home and takes care of a family will have to recognize that there are dull moments. I don't feel like women will ever be liberated. As long as there is marriage, the woman is going to have to answer the woman's responsibility which is still the home. I feel this way. Men were not reared, or most men in my age group anyway, to take care of a family. I feel it is a woman's responsibility no matter what else she does.

While many mothers are looking forward to resuming their careers after their children are older, others have returned to work out of necessity. Some of these mothers really prefer to be homemakers. In other families the husband resents the wife's job, but economic pressure necessitates the wife's employment. For example:

I've always liked cooking and baking and all the things that go with a family. And I really think that [among] most women that work, maybe there's some that want to be career women, but most of the ones I talk to would rather be home. But it's just a case where we have kids that are, you know, college age and you have to get out and help. I've been working for five years.

[My husband] hates it, but there's nothing he can say about it, because I wasn't a computer operator before. I was a clerk. This is a lot more money; and it's about as high as a person like me can go. And he insisted that I take the job. I debated taking the job because of the night shift, but he said that I should take it.

A number of mothers, however, desired to work because of the self-satisfaction gained from employment outside the home. It was this intrinsic value rather than extrinsic rewards that made their employment outside the home fulfilling. Among the mothers in these families there appears to be no systematic relationship between desiring to work and education levels. One wife, a waitress on the dinner shift, said she wanted to work "not just because of the money, but because I just wasn't satisfied sitting home in the house all the time; and, since I've gone to work the kids don't get on my nerves as much and we don't have as many arguments because I'm not as bored because I know I'm going to work and I know I have something to do." Another wife, a schoolteacher, expressed similar feelings: "My husband didn't like me to work. He wanted me to be a housewife, stay home and cook dinner. Well, that's not me. I felt I needed more than to be just a housewife. I should do something that's worthwhile and helpful to other people."

One mother, who has eight ex-mental patients as boarders, and is the economic provider in her home, described the advantages of developing one's own personal division of roles rather than unsuccessfully attempting to fulfill those prescribed by society, noting:

Who is to say that the man has to be the one to support the family? My husband and I have an arrangement that is agreeable to both of us. My children have grown up in this type of situation, and we have managed to raise them, support them, and help them, and feed them and clothe them this way. . . . He is good with the children. He is a good disciplinarian. He has the time to play with them. . . . We have a comparatively nice situation here where he takes the kids and gives them the attention they need and the guidance they need, and I run the [boarding] house. . . . I don't think our kids are going to suffer that much because of it. Yes, they are going to have some problems, but no worse than most kids, whose families are what you would call normal, where the husband goes to work.

Sharing Responsibilities

It appears that many families are devising alternative life styles that allow them to maximize individual development as well as benefit the entire family. Another alternative (in addition to role reversal) is utilizing shift work to allow both parents to share the child-rearing tasks. One father discussed the advantages of this option: "It's fine with me. She works because it doesn't interfere with the kids. When she is working, I am home, and when I'm working, she is home. I don't like to have my kids raised by somebody else. That's why we work the way we do."

This couple found an added advantage in that the father, who worked a night shift, was home during most of the day and was able to play with his young child, a rather unusual situation among families with small children in their neighborhood. With these additional responsibilities placed on the women who elect to work (or find it necessary to do so), many men are discovering that it is now incumbent upon them to don an apron and help with work previously defined as women's work. However, sharing these new roles is not a viable choice in some families. Unfortunately, emerging sex roles provide a source of conflict, rather than increased role flexibility in these families. For example, several wives reported that their husbands would not be willing to assume some of their chores, and they did not wish to hold two full-time jobs. The following two responses typified this:

> He wants me to go out to work and I think I have enough to do right here. He keeps telling me all the other women work. Now I'm talking about going to work, and he's not going to fix dinner. Right now he's starting to realize that maybe he doesn't want me working as much as he thought he did.

> [He] had this thing about women. He wouldn't pick up a dishtowel and dry a dish. This is a woman's job. This is what his mother did, and that's what I should do. He's unbendable.

Many wives were caught in a dilemma: they wanted to work but they felt guilty about the possible deprivation their children and husband would experience. They described an ideal situation as one where women could work part time and be with their family part time. For example, the following two responses:

> I think the thing that bothers me most is that I feel very guilty that I'm not home. My husband is great about helping me. He spends time with me . . . and even if I was home, I have a feeling she [the daughter] would be with her friends. But with the other two I was here, . . . if I had my druthers, I'd like to work part-time; so I could feel like a part of the world, you know, the community, and with adults, but still be home some of the time.

I would like to work, but I don't think I could do everything here and handle a full-time job. I am thinking seriously in the next few years of taking a part-time job, if I could find a part-time job with flexible hours or where I could stay home if I had a sick child.

Men's Liberation

It is not just women who are caught in this socially defined trap. If men are judged almost totally in terms of their occupational achievements, it places unnecessary strain on those men who are unable, or perceive themselves to be unable, to fulfill these socially defined goals.

Just because men have had it impressed upon them since early childhood that they must work and support a family does not necessarily mean that they will be able to fulfill this responsibility. One wife noted that her husband had a "fear of any responsibility for any length of time. It seems like the jobs that he went into, insurance and construction work, left him with as little time as possible around the children and the house. I have the feeling that he was getting away from the responsibility and I don't blame him for it."

Through counseling, another wife discovered that her husband felt that he had no future in his job and feared that the loss of job status would reflect a loss of "head of house" status. She related that any suggestion she made "was right away taken that I was trying to usurp his being the head of the household, which I wasn't doing at all."

Another wife reported that her husband was not happy in his job, and as many women found who are caught in this position, he was trying to develop new skills that would make his occupational role more fulfilling. His job as a maintenance man on a large estate was "not his main goal in life." The wife noted that "right now he is studying for the ministry and pastoring a small church. But the income is very small; it is not his main occupation."

Because a man's job is his major source of self-esteem, inadequacy in fulfilling this role, either actual or perceived, can be a "major family crisis." One wife reported:

We have talked about that [his job] and I have pleaded with him for about three years. I feel very guilty about it. Maybe if I were physically stronger and we didn't have constant medical expenses he wouldn't feel tied. To me that is about the saddest thing that can happen to us. It must be terrible to get up every day and face the job you hate.

In one family the only time the husband ever hit his wife was when the frustration and anxiety of being out of work resulted in a feeling of loss of status—a finding supported by O'Brien (1971).

Because society places on the husband the responsibility to provide for the family, he does not have the option of deciding between full-time or part-time work, or to take time off to develop new skills. This results in many men being trapped in jobs they can neither stand nor leave. This trapped feeling pervades all family interaction and results in strained marital interactions. Even when the wife urges and supports her husband in seeking a new job, his feelings of responsibility for the family's well-being hinder this change. One wife noted:

> I would be willing just to sell everything and start someplace else. For him it is easier said than done, because he feels that he is responsible for the rest of us and how we make it. . . . He is a very good father and a good husband, but he is just sort of lost.

Equalizing Resources

Utilizing a resource-theory framework (Blood and Wolfe, 1960), the wife's ability to find employment should provide her with an additional resource. This does not necessarily mean, however, that there will be fewer conflicts in a family because both husband and wife are more equally endowed with such resources as education, employment, or leadership qualities, that is, strong, dominant personalities. In fact, these families may find that they have more conflicts since the traditional role prescriptions no longer fit their circumstances.

In one family, a higher level of education and a dominant personality provided one wife with the resources needed to gain an upper hand at least some of the time:

> I think of the times I left him and I came back. I think we were separated about a year each time, and I came back and the problem just wasn't straightened out at all, [and] then the third time he left me with the three kids, no money, no job, nothing, so I borrowed money, went on welfare, I sold everything and made up my mind that I wasn't going to run back to my family again, that I was going to stand on my own two feet, which I did. I got substitute [teaching] work, and then I got the [regular-teaching] job at an elementary school and when he came back I told him I learned to get along without him. I learned that I could take care of myself.

There is some indication that in families with clearly defined traditional roles there may be fewer expressed conflicts, as long as participating in these assigned role obligations fulfills the mutually shared expectations of both husband and wife. As one husband in the study noted, "There is no conflict, I make all the decisions." In this family the husband has an advantage. His wife is not employed and he exercises complete control over her social life. And since his wife does not overtly question his authority, there is no conflict over roles.

It appears that many wives and husbands are willing to endure the inevitable conflicts occurring during this era of transition resulting from nontraditional allocation of familial, social, and occupational roles. As one wife suggested:

> I think women have become more aware of themselves, maybe women's liberation and the whole bit, you know. The whole thing that you can be outside the house and you can still be a good mother and wife. And that you should have interests outside. My husband was brought up where there was [a] totally husband domineered situation. The wife never did anything except to say "Yes, dear." Women have changed a lot and I think this is hard for men to realize, yet the women aren't going to go back again. This has ramifications for everybody's marriage.

Furthermore, many parents recognize that times are changing and are hopeful that their children will have more role options open to them. As one parent expressed it:

> K is lucky because she can either stay single and enjoy herself and do her own thing, or she can get married and support her husband, and nobody is going to say one way or the other. It is not going to be a cut and dry thing that the husband had to do this and the wife that. And in that respect, I think that it is good, I really do.

DIMENSIONS OF MARITAL CONFLICT
AND ITS RESOLUTION

Three sources of data were utilized to provide insights into the methods used to resolve marital conflict: interviews, questionnaires, and the diaries. These three sources are analyzed in an attempt to answer five questions: How are marital conflicts resolved?; How frequently did spouses use each method?; Who did more damage?; How successful was each method?; Are there life-cycle differences in marital conflict?

How Are Conflicts Resolved?

As was found for other intrafamily conflicts, a wide range of techniques are utilized in an attempt to resolve marital conflicts. Most families resort to verbal and physical force sometime in their marriage, but in only a few cases was physical force a frequent occurrence.

Utilizing the data from the in-depth interviews, the more typical aggressive and abusive methods of marital interaction are examined. It was found that some couples attempt to "outholler" each other. One husband described the interaction as follows: "Like when she starts, I will walk away. I can do that for about a half hour, and if she stops, then I'm okay. But if she keeps it up, then I will have to start hollering and screaming too."

Hitting is also used on occasion. However, this method frequently escalated rather than resolved the fight. One wife noted:

> I think things would bother us for so long, . . . he would let it go until he got sore and I think the same was true with me. Things would go on and on until we couldn't face it any more and then we would get into a big argument and I would just keep needling and pushing until he would slap me to shut me up.

When the interviewer inquired whether her husband's slap did shut her up, the wife responded, "No, I would hit him back. It just ended up in a bigger argument."

Some couples resorted to throwing things such as knives, loaves of bread, "Gino's giant hamburgers," pictures, plates, pillows. Either these couples had incredibly poor aim, for they all missed the target, or the object was to gain attention rather than physically attack the spouse.

Separation is usually seen as a final attempt to correct a bad marriage. This method was used by several wives as an attention-getting device. Serving one of the positive functions of conflict, it brings the problem out in the open as suggested by Coser (1966). When the wife leaves the house, this forces the couple to address the problem and reassess their marriage. A separation also provides a cooling-off period allowing the spouses to examine the conflict-producing issue in a more neutral environment. One wife explained the benefits of this approach:

> He was working shift work and holding a part-time job and never home. It was supposed to be all for us. . . . He'd have no time for conversation. . . . It drove me up the wall. . . . Finally, I just couldn't take it; I was ready for divorce. But three days [of separation] was all I could stand. After that, things were great. He had changed. I think a separation is the greatest thing in the world for a couple who are having problems.

Not all respondents felt this way, however. When asked by the interviewer if there was any hope for reconciliation, a recently separated wife in the study replied: "No, this isn't the first time we have separated. This is the fourth. For me it is going to be the last because it is just too much for the kids mostly."

The data recorded on the questionnaires regarding methods spouses used to resolve marital conflict provide further insights on spousal conflict resolution. Discussion and verbal aggression were nearly universally used by spouses to resolve marital conflict (98 percent used discussion, 93 percent used verbal aggression). Physical aggression was used by 60 percent of the families, at least once, to resolve marital conflict. In fact, a wide range of physically aggressive acts were used in an attempt to resolve marital conflict (see Table 6.1).

Some families had engaged in all of the forms of physical aggression indicated, while others had used only one form. In some families the wife

TABLE 6.1

Types of Physically Aggressive Acts Used to Resolve Marital Conflict

Type of Physical Aggression Used	Percent of Families
Throwing things	51
	(25)
Pushing, shoving, grabbing	31
	(15)
Hitting spouse with hand	22
	(11)
Hitting spouse with something hard	12
	(6)

Note: Number of families is given in parentheses; 49 famlies participated in the questionnaire part of the study recording marital conflict and its resolution.

committed the aggressive act, in other families the husband was the aggressor, while in many families reciprocal physical aggression was displayed.

The data presented above were obtained through in-depth interviews and questionnaires completed by a spouse. The marital interaction as indicated by these instruments tended to report generalities over the total duration of the marriage. In order to provide a more accurate measurement of specific techniques used to resolve marital conflict, the source of the conflict, method used to resolve it, and the perceived success of each method were recorded for all marital conflicts occurring during a one-week period. Forty-seven families participated in this part of the study and recorded 46 conflicts reported to be resolved by the methods shown in Table 6.2.

During the one-week recording period there were no acts of physical aggression between spouses recorded. One incident of withdrawal of privileges was noted—denial of sexual relations. This appeared to be a source of conflict rather than a method of resolving a conflict or a punishment.

How Frequently Did Spouses Use Each Method?

Table 6.3 suggests that there is considerable similarity between spouses in the type of physical aggression used. These data are computed separately for husbands and wives in the sample. Thus, only one spouse in a given family may use physical aggression, or each spouse could use a different method. For

TABLE 6.2

Methods Used to Resolve Husband-Wife Conflicts during a One-Week Period as Recorded in Diaries

Method	Percent of Families
Hollering, screaming, and yelling	26.1 (12)
Threats, asserting authority	10.9 (5)
Discussion	52.2 (24)
Ignoring	6.5 (3)
Compromise	4.3 (2)

example, the 10 percent of the husbands that "hit with something hard" were not, in all instances, the spouses of the 10 percent of the wives who used the same behavior. There was, however, a tendency for spouses to use similar methods, and to a similar degree.

Although the number of families in the study is fairly small, the data seems to indicate few differences between husbands and wives in the type and frequency of physically aggressive acts used.

Who Did More Damage?

The data from the interview part of the survey, supported by reports of wife beating, suggest that men do more damage. There are several possible reasons for this:

1. Through socialization, women are taught better impulse control and they stop aggressive behavior before any damage occurs.

2. Because women are more verbal than men, men resort to physical means to support their dominant position.

3. Men are physically stronger and therefore are capable of doing more physical damage to their spouses than spouses can do to them. The mating gradient (men should be taller, smarter, physically stronger, older, and so on) would support the notion that most men are probably stronger and physically larger than their wives.

The myth of women being prepared, through socialization, for greater impulse control appears to have little support in reality, at least as far as marital fights are concerned. The data provided in Table 6.3, plus insights gained from the in-depth interviews, suggest that women are as likely to select physical violence as are the men to resolve marital conflicts. Furthermore, child abusers are more likely to be women, and women throughout history have been the prime perpetrators of infanticide (Straus, Gelles, and Steinmetz, 1973). While it is recognized that women spend more time with children and are usually the parent in a single-parent home (which is prone to increased levels of stress and strain resulting in child abuse), and that fathers in similar situations might equally abuse their children, these findings do indicate that women have the potential to commit acts of violence and under certain circumstances carry out these acts.

The second of the above points is also questionable. Although the myth of the verbally abusing, nagging woman is perpetuated in the media—mainly in comic form—the data to support this myth are lacking. There appeared to be small random differences in the use of verbal violence in the families studies. Furthermore, Levinger (1966) in his study of divorce applicants found that wives were three times more likely than their husbands to complain of verbal abuse.

It appears that the third reason for men doing more damage than their wives is more plausible. The data reported suggest that at least the intention

TABLE 6.3

The Type and Frequency of Physically Aggressive Behavior Used by Husbands and Wives

Type of Physical Aggression Used	A Few Times		Sometimes		Almost Always		Total	
	Husband	Wife	Husband	Wife	Husband	Wife	Husband	Wife
Throwing things	20 (10)	27 (13)	18 (9)	10 (5)	0	0	39 (19)	37 (18)
Pushing, shoving, grabbing	20 (10)	12 (6)	6 (3)	6 (3)	4 (2)	4 (2)	31 (15)	22 (11)
Hitting with hands	14 (7)	14 (7)	6 (3)	4 (2)	0	2 (1)	20 (10)	20 (10)
Hitting with something hard	6 (3)	6 (3)	4 (2)	4 (2)	0	0	10 (5)	10 (5)

Note: Forty-nine families participated in this part of the study.

of both men and women to use physical violence in marital conflicts is equal. Identical percentages of men and women reported hitting or hitting with an object. Furthermore, data on homicide between spouses suggest that an almost equal number of wives and husbands kill their spouse, a finding which appears to be extremely stable over time. Indeed, Wolfgang (1958) found no difference between the number of husbands and the number of wives who killed their spouse, and during 1975, 7.8 percent of the homicides were committed by wives against their husbands and 8.0 percent were committed by husbands against their wives (Vital Statistics Reports, 1976). Thus it appears that men and women might have equal potential toward violent marital interaction, initiate similar acts of violence, and, when differences of physical strength are equalized by weapons, commit similar amounts of spousal homicide. The major difference appears to be the ability to do more physical damage during nonhomicidal marital physical fights. When the wife slaps her husband, her lack of physical strength, plus his ability to restrain her, reduces the physical damage to a minimum. When the husband slaps his wife, however, his strength, plus her inability to restrain him, results in considerably more damage.

Support for this position is provided by a newspaper article describing the beating a physically weaker husband had received from his wife. This article noted that a wealthy, elderly New York banker had won a separation from his second wife who was 31 years his junior. During the 14-year marriage the husband had been bullied, according to the judge in the case, by "hysteria, screaming tantrums, and . . . vicious physical violence practiced on a man. . . ill-equipped for fist-fights with a shrieking woman." The judge noted that the husband had worn constant scars and bruises. Once his wife had shredded his ear with her teeth, another time she had blackened both his eyes, and on still another occasion, had injured one of this eyes so badly that doctors feared it might be lost (Wilmington *Evening Journal*, April 21, 1976: 2).

How Successful Were the Methods Used by Spouses?

The interview data suggested that under extreme circumstances, a spouse considers it necessary to slap a husband or wife, or to throw something to "bring them to their senses." We also know from these interviews that in day-to-day interaction this behavior would not be considered successful and probably would not be tolerated. In order to obtain an indicator of the success for each method used to resolve day-to-day marital conflicts, the data from the daily conflict-resolution sheet (that is, the diary) were analyzed. About 65.2 percent of the marital conflicts were perceived to be resolved successfully. There were 15.2 percent of cases considered to be partial or temporary successes. Failure occurred in 17.4 percent of the incidents and the outcome of 2.2 percent was unknown. The perceived success of each method used for resolving marital conflicts is presented on Table 6.4.

TABLE 6.4

Percent of Marital Conflicts Resolved by Various Methods and Perceived Outcome

| Method* | Perceived Outcome | | | |
	Success	Partial Success	Failure	Unknown
H	36.3	27.3	27.3	9.1
(11)				
D	76.9	11.5	11.5	0
(26)				
A	100.0	0	0	0
(5)				
C	0	100.0	0	0
(1)				
I	33.3	0	66.6	0
(3)				

* H = yelling, hollering, arguing, screaming, etc.; D = discussion, talking it over; A = asserting one's will, threat; C = compromise; I = ignoring.

The data suggest that although discussion is the most frequently used method, it is only successful about three-fourths of the time. Arguing and asserting authority, however, are perceived to be successful all the time—at least for the week the spouses in this study recorded conflicts. A careful analysis of these cases reveals that a pattern exists in which one spouse announces, "We are leaving the party now" or, "I am buying a new truck," and the other spouse, while disagreeing with the dictum, goes along with it.

This is closely related to ignoring the situation. The difference probably lies in whether the spouse on the receiving end attempts to interject his viewpoint, or quietly buries his feelings. In those cases where a discussion (or argument) results over the dictum, it appears that authority is asserted and the issue labeled successful, even though the spouse receiving the dictum may still not be happy over the decision. When the dictum is ignored, the party attempting to ignore it feels that this method is a failure because it has not brought the issue out in the open. Being able to air one's wishes, even if these wishes will not alter the decision, is apparently considered more successful than keeping these feelings to oneself. Success is apparently not tied to the status of winner since the spouse receiving the dictum is a loser, in the sense of not obtaining one's wishes, in both situations.

Hollering and yelling, the second most common method used to resolve marital conflicts, does not appear to be very successful. It is considered successful

in less than half the times used. This method was also found to be fairly unsuccessful in resolving sibling and parent-child conflicts.

LIFE-CYCLE DIFFERENCES

The families were divided by the age grouping utilized in previous chapters.
Of the 46 conflicts recorded, 41.3 percent occurred in young families, 32.6
percent were recorded in adolescent families, and 17.4 percent occurred in
teen families. The remaining 8.7 percent occurred in the three families that were
not categorized by age. These families were deleted from analysis based on
stages in the family life cycle. The mean number of conflicts for each group is
listed in Table 6.5.

It appears that marital conflicts decrease as the age of the children
increases. This finding is contrary to the information reported during the interview, when many respondents indicated that their major conflicts with both
children and spouse developed when their children entered adolescence.

One explanation for this descrepancy might be that the types of conflicts
occurring with the onset of adolescence are more memorable. The friends one
chooses, schoolwork, drinking, smoking, and drug usage all begin to be issues
with this age group, and while the actual number of conflicts may decrease,
the perceived seriousness of the conflict may increase. Therefore, although the
number of marital conflicts decreases as the children mature, the severity of
the conflicts, as measured by the degree of success with which they are resolved,
appears to increase during adolescence. For couples categorized as members
of young families, 79 percent of the marital conflicts were considered to be
partially or totally successful in their resolution. Among teen families, 88
percent of marital conflicts were perceived to be successfully resolved. However,
couples in adolescent families reported success only 73 percent of the time.

TABLE 6.5

Mean Number of Marital Conflicts Occurring in Young, Adolescent, and Teenage Families

Age Group	Mean
Young	1.27
	(15)
Adolescent	1.00
	(15)
Teenage	0.57
	(14)

TABLE 6.6

Methods Used To Resolve Marital Conflicts in Young, Adolescent, and Teenage Families

Age Groups	Percent of Conflicts Resolved by Each Method				
	Discussion	Hollering	Threats	Ignoring	Compromise
Young (19)	84.2	0	5.3	10.5	0
Adolescent (15)	40.0	33.3	13.3	6.7	6.7
Teenage (8)	50.0	37.5	12.5	0	0

Note: Number of families in each age group is given in parentheses.

The resolution methods used also differed according to the family's stage in the life cycle as suggested in Table 6.6. These data suggest that couples with adolescent children are less likely to use discussion and more likely to use hollering and arguing as a method for resolving marital conflict than are couples with young or teenage children. This may result in a more emotionally charged environment in families with adolescent children.

Congruency of Spouses' Reports of Physical Aggression

Of 49 families responding, 29 reported the use of physical aggression to resolve marital conflict, and 11 reported hitting and slapping. The use of physical aggression reported during the interview was compared to that reported on the questionnaire. Since the interviewer asked specifically about hitting and slapping (not throwing things or pushing), those families in which this type of physical aggression occurred were examined. The congruency of the interview data and data provided by the questionnaire is summarized in Figure 6.1.

The data suggest that when the wife is reporting in both the interview and questionnaire, there is total congruency in the description of physical aggression occurring between spouses. It is not possible to determine if the same congruency would occur if husbands reported in the interview and questionnaire. When the wife is interviewed and husband completes the questionnaire part of the study, the data reported are also fairly congruent. The only systematic difference that appears is the slight tendency of the wife to play down her husband's physical aggression (or the husband to see himself as more physically aggressive than his

FIGURE 6.1

Congruency of Reports of Hitting and Slapping by Husbands and Wives in Questionnaire and Interview

Spouse Interviewed	Spouse Completing Questionnaire	Congruency	Comment
Wife	Wife	Total	Mentions wife beating fairly often.
Wife	Wife	Total	Mentions throwing things and pushing and shoving.
Wife	Wife	–	Not specifically asked about slapping in interview.
Wife	Husband	Total	Wife reports that she is more violent, hits and throws things, reports that husband is not violent; husband reports that he had hit (rarely) and wife is more violent.
Wife	Husband	Total	Wife mentions being severely paddled as a child, she hits and yells, and husband only hit once; husband's report in total agreement.
Wife	Husband	Almost total	Wife mentions no hitting, husband notes that it is a rare occurrence.
Wife	Husband	Some	Wife mentions being slapped but says she wouldn't dare slap her husband; husband reports slapping, but notes that they do it equally.
Wife	Wife	Total	Husband threw knife once, and slaps on rare occasions; she retaliates a bit.
Wife	Wife	Total	Mentions some beating during interview, supports in questionnaire.
Husband	Husband	–	Reports that both spouses had hit; was not specifically asked about hitting during interview.
Joint	Wife	None	Both report during the joint interview that they had never slapped each other; husband had been severely physically punished as a child; in questionnaire, wife reports that both have hit with hand (sometimes) and hit with something hard (rarely).

Note: Since the general topics covered during the interview only asked about hitting and slapping, not throwing things, or pushing and shoving, the questionnaire and interview data were compared only for the 11 families reporting hitting and slapping; they represent 22 percent of the sample.

wife does). Unfortunately, the data are lacking with which to compare the effect of husbands being interviewed and wives completing the questionnaire.

Niemi (1974), in a study of how family members perceive each other, found that rather than members being influenced by the social desirability of certain behaviors, respondents tended to describe other family members' beliefs in terms of how they themselves felt. In his study, students who considered themselves to be politically liberal tended to view their parents as liberal. Applying Niemi's findings to the data in this study, it is possible that wives felt that husbands should be calm, dominant, and in control (not given to verbal or physical outbursts) while women resort to verbal and socially acceptable physical outbursts. Husbands, however, might view the use of physical force to control their wife as necessary and acceptable. Therefore, respondents were reporting their spouse's behavior in a manner that was congruent with how they felt a spouse should behave. This is a different process than simply reporting behavior according to the generally accepted norms of social desirability. If the latter process were operating, we would expect all families to deny the use of physical force, and if such behavior were reported it would represent the husband's (rare) use to control his "disobedient" wife.

It is possible that norms regarding social desirability are influencing the respondents. If they view physical force between spouses as undesirable (and most respondents did, even when they reported that it was deserved, or that it solved the problem), then it is possible that they are quite conscious of their perceived deviation from the norm. Their reports of their use of violence may be attempts to be extremely honest and may provide for them the cathartic function of removal of guilt.

Only one family in which the husband and wife were jointly interviewed reported physical aggression. In this instance, both denied the use of physically aggressive methods for resolving marital conflict during the interview. In the questionnaire, which the wife completed, both spouses were reported to have "hit" and "hit with something hard." This was verified by the data provided by the questionnaires completed by the eldest child. Although it is not possible to draw any substantial conclusions with such a small number of respondents, the multitrait, multimethod approach to data gathering on physical aggression between spouses suggests that there is a considerable degree of congruency in the reporting of this phenomenon.

Interaction between spouses would appear to be the most intimate and private interaction of the dyads studied in this research. Furthermore, physical aggression between spouses is probably considered the most undesirable and possibly most embarrassing behavior for spouses to report. In support of this point, it is interesting that there was no mention of physical aggression between spouses during a joint interview, and yet a considerable amount was noted on the questionnaire. It is possible that the undesirability of this behavior, especially if it is a frequent and continued behavior (rather than one incident that happened years ago) makes it especially difficult to discuss in front of one's spouse. The degree of congruency of different reports and different data instruments for the most sensitive area of family aggression lends substantial support to the validity of data on nonphysical conflict-resolution methods and on all methods used by other family dyads.

SUMMARY

Many couples are realizing that traditionally defined roles are no longer suitable to their life styles. However, very few are engaged in radical changes in role allocation, most couples preferring a modification of traditional roles.

One-third of the sample contained working wives, and the larger number came from younger families. While many wives chose to work—to relieve boredom or to feel more useful as a citizen—others worked out of necessity. Men expressed dissatisfaction with their occupational roles, and this dissatisfaction with roles, on the part of both men and women, was often a source of marital conflict. Pregnancy, in-laws, and disciplining the children were all seen as major sources of marital conflict.

Based on the questionnaire data, discussion and verbal aggression were nearly universally used to some degree to resolve marital conflict. Physical aggression was used by 60 percent of the families with little difference shown between husbands and wives in the type and frequency of physical aggression used. Furthermore, couples recorded a wide range of techniques for resolving marital conflict during the one-week recording period. Discussion was used over half the time and hollering, arguing, and screaming over one-fourth of the time. Ignoring the incident, threats, and compromise made up the remaining percentages. Based on the questionnaires, there was a slight decline in reported conflicts with an increase in the ages of the children. Perhaps, as was suggested by many respondents, "you learn to keep your mouth shut" as your marriage matures. However, data from the interviews seem to indicate that having adolescent children increases marital conflicts.

Over 65 percent of the marital conflicts were perceived to be resolved successfully. Failure occurred about 17 percent of the time. The methods perceived to be most successful in resolving marital conflicts during the one-week period were assertion of authority and threats, 100 percent of the time; and discussion, over three-fourths of the time. Hollering, compromise, and ignoring the situation were successful only half of the time or less.

The ideal way to resolve conflicts, according to most all respondents, was to "keep the lines of communication open," to be able to "discuss everything, be honest" without the fear of hurting the other person's feelings. Most couples felt that almost any conflict could be resolved if they could talk about it. The problem becomes a real threat to the marriage when couples keep things inside themselves and are not willing to be honest with themselves and their spouse, according to the families interviewed.

If the method spouses use to resolve marital conflict becomes patterned interaction, will the spouses then use this method to resolve parent-child conflicts? Furthermore, since children's socialization results from both observation (of their parents interacting with each other) as well as personal experience (how their parents interacted with them), will they imitate the use of these methods first with their sibs and later with their own spouse and children? The following chapter will investigate intrafamilial patterns of conflict resolution in an attempt to provide answers to these questions.

THE CYCLE OF VIOLENCE:
FROM FAMILY TO SOCIETY

I haven't seen any battered women floating around. My parents didn't do it to each other. We don't and the children don't either. They are supposed to be carry-overs from the type of family they came from. Patterns are set, and you just repeat them again and again.

Mother of five daughters

It is easy for many people to simply ignore the existence of family-related violence because they feel that it is not important to them. After all, they don't abuse their children, nor do they abuse or experience abuse from their spouse. Furthermore, they ask: "Are child abuse and severe spouse beating large-scale phenomena?" Given our finite emotional and financial resources, should family violence be given a high priority relative to other societal concerns? There are over 300,000 reported cases of suspected child abuse each year, and an estimated 2,000 children in 1975 died of child abuse (Besharov, 1975). However, 5,000 children (8.2 per 100,000) between the ages of one and 14 die in auto accidents and about 3,000 (5 per 100,000) die each year of cancer (Vital Statistics Report, 1976: 11). Although about 60 percent of the couples in this study and several others (Steinmetz, 1977a; Straus, 1973) experienced at least one fight utilizing physical force during their marriage, survey data (Steinmetz, 1977c) suggest that only 7 percent of the wives (7,000 per 100,000) and just over 0.5 percent of the husbands (574 per 100,000) experienced physical violence from their spouse to a degree that could be labeled as battering. Homicide ranks twelfth as a cause of death among adults with a rate of 10.2 per 100,000 (Vital Statistics Report, 1976: 3). However, those occurring between husbands and wives are responsible for only 15.8

percent of the total homicide rate. Of this number, wives were offenders in 7.8 percent and husbands offenders in 8.0 percent of the cases (U.S. Documents, 1969).

Unfortuantely, these findings do not relate the degree to which physical violence between family members affects all members of our society. The following discussion will focus on the relationship between violence in the home and political assassination, criminal behavior, psychological disturbances, and a continued cycle of family abuse.

The importance of occupational, familial, and social life for the healthy development of the individual cannot be underestimated. This does not mean that if one is lacking adequate development in a single area, he is a potential danger to society. We know of many brilliant individuals whose devotion to their occupation was at the expense of their home and social life, and many individuals have an adequate family and social life but are lacking in the occupational realm. The importance of membership in a social group must also not be underestimated. Numerous studies, both of middle-class/working-class industrialized societies and a variety of subcultures, attest to the importance of a sense of belonging and of social enforcement of accepted norms that one gains by membership in a social group (W.H. Whyte, Jr., 1956; W.F. Whyte, 1943; Howard, 1966; Hostetler, 1968). As the group becomes more meaningful for its members, exclusion from group activities, for example, shunning by the Amish, is a powerful punishment. Thus an individual lacking in a social group does not have a set of standards by which to measure his or her attitudes and behaviors.

Inadequacy in only one area can bring with it problems of maladjustment, and this is intensified for the individual who is lacking in all three of these important areas—work, family, and social life. By examining these deficiencies we can better understand the factors that cause individuals to strike out against themselves, their family, and society.

Since the first contact a child has is usually with his parents or guardian, it is helpful to look at this aspect since a troubled adult often was a troubled child. The Harlow experiment showed us several generations ago that successful sexual and social relationships depend on adequate mothering. Although these studies were done on primates, studies on isolated or feral children (Davis, 1947), hospitalism (Spitz, 1964), or child abuse (Gil, 1970; Wasserman, 1967) all seem to indicate that a child needs a close stable relationship with an adult capable of fostering warm interpersonal relationships. These studies showed that children deprived of affectionate care, or having no care, react like animals and appear to be incapable of human behavior and responses, and, in extreme cases, die. The importance of warm, accepting models is shown in child-abuse studies. These studies suggest that the abusive or rejecting parent was often abused or rejected himself as a child and thus is using child-rearing techniques that resemble those with which he was raised.

POLITICAL ASSASSINATION

Although there have been relatively few acts of political assassination or attempted assassinations in the United States, the costs in terms of the country's social and emotional well-being as well as potential political disruption are incalculable. It is quite possible that the time and money expended for investigations, media coverage, tributes, and memorials, as well as the number of individuals who personally suffered the loss when John F. Kennedy was assassinated exceeded the total time, money, media coverage, and personal loss expended on all homicide victims occurring from 1963 to the present. Therefore, while political assassins and would-be assassins are few in number, the cost of political assassination for all U.S. citizens is immense.*

What is generally found in the group of political assassins and would-be assassins studied is parental rejection; homes broken by death, divorce, or desertion; lack of a strong male figure to emulate; parents only marginally integrated into the community; emotional stress, enough to prevent the individual from interacting successfully with others; and individuals who are described as loners or isolates. Under these conditions, these individuals experience normlessness or anomie and display symptoms of paranoia or schizophrenia. The lack of warmth combined with family disorganization certainly had deleterious effects on the assassins' ability to form close interpersonal relationships, familially, sexually, and socially. Although Ray, Zangara, Frome, Moore, and Bremer were raised in "intact" families, these could not be described as happy homes. Zangara was forced to leave school and was put to work when only six years old. Fromme had been kicked out of her home when barely 16 years old after numerous arguments with her father (Steel et al., 1975). Bremer received violent treatment from his mother who was described by a judge as "not knowing anything about handling children" and who treated her son like "an animal" (*Newsweek*, June 5, 1972). Bremer wrote in his diary "just call me a canoe, my mother likes to paddle me a lot" (New York *Times*, May 16, 1972). Ray's parents had minor criminal records, his mother was an alcoholic, and on several occasions, the Ray children had been placed in foster homes. Moore experienced severe discipline and, "stealing" her brother's paper-route money, ran away from home (Matthews et al., 1975).

---

* The sample consists of the following political figures and their assassins or would-be assassins: Andrew Jackson/Richard Lawrence (1835); Abraham Lincoln/John Wilkes Booth (1865); James A. Garfield/Charles J. Guiteau (1881); William McKinley/Leon F. Czolgosz (1901); Theodore Roosevelt/John N. Shrank (1912); Franklin D. Roosevelt/Giuseppe Zangara (1933); Harry S. Truman/Oscar Collazo, Griselio Torresola (1950); John F. Kennedy/Lee Harvey Oswald (1963); Robert F. Kennedy/Sirhan B. Sirhan (1968); George Wallace/Arthur Bremer (1972); Gerald Ford/Lynette Alice Fromme (1974); Gerald Ford/ Sara Jane Moore (1974); George L. Rockwell/John C. Patler (1967); Martin Luther King/ James Earl Ray (1968).

The assassins from broken families also had violent childhood experiences. Sirhan's parents were described as having terrible fights, and their father often beat the children with sticks and with his fists whenever they disobeyed him (Smith, 1968). At a very early age, Lee Harvey Oswald also "found that his mother was not easy to get along with and he had to learn to cope with her frequent outbursts of temper" (Oswald, Land, and Land, 1967). Shrank's mother, after remarrying, abandoned her son to an aunt and uncle (Donovan, 1955: 129).

As a result of a lack of close, stable family ties these individuals had not developed the ability to socially interact with others and were described as loners and isolates by acquaintances and neighbors. Frequently their parents were poorly integrated into the community and thus were not influenced by conformity to standards, which community ties demands. Although six in the group studied had married, the marriages were short-lived and, for Guiteau, Patler, and Oswald, filled with strife. When Moore's fourth marriage failed, she contemplated suicide. Although described as happy, it was the second marriage for Collazo. Thus only Torresola was living in a first, intact, marital situation at the time of his assassination attempt. Of the remainder, only Shrank and Bremer ever had a girlfriend and these relationships were of a short duration.

Assassins, even those who outwardly involved themselves in activities, were described as isolates. In both social and intimate contacts, the isolation was not, perhaps, the desired state but one sought to avoid the pain of rejection. The histories of these individuals are filled with rejections both from love objects (heterosexual and homosexual) and from membership in political causes with which they identified. Only Fromme obtained any prominence, and that was after Manson and others in his "family" were incarcerated. Although accepted at first by southern society, Booth, after a time, began to lose his appeal and his social and theatrical appearances dwindled (Hastings, 1965a: 98). Oswald was rejected first by a Russian girl to whom he had proposed, next by Russia when he was denied citizenship, and later by Marina, his Russian wife (Oswald et al., 1967: 110-11). His attempts to support the pro-Castro movement in New Orleans were a total failure since he was the only member to do so in his group. Patler gave up his family to become Rockwell's confidant, but Rockwell turned against him, isolating him from membership in the inner circle of the Nazi party. Bremer's only girlfriend dated him because she felt sorry for him, but finally told him that she no longer wanted him around. Guiteau's appeal to be an ambassador was rejected by Garfield. Sirhan was rejected by his peers when in grade school. Czolgocz's queer manner and ignorance of anarchism hindered his attempt to become a member of the anarchist group and forced the leaders to place a warning in the *Free Society* suggesting that he might be a spy (Donovan, 1955: 96-97). Furthermore, the assassins and would-be assassins had failed in the occupational realm. Generally, they had held low-prestige, blue-collar jobs and were marginally employed and frequently unemployed. Although Booth was an actor from a notable family, and Guiteau was a lawyer (the only professionals in this group), both these individuals were considered incompetent by other professionals in their fields (Hastings, 1965a: 97-98, 1965a: 157). Zangara, Lawrence, and Czolgocz, and Moore, who all previously had somewhat stable employment records, left their jobs and became chronically unemployed a few years prior to their act. Since occupation is the major role by which men (and most likely career women) receive their self-esteem, failure in this area is extemely detrimental to one's self-image. A picture now emerges of individuals who received inadequate, brutal, rejecting socialization as children, who were unable to form close interpersonal ties, either familial, sexual, social, or occupational, as adults. They desired and felt they had the right to be "someone," to be important, to be recognized, and rewarded. A poignant example is Moore's recollection of her starring role in the high-school senior play, which she said was her only bit of happiness (Matthews et al., 1975). Yet their lives had been a pattern of failure. They considered their act as one that would make them famous, make them remembered by society, and eventually turn them into martyrs and heroes, who had saved their country or cause.

As young adults, however, they were chronically unemployed, held low-paying, uninteresting jobs, were unable to pursue the needed education, and thus were unable to obtain their desired type of employment. They were unable to initiate and maintain intimate relationships either within or outside marriage, or even to develop close friendships. Their life had been one failure after another with the result of a large discrepancy between their desired goals and achievement of them. The brutality and rejection suffered during childhood resulted in a tremendous cost to society for the acts they committed as adults.

CRIMINAL BEHAVIOR

Curtis (1963), in a discussion of the battered-child syndrome, expressed a concern that the battered child might become tomorrow's murderers and perpetrators of other crimes of violence. His concerns unfortunately were well founded. In numerous studies of adolescents and adults who committed acts of criminal violence, brutal child-rearing techniques and witnessing parental violence during childhood emerged as common early-childhood experience. Satten, Menninger, and Mayman (1960) and Duncan et al. (1958) noted a consistent pattern of relentless brutality in childhood backgrounds of individuals who committed homicide. In a comparison of ten adolescents, who committed homicide, with a control group, a statistically significant proportion were exposed to parental brutality and to violence or murder in their home environment (Sendi and Blomgren, 1975), findings which were supported by Duncan and Duncan (1971) and Easson and Steinhilber (1961). A consistent pattern of personal experience with violent death, and extremely unfavorable home conditions were found to exist in the 25-year study of 33 adolescents who killed (Bender, 1959). Sargent (1962), in another study of children who committed homicide, found that not only was a parent guilty of extreme cruelty toward the child, but that other family members supported, unconsciously perhaps, the parent's behavior. He suggests (1962: 35), "The child who kills is acting as the unwitting lethal agent of an adult (usually a parent) who unconsciously prompts the child to kill so that he can vicariously enjoy the benefits of the act." Using a case study for illustrations, Sargent related the story of a 16-year-old who killed his stepfather with a shotgun when the stepfather, in a drunken rage, dared the boy to try and stop him from beating the boy's mother. In another case, a 14-year-old boy shot his father in an attempt to stop the father from beating the mother with a belt. During the beating the mother requested that the boy "get his rifle and put a bullet in it," a request she later reported was issued as a threat she hoped would stop the beating rather than as a suggestion to kill the father (1962: 38).

In some instances the murderous attack is a form of retribution. The victim had been the perpetrator of acts of brutality toward the child and other family members. The child, by murdering the parent, hopes to save his family and himself from further acts of brutality. An in-depth study of adolescents who committed parricide revealed that the parent was cruel, physically abusive to the perpetrator, and frequently beat other members of the family, particularly the child's mother (Tanay, 1975: Sadoff, 1971). In an evaluation of the backgrounds of 53 perpetrators of homicide, Tanay (1969) noted that nearly 70 percent had a history of violent child rearing. This lack of nurturing during childhood apparently hinders the formation by these individuals of close intimate relations as adults, since they frequently vent their hostility on those closest to them. Of their victims, Tanay (1969) notes, only 15 percent were strangers, 45 percent were a spouse or lover, 11 percent a relative, and 30 percent a friend. Furthermore, less than 60 percent of the time a quarrel immediately preceded the act and in nearly 30 percent of the homicides no emotional interaction occurred before the homicide.

In a study of 40 respondents who were brought to hospital emergency rooms as a result of violent altercation and 40 respondents who served as a control group, Climent and Ervin (1972) found that three-fourths of the violent group were assaulted by their fathers as compared with one-sixth of the control group. Furthermore, over one-seventh of the violent group (9 out of 31) were assaulted by their mothers while only one out of 39 of the control group experienced assault.

Palmer (1962), in a study of 51 murderers and their brothers, found murderers were more likely to have suffered severe physical beatings, serious illness, and traumatic incidents than were the control (brother) group. Albert DeSalvo, the Boston strangler, who confessed to raping, sexually mutilating, and murdering 11 women, was reported to be motivated by a "consuming rage . . . uncompromisingly directed against his drunken, brutalizing father who had regularly beaten him, his mother and the other children during a wretched youth" (Brownmiller, 1975: 204). Hartogs (1951: 167-68) noted that 92 percent of sex offenders studied had experienced frequent and severe beatings from their parents with "razor straps, sewing machine straps, electric cords, broom sticks and iron bars." In a comparison study composed of delinquents and criminals who were not sex offenders, 62 percent had experienced severe brutality. Finally, a study of Nazi war criminals suggests that they experienced a childhood of rejection and physical beatings (Bellak, 1970).

Not all violence is labeled as a criminal act as suggested in Chapter 3. Some violent acts are considered to be justified or even socially desirable behavior. Sears (1961) found that physically punitive discipline that produced antisocial aggressiveness in preschool children was frequently transformed into prosocial aggression (using aggression in socially acceptable ways) in adolescent children. In a study of the family backgrounds of Green Berets and war resisters, Mantell (1974) found that severe and frequent beating (between once a week and twice a month) from their fathers and threats or use of violence between spouses typified the family environment of members of the Green Berets. Furthermore, members of the Green Berets showed a preference for aggressiveness and violence during adolescence that was later transformed into prosocial aggression via Green Beret membership. War resisters, however, showed little adolescent aggressiveness. Their parents never used or threatened to use physical violence to resolve marital conflicts and they rarely used physical punishment as a child-rearing technique.

PSYCHOLOGICAL PROBLEMS

Schreiber (1973: 211) relates the following story that illustrates the psychological problems that can be created by violent childhood experiences:

> Hattie would "slap her daughter and knock the child to the ground . . . would fling Sybil across the room, once sufficiently violently to dislocate one of the child's shoulders . . . would give Sybil a blow on the neck with the side of her hand, on one occasion severely enough to fracture Sybil's larynx. A hot flat iron was pressed down on the child's hand, causing a serious burn. A rolling pin descended on Sybil's fingers. A drawer closed on Sybil's hand. A purple scarf was tied around Sybil's neck until she gasped for breath. The same scarf was tied around her wrist until the hand became blue and numb.

This horror story becomes still more frightening and repulsive when it is realized that it represents the real-life experiences of a woman so brutalized as a child that she retreated into 16 separate personalities for survival.

This is not an isolated incident. Retreating into another personality and suicide appear to be attempts to remove oneself from the brutality being experienced. Gayford (1975), in a study of wives who had experienced severe beatings from their husbands, found that half of the wives attempted suicide or self-mutilation. Bender and Curran (1940) note that suicidal preoccupations are often associated with a family background of violence and death. In a study designed to ascertain the likelihood of carrying out homicidal threats, MacDonald (1967) found that a childhood background of parental brutality, parental seduction, childhood fire setting, cruelty to animals, and arrest for assault were factors in the backgrounds of three groups studied. These groups selected for comparison consisted of patients admitted to a psychopathic hospital for verbal homicide threats; convicted criminal homicide offenders; and psychiatric patients at a veterans administration hospital. The findings suggest that violent childhood experiences are a factor in a wide variety of psychopathological, psychological, and criminal behaviors. And, further, that when homicidal threats were accompanied by suicidal threats or attempts, they were less likely to be carried out. This suggests that physically violent early-childhood experiences result in violent aggressiveness in adulthood either toward oneself or others.

Family Violence: Continuing the Cycle

In an extensive study of psychological and sociological factors in the backgrounds of children and adolescents who kill, Bender and Curran (1940: 321) note: "If the reaction pattern of the whole family is one of violence and aggression with which the child both identifies himself and must defend himself against, the child may react with overt acts of violence calculated to cause death."

The backgrounds of 100 battered wives studied by Gayford (1975) revealed that 51 percent of their husbands had been exposed to models of family violence; 54 percent were violent toward their children; and 33 percent had been in prison for committing violent acts. Twenty-three percent of the wives in this study had experienced violence in their childhood and witnessed marital violence between their parents, and 37 percent of them were violent toward their children. A secondary analysis of a large national representative sample (Owens and Straus, 1975) provides evidence to support the assumption that the more an individual is exposed to violence both as an observer and a victim during childhood, the more likely the individual is to be violent as an adult. Gelles (1976) reported that 66 percent of the women who had observed spousal violence in their family of orientation were victims of wife beatings in their family of procreation. However, 46 percent of the women who had never seen their parents fight physically also experienced violent attacks from their husbands.

In a study covering three generations, Silver, Dublin, and Lourie (1969) noted that in 34 cases of child abuse, physical violence between spouses or toward another child was found in more than half the cases. In 20 of the 34 cases multiple episodes were recorded. The researchers noted that these abused children were already known to the courts for truancy, delinquency, and assault with a deadly weapon. The authors also suggest that in some cases the abused child, who identifies with the victim, later becomes the wife-beater's wife, the person attacked and beaten. Oliver and Taylor (1971) studied the backgrounds of 49 family members who were related to a three-month-old, severely battered infant. Their investigation, which covered five generations, revealed that a majority of these individuals had suffered physical and emotional abuse. Milowe and Lourie (1964) note that the personality of the child may actually result in the child's inviting others to hurt him.

There is much data supporting the premise that abusive parents were often abused as children. Wasserman (1967), Bryant (1963), Craft (1969), and Zalba (1966), in studies of abusive parents, found that many abusive parents not only had witnessed violence in their homes while growing up but were also victims of parental brutality as children. There is an accumulation of support for the thesis that the aggressive and abusive behavior learned by children in their family of orientation provides the foundation for many physically abusive acts as adults. As the data above suggest, not only does this behavior frequently occur in the form of abusing one's own children or spouse, but it also constitutes other violently aggressive crimes such as rape, assault and battery, and murder.

One problem with these studies is that the phenomena have been studied on a sample of respondents who have committed these acts, and therefore do not accurately reflect the effect of generational transmission of physical abuse on a more representative sample. For example, we know that a certain proportion of child abusers were abused as children. We do not know, however, how many abused children grow up to be loving parents. We also have a paucity of information on the conditions that would cause a parent who had not been abused as a child to use this method on their own child. Evidence from clinical studies as well as insights provided by the respondents in this study suggest that behavior may not be used by adults in the same context as this behavior was witnessed or experienced as a child. For example, an individual who had been severely beaten as a child may abhor the idea of beating his own child, and yet beat his wife. Similarly, one who had received moderate punishment but witnessed physical aggression between his parents may avoid physical aggression with his spouse, but use it liberally on his child. Therefore, it is necessary to investigate the extent to which a variety of conflict-resolution methods appear to be transmitted intragenerationally and intergenerationally among a representative sample of families rather than a sample composed of families labeled as deviant.

THE EXISTENCE OF PATTERNS OF INTRAFAMILY
CONFLICT RESOLUTION

The following research question will provide the focus for examing these intragenerational and intergenerational patterns of conflict resolution: Is there a similarity between the methods husbands and wives use to resolve marital conflicts, the methods they use in disciplining their children, and the methods their children use to resolve sibling conflicts?

There was much descriptive data from the interviews to provide supporting evidence for the existence of family patterns of conflict resolution. For example, one mother, while discussing her daughters' interaction with each other, related:

> We never spanked very much, though we have on occasion when they were little. . . . We probably spanked C more than the others, and maybe that's the reason she is taking it out on her younger sister. I hadn't really thought about it before but it might very well be.

Another respondent noted how her yelling at her husband developed into a pattern she then used on the children: "He just didn't understand me. I had to yell at the top of my voice before I would get his attention. It just developed from that and I just carried it on with the kids."

Literature on child abuse and role modeling suggests that the disciplining techniques used on parents when they were children are often the techniques they resort to when disciplining their own children. This idea was commonly expressed by parents as indicated by the following:

> When I was a child, my father would warn us two times, and after the second time there was no more warning. We would get it with the hand. Maybe that is the principle that I have picked up, but that is the way I feel, that if you are warned at least twice, then the third time something has to be done about it.

One woman, when asked if her husband's family used slapping or screaming to resolve family conflicts, stated "none whatsoever." She described the verbal and physical aggression on her side of the family as follows:

> Oh, I had my fair share of lickings from my mother. She is short tempered like I am. I am a yeller. My husband will sit and talk with them [the children]. He will try to reason as to why they can't do everything they think they can; whereas, I just go around blowing off.

There was also evidence to suggest that the way respondents had seen their mother and father interact had an influence on the way they interacted with

TABLE 7.1

A Comparison of the Percent of Parents and Percent of
Children Reporting the Use of Discussion, Verbal
Aggression, and Physical Aggression to Resolve
Conflicts in Family of Orientation (G_1) and
Family of Procreation (G_2)

Methods Used by Each Dyad	Family of Orientation (G_1)[a]	Family of Procreation (G_2)[b]
Husband-Wife		
Discussion	95.8	98.1
Verbal aggression	89.6	92.5
Physical aggression	45.8	64.4
Parent-Child		
Discussion	97.9	98.1
Verbal aggression	95.7	96.2
Physical aggression	61.7	69.2
Sibling-Sibling		
Discussion	97.6	98.1
Verbal aggression	95.1	96.2
Physical aggression	65.9	94.3

[a] Reported by parent.
[b] Reported by child.

their spouse. In a discussion on physical aggression between spouses, one wife
noted: "I have thrown things. My mother used to throw things." Her husband
did not seem to find this interaction out of line, noting that his mother also
resorted to throwing things.

In order to empirically test the research question stated above, the data
obtained from the parents and child were analyzed. The conflict-resolution
techniques used by the respondents were measured by a series of statements
regarding conflict resolution between mother and father, mother and child,
father and child, and child and each sibling (see Appendix A).

These data were provided by the parent on the methods used in their
family of orientation (G_1), and the child on the methods the parents used in the
family of procreation (G_2). Thus, data for three complete generations—grandparents, parents, and child—were obtained to enable comparisons of both
intergenerational and intragenerational patterns of conflict resolution.

Table 7.1 compares the percentage of each generation using discussion,
verbal aggression, and physical aggression to resolve intrafamily conflicts as
reported by parents and children. These percentages reflect families who noted

on the questionnaire that they had used, at least once, a particular method, but do not, however, reflect the frequency or the degree to which each method was used.

The findings suggest that nearly all families in both the grandparent and parent generation have used discusssion and verbal aggression to resolve conflicts. The physical-aggression scores appear to have the widest variability. Nearly 95 percent of the respondents in the parent generation (G_2) reported use of physical aggression to resolve a sibling conflict; 69 percent of the children reported the use of physical modes to resolve parent-child conflict, and 60 percent reported that their parents had used some form of physical aggression. The percent using physical aggression in the grandparent generation (G_1) followed a similar trend, with highest physical-aggression scores reported for resolving sibling conflict, the lowest for resolving marital conflict.

One interesting finding is the similarity between the percentages reported by the parent for (G_1) and those reported by the child for (G_2). The only large differences between generation occurred in the use of physical aggression to resolve conflict. Rather than indicating that families are becoming more physically violent with each succeeding generation, these differences probably reflect the greater time between occurrence of the behavior and reporting the behavior. While the parents are reporting retrospective data on events that occurred perhaps 20 or 30 years ago, children are reporting relatively current events. It is possible that the minor incidents of physical aggression are more likely to be forgotten over time.

It is important to note the influence of social sanctions on the percentage of families, in both generations, reported to have used physical force to resolve intrafamilial conflict. It appears the fighting between children is considered inconsequential and, as illustrated in preceding chapters, is likely to be considered normal (or even expected) behavior. Therefore, in the United States, sibling aggression does not have strong social sanctions against it. It is not surprising that physical aggression between siblings has the highest percentage, with 94 percent of the children reporting that they have used physical means to resolve conflicts between their brothers and sisters.

Social sanctions discouraging the use of physical force to resolve parent-child conflicts apparently are also weak. Nearly 70 percent of the children reported that their parents used physical force to discipline them. As one mother suggested "There are little mean streaks that I think have to be spanked out."

Although the percentage of children reporting that their parents use physical modes to resolve marital conflicts was the smallest percentage recorded, over 60 percent of the spouses had used physical aggression to resolve conflicts in G_2. It appears that even among spouses, sanctions prohibiting the use of physical force are weak since a considerable number of families have resorted to verbal and physical aggression to resolve conflict. Findings similar to those reported above were found in other studies (Steinmetz, 1974b, 1977a) using both a U.S. and a Canadian sample.

TABLE 7.2

A Comparison of Methods Used to Resolve Marital and Filial Conflicts as Reported by Child and by Parents (in percent)

		Method	
Relationship	Discussion	Verbal Aggression	Physical Aggression
Husband-Wife[a]	98.0	93.9	61.2
Mother Father[b]	98.1	92.5	60.4
Parent-Child[a]	96.2	96.2	84.6
Child-Parent[b]	98.1	96.2	69.2

[a] Reported by parent.
[b] Reported by child.

Similarities Between Parents' and Children's Report

Using the data from the two questionnaires, it is possible to compare the parents' report of how they resolved marital conflict with the children's report of how their parents resolved marital conflict. In addition, it is possible to compare the parents' and children's report of how parent-child conflicts are resolved within the same generation. The findings for marital-conflict resolution as reported by both the parent and the child suggest amazing congruency. Parent-child interaction as reported by both the parent and child also show considerable similarity as indicated in Table 7.2.

The only dissimilarity was in the reporting of physical aggression, and probably can be accounted for by the child's inability to recall events that occurred in early childhood, for example, spankings received before age three or four years. It should be noted that comparing group percentages has limitations. Although percentages for the total group as reported by the children may be similar to group percentages reported by parents, the similarities in percentages may be the result of different members within the groups, but not necessarily members of the same family, who are reporting the phenomena.

Since nearly the total group of both children and parents reported the use of discussion and verbal aggression, and a high proportion reported physical aggression, the degree of potential error is most likely small. This is supported by the analysis of husband-and-wife violences (see Figure 6.1) and additional analyses, below, which suggest congruency between reporters.

Intergenerational Similarity of Conflict
Resolution Methods

In order to ascertain intrafamilial patterns of conflict resolution, the husband-wife scores were dichotomized, using the midpoint, into high and low group for each of the three major categories of conflict resolution: discussion, verbal aggression, and physical aggression. The dichotomization for discussion (items A-D in the questionnaire), verbal aggression (items E-H), and physical aggression (items I-N) was independent (see Appendix A for questionnaire).

TABLE 7.3

Mean Parent-Child and Sibling-Sibling Discussion, Verbal Aggression, and Physical Aggression Scores for Families with High and Low Husband-Wife Discussion, Verbal Aggression, and Physical Aggression Scores, for G_1 and G_2

Generation	Low Group	High Group	p (two-tailed)
Husband-Wife Discussion Scores			
G_1[a]			
Parent-Child	6.22	7.64	.10
Sib-Sib	6.53	6.62	ns
G_2[b]			
Parent-Child	7.87	8.25	ns
Sib-Sib	6.10	6.90	ns
Husband-Wife Verbal Aggression Scores			
G_1			
Parent-Child	3.55	5.78	.01
Sib-Sib	5.24	5.67	ns
G_2			
Parent-Child	5.50	6.51	.10
Sib-Sib	6.90	7.48	ns
Husband-Wife Physical Aggression Scores			
G_1			
Parent-Child	1.04	3.10	.02
Sib-Sib	2.36	5.13	.05
G_2			
Parent-Child	1.45	3.27	.01
Sib-Sib	6.36	9.60	.02

[a] Reported by parent.
[b] Reported by child.

The mean scores for parent-child conflicts and sibling-sibling conflicts were then calculated within each of the above groups. This procedure was used for both the grandparent (G_1) and parent (G_2) generation.

Although not all findings were at the generally accepted levels of significance, the patterns shown in Table 7.3 support the thesis of intragenerational patterns of conflict resolution. Those grandparents (G_1) who used low amounts of discussion to resolve marital conflict, also used lower amounts of discussion to resolve parent-child conflicts than did grandparents who use high amounts of discussion in resolving marital conflicts (6.22 versus 7.64). Their children also used lower amounts of discussion to resolve sibling conflict as compared with the sibs whose parents were categorized as high in discussion (6.53 versus 6.62). These same patterns were found in the parent generation (G_2) and held for verbal and physical aggression in both generations. The strongest relationship appears to be in the use of physical aggression. Perhaps all families use discussion and verbal aggression to a similar degree, while the use of physical aggression clearly identifies two distinct groups of families.

It would appear from the data in Table 7.3 that the method spouses use to resolve marital conflict is similar to that which they will use to discipline their children, and to that which their children will use when interacting with siblings. If this pattern continues, it would be expected that the methods sibs use to resolve conflicts within their family of orientation would be similar to that which they will use to resolve marital conflict when they marry, or to that which they will use to discipline their children, and to that which their children will use when interacting with siblings, thus continuing the cycle.

Correlations

The above analysis focused on group trends, and may not account for differences in families whose scores are close to the midpoint (the method by which the groups were dichotomized). In order to provide additional support for the thesis that there exist intrafamilial patterns of conflict resolution, Pearsonian product-moment correlations between husband-wife and (1) mother-child, (2) father-child, (3) sibling-sibling were computed for discussion, verbal aggression, and physical aggression scores in G_1 and G_2. These results, presented in Table 7.4, are in the predicted direction and are highly significant for most relationships.

The higher correlation for both G_1 and G_2 on the dimensions of verbal and physical aggression tend to occur between husband-wife and mother-child, and husband-wife and father-child. This indicates a direct transfer of mode of conflict resolution by the actor from one object (spouse) to another (child). The correlations between husband-wife and sib-sib tend to be lower and possibly reflect imitation, that is, using the modes of conflict resolution that have been

TABLE 7.4

Correlation Between Husband-Wife and Mother-Child, Father-Child, and Sibling-Sibling on Measures of Discussion, Verbal Aggression, and Physical Aggression, for G_1 and G_2

Relationship and Method Used, G_1 and G_2	Husband-Wife Discussion	Husband-Wife Verbal Aggression	Husband-Wife Physical Aggression
Discussion			
Mother-child			
G_1[a]	.40 (.002)		
G_2[b]	.34 (.01)		
Father-child			
G_1	.40 (.003)		
G_2	.51 (.001)		
Sib-sib			
G_1	.41 (.005)		
G_2	.22 (.07)		
Verbal aggression			
Mother-child			
G_1		.55 (.001)	
G_2		.27 (.04)	
Father-child			
G_1		.25 (.05)	
G_2		.36 (.006)	
Sib-sib			
G_1		.09 (ns)	
G_2		.14 (ns)	
Physical aggression			
Mother-child			
G_1			.48 (.001)
G_2			.34 (.009)
Father-child			
G_1			.63 (.001)
G_2			.55 (.001)
Sib-sib			
G_1			.44 (.003)
G_2			.32 (.02)

Note: Levels of significance are in parentheses.
[a] Reported by parent.
[b] Reported by child.

TABLE 7.5

Correlation Between Mother-Child, Father-Child, and
Sib-Sib on Measures of Discussion, Verbal Aggression,
and Physical Aggression, for G_1 and G_2

Method	G_1[a] Sib-Sib	G_2[b] Sib-Sib
Discussion		
Mother-child	.51 (.001)	.43 (.001)
Father-child	.53 (.001)	.46 (.001)
Verbal aggression		
Mother-child	.17 (ns)	.41 (.001)
Father-child	.54 (.001)	.32 (.01)
Physical aggression		
Mother-child	.41 (.004)	.53 (.001)
Father-child	.40 (.008)	.38 (.003)

Note: Levels of significance are in parentheses.
[a] Reported by parent.
[b] Reported by child.

observed being used by others (the parents). This suggests that experiencing
verbal or physical aggression directly either as perpetrator or victim has a greater
influence on the subsequent use of aggression with another person. This thesis
is supported by comparing the correlation for discussion, verbal aggression, and
physical aggression between parent-child and sib-sib for each generation (see
Table 7.5).

Correlations were also computed between the generations on the combined husband-wife, parent-child, and sib-sib scores, providing a measure of
relationships between generations. The intergeneration correlation for discussion
was .27 (p = .02); for verbal aggression, .44 (p = .001); and for physical aggression, .24 (p = .04).

These data suggest that conflict-resolution methods are transmitted intergenerationally, as well as intragenerationally, thus continuing the trend for the
three generations measured in this sample.

A Typology of Family Patterns of Conflict Resolution

Since it is likely that some parents might use a combination of methods,
for example, high verbal aggression, but low physical aggression, the sample
was categorized according to the husband-wife scores on both the verbal- and

physical-aggression dimension. Unfortunately, the sample was too small to develop a typology utilizing all three modes: discussion, verbal aggression, and physical aggression. In another study (Steinmetz, 1977a) discussion was included and most patterns were found to be highly significant. Using verbal and physical aggression resulted in four basic types of problem-solving families: screaming sluggers—parents who are both highly verbally and physically aggressive; silent attackers—parents who are not verbally aggressive but use high amounts of physical aggression (the actions-speak-louder-than words type); threateners—parents who use verbal aggression and threats, but are low users of physical

TABLE 7.6

Mean Parent-Child and Sibling-Sibling Verbal and Physical Aggression Scores When Categorized According to Husband-Wife Verbal and Physical Conflict-Resolution Scores, for G_1 and G_2

Family Type	Type of Aggression	Parent-Child Score		Sib-Sib Score	
G_1[a]					
Pacifists	verbal	3.17	(22)	5.32	(16)
	physical	0.74		4.14	
Threateners	verbal	5.43	(7)	5.50	(6)
	physical	1.25		1.03	
Silent attackers	verbal	3.50	(3)	2.33	(1)
	physical	0.42		0.33	
Screaming sluggers	verbal	5.29	(17)	5.41	(15)
	physical	3.16		5.22	
G_2[b]					
Pacifists	verbal	4.81	(18)	6.70	(18)
	physical	1.08		5.45	
Threateners	verbal	4.99	(8)	7.13	(8)
	physical	1.45		8.42	
Silent attackers	verbal	5.72	(11)	7.27	(10)
	physical	2.08		6.68	
Screaming sluggers	verbal	6.98	(12)	7.66	(12)
	physical	3.76		11.54	

Note: Number of cases is given in parentheses.

[a] Because of the small cell size, anova was possible only for parent-child verbal (p = .01) and parent-child physical (p = .08).

[b] Anova: Parent-child verbal = ns; physical, p = .01; sibling-sibling verbal = ns; physical, p = .08.; t's were computed between the two extremes: pacifists (low verbal, low physical) and screaming sluggers (high verbal, high physical). For parent-child, verbal, p = .01; physical, p = .01. For sibling-sibling, verbal = ns; physical, p = .011.

aggression; and pacifists—parents who are low in both verbal and physical aggression. It should be noted that these titles for types of problem-solving families are only offered as illustrative aids and are not to be interpreted as negative (or positive) descriptions of family behavior. In order to ascertain the relative positive or detrimental effect of each type of interaction, considerable additional research is needed.

The mean verbal and physical scores for parent-child and sib-sib were then computed within each of the four types of conflict-resolution patterns. The findings presented in Table 7.6 are most impressive between those families who use high amounts of both verbal and physical aggression (screaming sluggers) and those families who are low users of verbal and physical aggression (pacifists).

For screaming sluggers in G_2, the parent-child verbal and physical scores were 6.98 and 3.76 respectively, while parent-child verbal and physical scores of 4.81 and 1.08 were computed for pacifists. The sib-sib scores for these two groups also differed significantly, with the screaming sluggers receiving verbal scores of 7.66 and physical scores of 11.54 while the pacifists' scores were 6.70 and 5.56 for verbal and physical aggression.

All scores followed the predicted pattern. High verbal husband-wife interaction resulted in high verbal parent-child and sib-sib interaction. The same patterns held for low verbal interaction and high and low users of physical aggression, in both the grandparent (G_1) and parent (G_2) generations and represent data provided by two distinct sets of informants, that is, parent and child. Furthermore, this is the third study to use this checklist for developing intergenerational patterns, both with a U.S. sample and cross-culturally (see Steinmetz, 1974b, 1977a). The items and methods of administration fulfill the criteria of "face," "pragmatic," and "concurrent" validity (Campbell and Fiske, 1959; Seltiz et al., 1959). In addition, the conflict-resolution items were found to have an adequate level of internal-consistency reliability (Straus, 1974: 18).

Continuity of Family Patterns of Conflict Resolution

Correlations provide support for the transmitting, generationally, of conflict-resolution methods between specific dyadic units. If, however, the methods used are part of a whole matrix of family interaction, then a measure is needed that simultaneously compares the relationship between all dyads. Osgood's and Suci's (1952) D statistic provides such a measure. The D statistic is a measure of relationship that takes into account the absolute discrepancy between sets of measures as well as their profile similarities. The mean scores for discussion, verbal aggression, and physical aggression between husband-wife, parent-child, and sib-sib for the grandparent generation (G_1) was compared to the husband-wife and parent-child scores for the parent generation (G_2).

The D statistic compares the profile of conflict-resolution techniques used by the grandparents in their marital and parental roles with the techniques

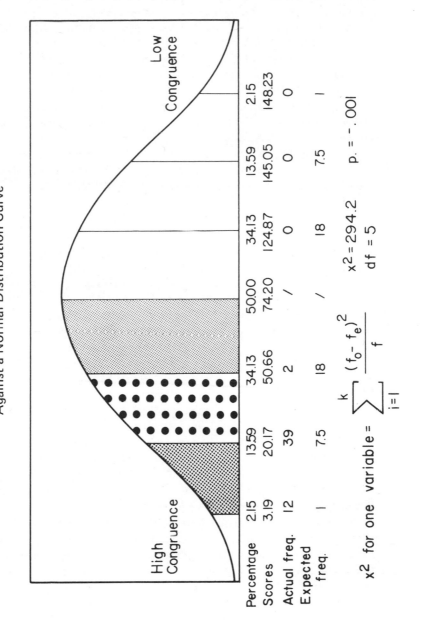

FIGURE 7.1

Observed Intergenerational Family-Conflict Profiles Reported as D Statistics Plotted
Against a Normal Distribution Curve

Percentage	2.15	13.59	34.13	50.00	34.13	13.59	2.15
Scores	3.19	20.17	50.66	74.20	124.87	145.05	148.23
Actual freq.	12	39	2	/	0	0	0
Expected freq.	1	7.5	18	/	18	7.5	1

$$x^2 \text{ for one variable} = \sum_{i=1}^{k} \frac{(f_o - f_e)^2}{f}$$

$x^2 = 294.2$ p. = -.001

df = 5

used by the child in sibling roles and later in marital and parental roles, for each family. The possible range of D-statistic scores was from 0 (totally congruent pattern between generations) to 148.43 (completely dissimilar patterns). There were four measures combined in the G_1 scores: mother-father, mother-child, father-child, and child and sibs, all reported by parent. There were five measures making up the G_2 scores: mother-father, mother-child, father-child as reported by the child, and husband-wife and parent-child as reported by the parent. The maximum D statistic was computed by obtaining a D statistic when $G_1 = 0$, and $G_2 = 20$ (verbal), 20 (discussion), 30 (physical), and averaging it with a D statistic obtained by letting $G_1 = 16$ (verbal), 16 (discussion), 24 (physical), and $G_2 = 0$.

Plotting the theoretically possible scores on a normal curve enables comparison with the actual dispersion of scores (see Figure 7.1). All observed scores fell below the fiftieth percentile, with a range of 5.48-52.87, suggesting a high degree of congruency between the scores of different family dyads. Twenty-two percent of the observed scores were three standard deviations away from the median, 74 percent of the scores were two standard deviations away. Only 4 percent of the scores were within one standard deviation away from the median. When the observed frequencies were plotted against a hypothetical normal curve, X^2 was significant at the p = .001 level. This would suggest that there is a strong intergenerational pattern of conflict resolution, considerably more than would be expected by chance. It is not possible by this method, however, to ascertain the type of conflict resolution selected by these families. Thus a family in which husband-wife scores are highly congruent with parent-child scores, may be characterized as either high or low in use of discussion, or verbal or physical aggression.

SUMMARY

The data presented strong support for the research question stated earlier in this chapter. The conflict-resolution methods used by husbands and wives to resolve marital conflict were found to be quite similar to the methods these individuals will use when disciplining their children. These same methods are imitated by their children much in the "monkey see, monkey do" manner when these children interact with their siblings. Furthermore, when these children mature and marry, they appear to use these methods, which are a firmly entrenched part of their behavior repertory, to resolve marital conflict, and, continuing the cycle, transfer this method to their children in the form of the disciplinary techniques they utilize.

Both intragenerational (for G_1 and G_2) and intergenerational patterns were found for the use of discussion, verbal aggression, and physical aggression. By means of correlational analyses and the D statistic, which provides a comparison of profiles, congruent intergenerational patterns were found to exist, thus providing support for a transfer of conflict-resolution modes over three generations. Finally, a typology of family conflict resolving modes was developed that identified four distinct types: screaming slugger, silent attackers, threateners, and pacifists.

Considering the evidence on the relationship between the use of physically aggressive or abusive interaction between family members and subsequent physically aggressive crimes in adulthood, it appears that all citizens are affected by higher crime rate, fear for the lives of political leaders, and a fear for one's own personal safety. Remedies such as fleeing from the urban area provide only temporary relief as crime rates spiral in suburban areas. Elaborate security systems, attack dogs and guns, while possibly providing a superficial sense of security in one's home still do not attack the roots of the problem. The conditions that seem to foster family violence, such as unemployment, inadequate role fulfillment, insecurity, lack of family- or community-support systems, isolation, are also found in the background of individuals who commit other acts of violence. It would appear that removing the sanction for using physical force on family members might be a first step in reducing other physically violent acts. A summary of the study's findings and some possible solutions for changing family-interaction patterns are presented in the concluding chapter.

8

QUESTIONS, ANSWERS, AND
THEORETICAL AND POLICY
IMPLICATIONS

The goal of this concluding chapter is to tie together the study's diverse findings and to assess the adequacy of these findings in providing answers to the research questions posited in Chapter 1. Theoretical and policy implications suggested by this research are also considered.

RESEARCH QUESTIONS

Much evidence was accumulated that provides insights into the following two research questions:

1.   Is there a similarity between the methods husband and wife use to resolve marital conflicts, the methods they use in disciplining their children, and the methods their children use to resolve sibling conflicts?
2.   Does the use of violence to resolve conflicts mirror the general societal attitude toward the use of verbal and physically aggressive and abusive resolution modes?

Evidence from the in-depth interviews suggests that verbally and physically assertive and aggressive modes have much normative support from society. For example, during the in-depth interviews, parents told us how normal they considered such interactions as spanking or slapping a child, or screaming or throwing things at a spouse, or having their children scream, hit, and throw things at each other. They frequently reinforced their belief about the normalcy of this interaction by noting that their friends all used similar methods.

Data from diaries and interviews support the notion that the family, through the child-rearing techniques they use as well as their tolerance of aggressive and abusive interaction between siblings, provides the initial setting for the learning of assertive, aggressive, and abusive behavior. As one mother noted: "I am only teaching my children to hit if I hit, . . . if it is alright for me to hit, then they are going to feel it is alright for them to hit."

Parents, police, and the military were presented as examples of three levels of social interaction that encompass the use of sanctioned control over others. Evidence was presented suggesting that the sanction to use physical force as one's right and duty to control others, for example, enemies, criminals, children, frequently results in the overstepping of the normally imposed controls and becomes abuse.

Empirical evidence in addition to descriptive material from the in-depth interviews, presented in the preceding chapter, considerably support the existence of both intragenerational and intergenerational patterns of conflict resolution. Four patterns of intrafamilial conflict resolution were identified: screaming sluggers, users of high amounts of both verbal and physical aggression; silent attackers, users of low amounts of verbal aggression but high amounts of physical aggression; threateners, users of high verbal but low physical aggression; and pacifists, users of low verbal and physical aggression. These patterns were found to accurately describe not only marital interaction but parent-child and sibling interaction as well. Both the family typology, as well as family profiles defined by the D statistic, suggest that spouses tended to interact with their children in a mode similar to that which categorized their marital interaction. Sibling interaction also tended to be similar to the mode characterizing husband-wife and parent-child interaction, but was stronger when the relationship being tested was a direct transfer of aggression, that is, when one was a perpetrator of aggression and later used this method in another setting. For example, the methods used between spouses were used by these spouses when disciplining their children. Likewise, the methods used by parents to discipline their children were imitated by the children when interacting with their sibs. The relationships tended to be weaker when the transfer of the method of conflict resolution was indirect and represented witnessing rather than experiencing aggression, for example, the relationship between marital interaction and interaction occurring between sibs. Although not all relationships were found to be statistically significant, they were all in the predicted direction and held for both generations (G_1 and G_2).

PROPOSITIONS

A better understanding of the mechanisms of family violence is obtained by comparing these data with the propositions derived from an examination of child, police, and military abuse. These propositions are concerned with the conditions that appear to be related to crossing the boundary from sanctioned or legitimate physical force to unsanctioned or illegitimate physical violence.

The conditions found to relate to an increase in family violence described in the following five propositions are similar to those found in the background of individuals who commit other acts of violence, such as homicide, assault and battery, rape, and political assassination (discussed in the previous chapter):

1. The frequency of assertive, aggressive, and abusive interaction will increase as the acceptance of violence to obtain socially desirable goals increases.
2. Assertive, aggressive, and abusive interaction will increase as frustration and dissatisfaction with jobs, one's role, and one's family setting increases.
3. Assertive, aggressive, and abusive interaction will increase as the individual's lack of understanding of, or inability to cope with, family demands increases.
4. Assertive, aggressive, and abusive interaction will increase as communication barriers increase.
5. Assertive, aggressive, and abusive intrafamily interaction will increase when the traditionally assigned role of authority is questioned by the individual(s) in the traditionally assigned subordinate roles.

On the descriptive level, parents reported the use of more severe punishment when they perceived the goals to be absolutely necessary for safety reasons. For example, parents who used very little physical punishment did so to punish their children for playing in the streets. Preventing this behavior was seen as an extremely desirable (absolutely necessary) goal. Other parents noted that they rarely used physical punishment, but did so to prevent their child from hurting himself (herself) or another child.

Many parents also reported an increase in the use of verbal and physical aggression when their frustration point was reached. Caring for small children, housework that never stays done, and jobs that are demanding often resulted in parents arriving home tired and unable to cope with the normal stresses and strains of family life. Mothers with several small children, who were housebound, also reported similar feelings of frustration and increase in the use of verbal and physical aggression.

Spouses' inability to cope with increases in family demands such as those brought on by pregnancy and its expected increase in responsibilities also led to increases in verbal and physical aggression. In a few families, the wife's pregnancy resulted in the husband becoming violent, having a mental breakdown, or deserting the family. In other families, increased demands resulted in more yelling at and slapping of children. The children, who were victims of this higher-than-usual level of verbal and physical aggression, reacted with increasing amounts of sibling conflict, which further escalated the level of stress in the family.

Probably the single most frequently mentioned complaint relating to marital interaction was that one spouse would not discuss the problem. Although several husbands noted that women tend to "suffer in silence," many wives listed, as a typical male reaction, "ignoring the issue." The reaction to this lack of communication tended to be dramatic: throwing things, slapping and hitting, screaming, talking to the wall, or sending notes; none of these were considered productive, all done out of desperation.

A common complaint among parents of teenagers is lack of communication, as one parent noted: "I think our biggest conflict with our son is that he keeps telling us we don't understand him, and we try to talk with him and ask him questions and he doesn't want to tell us what is going on."

Finally, the wife's questioning the authority of her husband, or children questioning the authority of parents was found to be a condition of family-related violence. In several families, the only physical aggression between spouses occurred when the husband was temporarily unemployed. In other families, the wife's desire to become more socially active, or to return to work resulted in verbally aggressive marital interaction. Another source of verbal and physical aggression results from the mouthy adolescents who question the traditionally assigned parental authority, or the small child who willfully disobeys.

These propositions, drawn from data pertaining to the causes and conditions of parental, police, and military abuse, were found to hold for family interactions between spouses, parent and child, and siblings.

HOW IS CONFLICT RESOLVED?

The first question most individuals will want to consider in a study investigating conflict between family members is, How much conflict exists and how do family members attempt to resolve it? Based on the data provided by the two sets of questionnaires, it can be reported that intrafamilial conflict exists to some degree in all families. Nearly 98 percent of G_2 (as reported by the eldest child) used discussion, 93 percent used verbal aggression, and 60 percent used physical aggression to resolve marital conflict. Discussion was used by 98 percent, verbal aggression by 90 percent, physical aggression by 69 percent of the families to resolve parent-child conflicts. In resolving sibling conflicts 98 percent used discussion, 96 percent used verbal aggression, and 94 percent resorted to physical aggression.

Similar trends were found for the G_1 generation (as reported by the parent) with the exception of a lesser amount of physical aggression for this group. This difference can probably be accounted for by the greater time span between occurrence of the behavior and the reporting of the behavior.

Causes and Resolutions of Conflict, and Perceived Success

The causes of conflict were also a concern of this study. Utilizing the data on the conflict-recording sheets, it was possible to have some ideas of the causes of conflict, the modes used to resolve these conflicts, and the perceived success of each method.

Sibling Conflicts

The data provided by the conflict-recording sheets and substantiated by the in-depth interviews suggest that sibling conflicts decrease, or at least are less likely to be observed and reported by parents, as children moved from the younger to adolescent to teenage years. With the younger siblings (all children with a mean age of eight or less) the conflicts usually revolve around possessions such as toys. In the adolescent group (mean age, nine through 13) conflicts tend to deal with infringement of personal space—touching or making faces or in some way violating personal-space boundaries. There were very few sibling conflicts recorded for the teenage groups (mean age, 14 or over). Those conflicts that were recorded tended to center on obligations, responsibilities, and social graces.

The modes of resolving conflicts also differed by the age grouping of the children. With younger children there are considerably more physical means utilized while verbal modes are more frequently used for the adolescent group. The teenage group also relied on verbal means for resolving sibling conflicts. The perceived success of each method also varied by age group. Compromise, threats or asserting authority, and restricting privileges are fairly successful with the young children. These findings, however, really represent the success of the method the parents use to resolve sibling conflict. Among the adolescent group, ignoring the conflict is most successful, possibly because these conflicts tend to revolve around personal-space boundaries and need the reaction of the victim in order to provide a reward for the perpetrator. Among teenagers, all modes, except yelling and hollering, the most emotion-laden response, were considered successful.

Parent-Child Conflicts

Most parent-child conflicts tended to revolve around power struggles, with a consistent decrease in the number of conflicts recorded as the age of children increases. A note of caution must be interjected, however. While the number of reported conflicts may be lower, it is possible that the perceived seriousness of the conflict may increase with teenagers. For example, a family with small children may have recorded a half-dozen conflicts per day, none more serious than requiring a child to give back a toy or get back to bed. A family with adolescent or teenage children may not have recorded any conflicts for the one-week period, yet have mentioned during the interview that a child had run away or taken up with undesirable associates. Thus the number of conflicts recorded may not necessarily reflect the frequency or intensity of major problems.

Mother-child conflicts accounted for over 60 percent of the parent-child incidents recorded; only 15 percent of the conflicts specifically involved the father with the remaining 15 percent involving both parents. This probably reflects the mother's increased availability, since in the one family where the mother did shift work, a predominance of parent-child conflicts were father-child ones.

The modes used to resolve conflicts also differed. Mothers reported more use of threats and discussion with each age group. Fathers reported the use of threats and restriction with younger children; yelling and screaming with adolescents; and discussion, threats, and withdrawal of privileges with teenagers. Fathers are more likely to be perceived as successful when disciplining younger children, but this perceived success consistently diminishes with each older group. Mother's perceived success is extremely high for adolescent groups, but decreases with teenagers (although it remains higher than father's success for this group).

Marital Conflict

The marital conflicts recorded can be divided into two major categories: picky, annoying, individualistic conflicts, such as arguments over keeping a jug of water in the refrigerator; and major conflicts over children, roles, in-laws, and decision-making prerogatives. Over 65 percent of the marital conflicts recorded were perceived to be resolved successfully. Communication was seen as the most ideal way to resolve conflicts and prevent major ones from occurring. The lack of communication was considered the real threat to marital happiness and stability.

There was a slight decline in the reporting of marital conflict with length of time married. This also reflects in most instances an increase in the age of the children, so that it is difficult to ascertain how much conflict is directly related to problems with children. This may reflect the tendency, with maturation, to learn how to avoid an argument or how to deflate a conflict. It is also possible that this may be a mechanism developed in order to make marital relations tolerable. Some evidence supporting the latter is provided by the in-depth interviews. Many parents noted that their major marital problems concerned children. Furthermore, these problems started when children entered adolescence and decreased when the children neared the latter teenage years. This is congruent with studies suggesting a curvilinear relationship between marital satisfaction and length of time married; high satisfaction in early marriage and after children are launched; and lowest around 20 years of marriage (when most families have adolescent children) (Miller, 1976).

Effects of Social Class and Education

The goal of this research was to identify patterns of conflict-resolution modes within families rather than the effect of independent variables (income, family size, education) on family-conflict resolution.

Because social class and education have been linked on both a theoretical and empirical level to such phenomena as physical punishment (Sears, Maccoby, and Levin, 1957; Kohn, 1969) and spouse beating (Gelles, 1974; Levinger, 1966), the relationship between these two variables and family-conflict-resolution modes was investigated. The data suggest that an increase in husband's and wife's education, and in social class will result in an increase in the use of discussion and a decrease in verbal and physical force to resolve marital conflict (see Table 8.1).

Extremely small (nonsignificant) correlations were found between mother's education and her disciplinary techniques. Higher correlations were found between father's education and social class and the modes fathers used to resolve father-child conflicts. These correlations seemed to indicate a slight, barely significant decrease in verbal and physical aggression with an increase in education and social class. A similar decrease in use of discussion, however,

TABLE 8.1

Correlation Between Education, Social Class, and Conflict-Resolution Scores

Conflict-Resolution Method	Husband's Education	Wife's Education	Socioeconomic Status (based on Husband's education and occupation)
Husband-Wife			
Discussion	.27 (.03)*	.24 (.05)	.21 (.08)
Verbal	-.30 (.02)	-.26 (.04)	-.33 (.01)
Physical	-.35 (.007)	-.26 (.04)	-.36 (.006)
Mother-Child			
Discussion		-.11 (ns)	-.05 (ns)
Verbal		-.08 (ns)	-.13 (ns)
Physical		-.04 (ns)	-.29 (.01)
Father-Child			
Discussion	-.004 (ns)		-.01 (ns)
Verbal	-.19 (.10)		-.17 (.11)
Physical	-.19 (.10)		-.27 (.03)

* Levels of significance are in parenthesis.

was also found. These findings suggest that although a relationship exists between measures of socioeconomic status and spouse's use of conflict-resolution methods, there appears to be extremely weak evidence that a relationship exists between these measures and methods of conflict resolution used in child rearing. This finding probably reflects the concern expressed by nearly all parents in this sample regarding proper parenting and the wide variety of sources available and used (especially by mother) on the topic of improving parent-child relations.

THEORETICAL AND POLICY IMPLICATIONS

Although a predominant theoretical approach for explaining family inter-action has been a structural focus, the findings from this reaearch indicate the importance of viewing family relationships as a dynamic process. For example, it is apparent that conflict is not defined similarly by all families. In order for a particular family interaction to be defined as a conflict, two major conditions must be met: first, the resolution or outcome must be considered to be of major importance; and second, the obtaining of the resolution must be perceived to be problematic. Therefore, if the incident is defined by the participants as unimportant, or the method of resolving it nonproblematic, the incident tends not to be perceived by the actors as a conflict. Furthermore, while a structural perspective is able to identify the existence of generational patterns, a process perspective attempts to explicate those dynamic aspects, such as role modeling, perception of success of conflict-resolution methods, social learning, and explicit transmission of attitudes and values, by which intergenerational and intragenerational patterns emerge.

A process approach also suggests that rather than viewing the resolution of conflicts as unidimensional action-reaction phenomena, these resolutions are constantly being negotiated by the actors. Families, through a process of negotiation, legitimize certain techniques that are then utilized in the management of conflict, rather than the total resolution of the conflict (Sprey, 1969, 1971). Since the occurrence of conflict and its management is a dynamic process, the techniques are constantly reevaluated on the basis of the perceived importance of the outcomes as well as the perceived success of previously utilized modes.

THE EFFECT OF PERCEPTION ON CONFLICT-RESOLUTION METHOD AND PERCEIVED SUCCESS

A crucial theoretical and methodological consideration in investigating choice of conflict-resolution modes used by family members and the perceived success of these interactions is the individual's perception of the situation.

Rogers (1965) suggests that an individual reacts to the field or situation as it is experienced and perceived and for this individual this perceptual field is "reality." Therefore, the best vantage for understanding the interaction taking place in socialization would be from the internal frames of reference of the individuals involved.

As W.I. Thomas noted in his "definition of the situation," if a situation is perceived to be real, then it is real in its consequences for the individuals involved. For example, one respondent, after denying the existence of conflict between parents and children in their family, noted that there were problems over who did the chores. This respondent had not defined "problems over doing chores" as a conflict.

This study has been concerned with what is considered aggressive or abusive interaction by the participants as well as with identifying and describing the frequency of such interaction. The parent who does not see siblings fighting, even when it results in fairly severe physical injury, as a problem or a family conflict will see no reason for modifying this sibling interaction. Likewise, if family members do not perceive a particular behavior to be aggressive or abusive, then social agencies will not be able to alter interaction patterns that are detrimental to family functioning.

The model presented in Figure 8.1 attempts to link family-conflict resolution with an awareness of the respondent's perception of the situation, a major theoretical perspective on which this research is grounded. The broken lines in Figure 8.1 indicate a possible linkage between the social structure, how it affects family conflict, and its resolution, and perceived success of the method used. Using as an illustration the disciplining of a child, it can be shown that depending on the definition of the situation by the participants, differential, stepwise processes and outcomes will occur.

Social-Structure Variables

Boxes A, B, and C in Figure 8.1 contain the social-structure variables that have been linked, in the illustrative example, to a parent's decision regarding socialization techniques. As the dotted line to box D indicates, it is important to consider the individual's perception of these variables, not to impute the social scientist's meaning to their importance. For example, we assume, given a specific social-class ranking, that a person will see the world in certain terms—that he sees himself and is seen by others as having certain competencies. We label, for example, the welfare mother as incompetent (in middle-class standards), as a less-valued person because of her social position relative to others.

Family members may be incompetent in the sex roles society assigns them but may be quite competent in fulfilling other roles. This study had one middle-aged couple in which the father provided the mothering and the mother financially supported the family and adopted the breadwinner role. This change in

FIGURE 8.1

Theoretical Model for the Effects of Perception on Choice of Conflict-Resolution Modes and Determination of Their Success

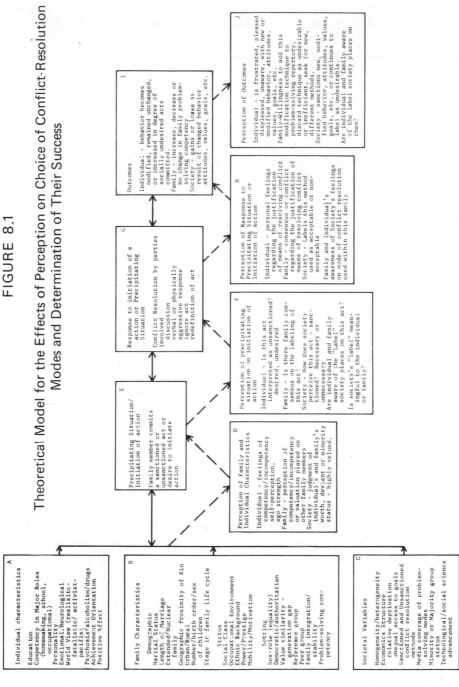

roles occurred when the couple realized that the husband did not want to (and was unable to) fill the socially sanctioned roles assigned to men. He was, however, demonstrative, patient, and loving, and enjoyed interacting with the children on a level that the wife did not enjoy.

Precipitating Situation

Typically, when discussing the act of disciplining a child, or a marital conflict, we assume that there is a precipitating situation (box E): the child or spouse does something objectionable, or there is some form of action initiation such as an attempt to change views, habits, goals, or attitudes. The researcher rarely questions how this action is interpreted by the participants, as suggested by box F.

How does the individual view this act—as welcome advice, or an invasion of privacy? Does the child feel the unsanctioned act was or should be unsanctioned? Perhaps the child was forbidden to leave his yard or wear certain clothing. His peer group, however, all have been given these privileges and the child feels that he is now old enough to have this privilege also. He is likely to view leaving the yard not as an act of direct disobedience, but rather as a lack of communication or awareness on the part of his parents. By doing the forbidden act the child may be able to convince his parents of their error, just as civil-rights sit-ins aimed to show the citizenry the unjustness of racial discrimination. Family consensus is also important. Do all adults in the household share similar feelings in regard to the action? How does society perceive the act, and more importantly is the label society places on the act meaningful to family or individual? This same process must be considered in examining interaction between all family dyads.

Response to Situation

The next link in the socialization scheme is the response to the precipitating situation, or initiation of action, for example, spanking the child (box G). The link frequently overlooked is the perception of this response (box H). Does the individual feel the response was justified? Does the individual feel guilty? How do other members of the family feel about the response? How does society label the response—a sanctioned or unsanctioned one?

In our society spanking is experienced by nearly every child. In this study only one family stated that they never spanked, even when their children were young. Likewise 60 percent of the families had used physical force to resolve a marital conflict. The occurrence of an act may not necessarily indicate sanction, and sanction may not necessarily indicate the desirability of the behavior. Premarital sex and drunkenness are probably not sanctioned by the majority of society, but reports from surveys (Reiss, 1967; Bell, 1971) would indicate that these acts occur frequently. Although slapping a child and slapping between spouses is sanctioned and may occur frequently, the definition of the desirability of this method may vary.

For example, one mother, during a joint interview, suggested that a slap in the face was the best cure for a smart mouth. However, her husband "absolutely forbade" her to slap their children around the face because he had grown up "as a kid whose mother put his eye out by doing it, and I've never gotten over it, and I never will." Therefore, this parent perceived a fairly common, sanctioned, and somewhat desirable (because it is perceived to be effective) method to be undesiarble and unsanctionable based on his personal experiences.

One must also view the act of slapping a child from the perspective of society. Is slapping a behavior that is expected from parents and would avoiding slapping a child be seen as a nonnormative response indicating weakness or indecisiveness on the part of the parent? Certain closely-knit ethnic groups, such as Greek communities in the United States, require absolute respect from their children, and to disobey or question this respect is to guarantee the administering of corporal punishment. However, it is also quite possible that the social control exerted over youth in these communities is so strong and well integrated that the likelihood of disobedience of the degree requiring corporal punishment is small.

Outcome: Success or Failure

The last link in the usual scheme of socialization is the outcome (box I). Have the individuals involved modified their behavior congruent with the expectation of those administering the response? In the example being used in this chapter, did the child's behavior change as a result of the slapping? Has this problem-solving approach increased or decreased (or left unchanged) the family's problem-solving competency?

What society has gained as a result of this change or modification in behavior, goals, attitudes, and so on, must be considered. For example, in several studies (Sears, Maccoby, and Levin, 1957; Sears, 1961; Eron, Walder, and Lefkowitz, 1971) the parents administered physical punishment in an attempt to reduce aggressive acts on the part of their child. This form of discipline, however, increased rather than decreased the aggressive acts of the child. In a study of the relationship between disciplinary practices and the child's aggressiveness, conscience development, and dependency (Steinmetz, 1977b), the strong positive relationship between parent's use of physical punishment and child's aggressiveness was the most consistent of all findings in the studies examined. Therefore, society did not gain a less aggressive child, but instead a child whose aggressive tendencies had increased.

The last step in this model is the perception of the outcome (box I). Do the parents in this study perceive success or frustration as a result of the attempts to reduce their child's aggression by means of physical punishment (box J)? Likewise, does the spouse administering the slap feel the behavior was necessary and therefore justified?

There are indications that verbal and physically aggressive modes do not produce the desired results. (The perceived success of different methods of resolving sibling, parent-child, and husband-wife conflicts are discussed in Chapters 4, 5, and 6). It may be, however, that while the parents were not rewarded with total success in reducing aggression in their children, they feel that without the use of physical punishment their child might have exhibited considerably more aggressive behavior than presently displayed. How does society perceive the outcome—as successful or unsuccessful? Will the individuals and families be aware of the label society places on them as a result of the outcome? Will soceity see an aggressive child and assume that either his parents don't care about his behavior or they are incompetent child rearers?

Although this research has not attempted to empirically test each linkage, an effort was made to analyze and interpret the interview and daily-conflict-sheet data utilizing the linkages suggested in the model. It is possible that for a majority of individuals the selection of conflict-resolution methods, especially those pertaining to parent-child interaction, may be a random procedure. It is quite possible that even in view of the large number of child-rearing books and mass-media exposure, differential life experiences will result in a wide variety of interpretation of the information presented.

There appears to be sufficient evidence from the parents interviewed to suggest that given the best intentions, parents do not always succeed with all children to produce the type of individual they desire.

ALTERNATIVE MODES OF INTERACTION

The emphasis on process also has major policy implications. Intervention programs must not only be concerned with changing structural variables that have been linked to aggressive interaction, but must also be concerned with the individual participant's definition of a conflict and the family members' legitimization of particular techniques. If a family member does not define a given set of behaviors as conflict, then there will be no attempt by the members to change them. Likewise, if a family legitimizes the use of certain management techniques, regardless of the dysfunction, it will be difficult to convince them to develop alternative ones.

Although most of the verbal and physical assertive and aggressive acts reported by the participants in this study would not be considered abusive, the persistent use of these forms of interpersonal interaction does raise the level of tolerance toward aggressive and abusive family interaction. As this level of tolerance increases, it becomes increasingly easier for individuals to define aggressive-abusive acts as socially sanctioned. And, as the data suggest, these patterns will be transmitted both intergenerationally and intragenerationally.

Although a slight differentiation exists among classes, with the lower class reported to have used more aggressive modes (Sears, Maccoby, and Levin, 1957; Toby, 1966), those conditions that are seen as causal within the lower class, such as unemployment, lack of a status-conferring role, and frustration, are unfortunately becoming part of all social-class environments (see *Time*, March 17, 1975: 88, for a discussion of the reported increase of family-related violence among the middle classes).

Therefore, a major emphasis of institutions concerned with the reduction of levels of family aggression as a mode of conflict resolution must be on redefining tolerable, sanctionable modes of family interaction to exclude physically and verbally aggressive modes.

Based on the findings of this study, potential conflict-management mechanisms can be identified that may facilitate lower levels of family aggression. These mechanisms can be instituted at three major levels.

Societal Level

Changes in the social structure that foster equality in roles, full employment, adequate social-health benefits, and reduction of violence in the mass media are needed. Over six million children have problems that limit their ability to cope with society. A disturbed child who received proper treatment may grow up to lead a productive and useful life (Gallagher, 1972). When calculating the cost-benefit analysis, the long-range outlook of the social cost of not instituting changes in the social structure must be considered.

Community Level

Conflict-management mechanisms can also be instituted at the community level through expansion of third-party intervention systems, such as training police to engage in positive (helpful) modes of defusing marital conflicts (Bard, 1971); or training bartenders, taxi drivers, and beauticians as lay psychologists (Philadelphia *Sunday Bulletin*, October 13, 1974: 24). Since teachers spend a considerable number of hours with their students, they should receive adequate training in identifying a battered child and recognizing personality changes and disturbances that might be indicative of family disruption. These teachers should be familiarized with mechanisms for protecting the child from further abuse, and have available professionals to which they can send troubled students. Physicians, ministers, and social-service professionals need a greater awareness of the causes of family-related violence, adequate training in dealing with these problems, and better utilization of existing resources. Many local groups, such as the National Organization for Women (NOW), have made the battered spouse a major concern and are lobbying to change laws to provide better protection for the victim by sponsoring counseling and safe shelters for emergency care. Crisis lines for reporting, as well as seeking help for child abuse, exist in many cities, as well as 24-hour emergency foster care for the abused child. Crisis-hot lines sponsored by church-related groups, women's groups, NOW, and child-abuse workers provide a valuable (frequently 24-hour) device where abusers as well as victims can receive emotional support and referral to existing professional services.

Family Level

The plethora of how-to books on parenting, the large number of articles in women's magazines, and the growing interest in courses on parenting through academic institutions, church groups, Y's, and private family-service groups indicate that parents want to improve their parenting techniques. Unfortunately, it appears that parents often wait until after a problem arises before seeking help. There is a need for improved parent education, emphasizing less aggressive methods for resolving interpersonal conflict, starting in grade school. These courses need to prepare youth for the realities of marriage and parenthood, not reinforce the romanticism often expressed by youth. Youth should be made aware that conflict is a normal part of family life, and that aggressive methods not only do not resolve the problems, but tend to escalate them. Certainly as much concern, if not as much formal education, should be provided for marriage and family preparation as is provided for occupational and social endeavors. It is crucial to prepare today's youth—the parents of tomorrow—for their potential roles as spouses and parents.

However, when living in a social system that requires competition and aggressiveness for social survival, training one's children to be nonaggressive and nonviolent may be dysfunctional. Therefore, if we value nonviolence and desire lesser amounts of aggressive interaction at all levels of society, perhaps the question to be asked is, not "How can we change family interaction?" but rather, "Are we willing to change the social structure?"

In a society where two out of three marriages end in divorce and where countless youngsters run away from home each year, one can ask, "What kept the families in this study together?" Many of them suffered crises such as unemployment, illness, deaths, children running away from home, and alcoholism. Furthermore, almost all families experienced conflicts and used considerable amounts of verbal and physical aggression in an attempt to resolve these conflicts. Yet, what keeps families together is a question not nearly so often posited as the question, "What causes dissension or conflict, or what are the causes of family dissolution?" Perhaps we only become concerned about family life when problem areas are defined, for example, divorce, abortion, and desertion. The following discussion will briefly examine some of the insights provided by these families on what kept their family together.

Throughout the collection of data for this research, participants were encouraged to add information they considered important for understanding how their family resolved (or prevented) conflicts, but was perhaps not covered during the interview or in the questionnaire. Many families expressed their philosphy of how and why they worked at their marriage, and took the interviewer to task for overlooking the importance of religion, love, or a sense of responsibility—factors guiding a lot of their decision making and conflict resolution. The following comments provide insight on how many wives regarded their marriage:

> A couple of times I felt like I'm just going to walk out this door and chuck it. Who needs all this moving? I thought, no, because my idea of marriage is, I'm going to do something and I am going to do it. It may not be easy, but I made a promise. This had a religious significance to me.

> You know, it's a shame, you never get to see the love and kindness— only conflict. You really miss the whole picture. . . . All love begins in Christ.

There was a general feeling among respondents that marriages mature and become "better" with age—after about ten years. For example:

> I think it depends on how long you've been married. When we were first married, we had an argument and would stay mad. Now we say whatever we have to say and go pick up where we left off. When we were first married, I'd cry, and lock him out of the house. We've

135

been married 24 years, and I don't think I've done anything like
that for 12 years or more.

Perhaps, as one respondent suggested, a lack of experience and prepared-
ness for marriage and child rearing may be an explanation for the lower level
of marital satisfaction that occurs after the children arrive:

> I think it is really sad that they don't teach girls more in high school
> about what most of them are going to end up doing, and that's
> being a wife and mother. . . . I just wish there was some way to get
> instant knowledge. I'm sure my kids are going to make the same
> stupid mistakes I did, you know, as they start to raise their children.
> But it's like anything else, you just learn as you grow.

Research findings suggest that child abuse and physical aggression between
spouses appear to be related to social isolation (Gil, 1970; Gelles, 1974). Whitehurst (1974), in a theoretical essay, suggests that alternative family forms such
as extended or communal families may reduce family violence because of the
greater number of kin for support and social control.

Many families in this research expressed a strong desire for privacy and
independence. The family's home is their castle, guarded against invasions
from outside. Not all families, however, shared this feeling and noted that a
lack of concern for others' problems and a desire to escape from less desirable
social environments is contributing to social problems such as crime in the city.

During a joint interview, one wife, who is active in local politics, expressed
this feeling:

> Everybody needs other people. No family is sufficient unto itself. . . .
> I need more than me, and our children need more than us. . . .
> This is where our country has gone wrong! It has gone from the
> period where everybody helps everybody else when you need
> help, because they themselves might need help sometime. . . .
> And we are all paying for it.

Her husband added that in our desire to escape the cities, we've left them for
the isolated suburban plots and allowed the cities to become unsafe, crime-
ridden areas. He noted:

> The trouble with society is the lack of row houses. People are
> distant today. When we had row houses, if you had a fight here the
> people on the side knew it but at least you felt you were close
> together. . . . Today, the neighbors get together, put up a fence
> together and two weeks after the fence is up they say, "That quarter
> is mine, this is yours. You do what you want with yours." We've
> come to the point where the old barn raising days are gone—every-
> body, each family is sufficient unto himself. I disagree with this.

Throughout the study it became evident that many of the families tended to be described by the interviewers as warm, loving, caring, fun-filled families. The feelings expressed by the interviewers were substantiated by comments respondents made on the conflict-recording sheet. These families had their share of illness, disappointments, and hardships, but they had a quality that indicated a togetherness or family spirit rather than a group of related individuals sharing a house. There was a common theme among these families suggesting, as one mother put it, "I think every family has to have a generation gap, but there isn't any big communication gap in our family."

These families tended to share activities and take a sincere pleasure and pride in the accomplishments of other family members. Some families centered their life on church-related activities, other families raced horses or motorcycles, and still others planned expensive but family-oriented vacations and trips.

Perhaps this quality is a special form of love and a sincere enjoyment of interaction with family members. As one mother noted, "You know, 'The family that prays together stays together'; well our family is, 'The family who races together stays together.' "

It seems fitting that a book dealing with the more unpleasant aspect of family life—conflict—should end on a light note, that of humor. This appears to be another important quality shared by families possessing that special family spirit. These families have the ability to see the bright side in family conflicts, place them in their proper perspective, and be able to laugh at their own and other family members' shortcomings, while working on conflict resolution.

Many parents were able to smile at their attempts to outsmart their children. These attempts, which displayed ingenuity as well as their sense of humor, were taken from the in depth interviews and comments on the conflict-recording sheets. A parent who is able to report on a topic as sensitive as family conflict, in a light-hearted, humorous way, noting all participants' faults, is most likely a parent who is tolerant, understanding, able to roll with the punches and keep all family interaction in proper perspective.

One heartwarming incident was noted concerning bed switching:

Conflict: Youngest two children swapped beds for the night. After the youngest was asleep the other wanted his own bed back.
Method of resolving conflict: Each remained in the other's bed. Son said he'd "remember that 'Happiness is sleeping in your own bed.' "

Parent-child struggles often were resolved in unexpected ways. One family used "false time," by turning the clock ahead, to prevent bedtime hassles:

He [6-year-old] knows when it is 8:30 he is supposed to go to bed. Rather than keep hassling, I keep turning the clock ahead. He has really been going to bed around 7:00. . . . I have to threaten the two bigger ones . . . not to dare say "Gee, how come that show is on television right now."

Marital conflict is also apparently easier to take if a measure of humor is interjected. One wife noted that she became very irritated and complained to her husband about his habit of acknowledging each child in a bright and spirited tone: "He acknowledged the kids with a bright 'hi M! hi G! hi L!' and dragging 'hi dear.' I complained so now he comes in and drags 'hi kids' and shouts 'HI DEAR!' "

Perhaps the most humorous tale revolved around lying as a source of parent-child conflict. The incident is presented below as it was recorded on the conflict-recording sheet.

> Conflict: C brought home a family of 6 baby black snakes several weeks ago and put them in an empty 30 gallon fish tank. He came down for breakfast and said one of them got out and he couldn't find it. I told him to go find it or he could not have his breakfast. He left the table, went upstairs and said he found it on the toilet paper roll. O.K. Monday is wash day here. I pick C's dirty clothes off the floor, separated the clothes in their respective piles. I had thrown in all the jeans and went upstairs to finish beds. I found another pair of dirty jeans and took them down to put in the washer. Well, there's a snake in the washer. I quick grabbed him out because I didn't want him drowned or be in pieces all over my clothes. When C came home from school I jumped him again for lying to me. He's quick. He said, "Well, there must have been two of them out because I did put one in the tank."

Some components of family interaction were not objective, tangible measures but seemed to be expressed by the respondents as love, happiness, enjoyment of other family members, a desire to extend love and supportiveness beyond the family boundaries, and a sense of humor. We know that some individuals survive brutal childhood experiences. Thomas Edison was beaten so frequently as a child that his hearing was impaired (*Family Weekly*, January 16, 1977: 22), and Jimmy Carter's father "whipped him on six occasions with such thoroughness that Carter vividly recalls every datail" (*Time*, January 14, 1977: 14). A famous expert in the field of child development, herself a beaten child, related to the author that she is often asked, "Do all children who are abused grow up to be abusing mothers?" to which she replies, "No, some of us grow up to study empathy" (personal communication).

If we view the pluses and minuses of any family unit as weights on a balance scale, we can then posit: "How much love, happiness, enjoyment of family life, sense of humor, and so on, is necessary to offset family conflict, unhappiness, and disappointment as well as the verbal and physical aggression experienced by these families?" Prescott (1975), in a study of 49 societies, found that those societies that provided sparse physical affection to their children tended to be societies in which adults expressed a high level of inter-personal violence. However, this does not provide answers to just how little physical affection or how much physical aggression, or the particular com-bination of these child-rearing environments produces violent adults.

Although this study focused on how families resolved conflicts, the respondents in this study wanted to make it quite clear that other factors, not just how conflicts are resolved, made up the total family environment.

IN-DEPTH SEMISTRUCTURED INTERVIEW: PROCEDURE AND GENERAL TOPICS

1. Background data to be explained to respondents. "Today society presents many conflicts such as the high costs of living, the shrinking pay checks, how to raise one's children, whether the wife should work or stay home, etc. The Delaware family study is interested in knowing just how families resolve these conflicts. Usually research of this type is handled through a questionnaire or a single interview, and what happens is the people tend to report only the more dramatic crisis. This study will attempt to have the participants actually become part of the research team. So if I overlook any aspect which you feel is important, please feel free to add comments."

2. Ask permission to tape the interview. "It will allow me to concentrate on our discussion instead of trying to take notes. All information will be strictly confidential—no names will ever be used."

3. Go into the topics.

Do's and Dont's

DO

Check tape recorder before entering the home—make sure it is ready to go—
   test to see that it is recording properly and that volume is OK.
Ask permission to tape the interview—be friendly and sincere—but positive.
   ("You don't mind if I tape this—it will save me a lot of time trying to
   write down what you say.")
Assure confidentiality—only the researchers will know the respondents inter-
   viewed. No names will be used.
Do probe for answers—ask why? Why not? Suggest examples if they seem
   stumped—reword the question if necessary.
Remember the object of this interview is to find:

1. *What causes conflict between different members of the family?*
2. *How different members attampted to resolve the conflict—discussion,
   screaming, ignoring, threatening physical force, etc.*
3. *Their feelings as to the success or failure of this method.*
4. *Would they use this method again? Why or why not?*

After the interview—after you have left the area (drive around the block, etc., don't sit in front of their window) write down any impressions about the family which you had that might be helpful. You may want to dictate this on the recorder.

Did the parents show warmth towards the children?
Husband/wife interaction—kidding, supportive, aggressive, etc.
How were kids interacting with each other?
General appearance of family members, house, neighborhood, etc.

Note any unusual family patterns—is the husband out of town, a child sick, preparing to move—anything which might indicate that this visit and the week following might be atypical.
Take a positive attitude—*normal families are not conflict-free families.*
Some helpful data to reassure respondents that their behavior is normal: National survey: 94 percent of respondents had been spanked; 20-25 percent of respondents felt that it is OK for husband to slap wife and wife to slap husband on some occasions.

Be sure to explain the importance of recording the conflicts on a daily basis as soon after the occurrence as possible. Even the most trivial conflict—a small disagreement, kids yelling or hitting each other—is very important information. If kids are old enough, you might even suggest this as a family project and the kids can help to remind or even record incidents.

Assume that most families do engage in family "fights" and you are interested in frequency rather than whether or not they occur, e.g., "How often have you and your husband had what you would consider a big fight?" rather than "Have you and your husband ever had a fight?"

Be sure to label the tape as soon as it is complete. Use only 1 interview per tape.

DON'T

Don't show shock or surprise over an answer—remain non-committal, but supportive in your stance.

Control facial expression—don't register shock or disapproval. Prepare some stock replies—head nods, "I know how you felt." *Don't interrupt.*

Don't mention the word violence—use conflict resolution, problem solving or specific terms such as hit, slap. Violence is a label (what is violent to you may not be considered violent to some one else).

Talk as little as possible—only enough to feed respondent(s) new topics.

Don't rush the respondents—allow them adequate time to express their feelings but try to keep the interview to a period of about 1-1½ hours.

Don't stick strictly to the schedule—but try to cover all topics on it. Remember—even tangential information may be important—such as argument over in-laws or friends.

Topics For Interview

1. GENERAL

Family members, ages, occupations

Likes or dislikes of major occupation (job, housewife, student)

General feelings towards aggression (yelling, screaming, slapping) among family members

2. SIB/SIB

Causes of conflicts among brothers and sisters

Is this a new source—different from earlier conflicts—a particular stage?

How do parents cope with this?

Do your children have (more, less, same amount) conflicts than do your friends' and neighbors' children?

3. PARENT/CHILD

Causes of conflicts, more or less than at an earlier time (for each child)

How are conflicts resolved?

Do both parents agree on this method?

Are parents successful? Yes. No. Why, or why not?

4. HUSBAND/WIFE

What are the major sources of conflict between you and your spouse?

Do any of your friends or neighbors have similar problems?

Do you know if any of your friends were ever slapped or ever slapped their spouse? Why? Describe circumstances.

Do you think this solved the problem?

Have you ever slapped or been slapped by your spouse?

Describe circumstances and outcomes.

At what point in your marriage did this occur?

Is this a frequent or relatively rare occurrence?

Do you consider this action justified? Did your spouse?

Do you feel you and your spouse have (more, less, or same) amount of conflicts as other couples you know?

Do you use about the same amount of screaming or hitting as other couples you know?

Do you think that you and your spouse could prevent a marital conflict.

What would be an *ideal* way to resolve conflicts? How close do you think you and your spouse come to this ideal?

FAMILY PROBLEM-SOLVING QUESTIONNAIRE—
SHORT FORM

The following questionnaire is designed to find out how different family members resolve conflict. Please answer all questions carefully. Feel free to add comments and any other information which you feel is important and may not have been covered in the questionnaire. All information will be confidential.

Age _____ Sex _____ Year in School _____
Mother's highest level of schooling _____
Mother's job description _____
Father's highest level of schooling _____
Father's job description _____
Check correct one for each parent.
Do your parents supervise others as a part of their job?

	Mother	Father
No	_____	_____
1-4	_____	_____
5-9	_____	_____
10-19	_____	_____
20 or more	_____	_____

Please rate the 8 items below according to the importance your mother and father place on *your* having each of the traits. Give the trait your parent considers most important a rank of "1", the next important trait a rank of "2", and so on. The least important trait would be ranked "8". Rank the traits separately for your Mother and Father.

Mother	Father
_____ That I work hard	_____ That I work hard
_____ That I think for myself	_____ That I think for myself
_____ That I be considerate of others	_____ That I be considerate of others
_____ That I obey my parents well	_____ That I obey my parents well
_____ That I be dependable	_____ That I be dependable
_____ That I have self-control	_____ That I have self-control
_____ That I be popular with other children.	_____ That I be popular with other children
_____ That I be able to defend myself	_____ That I be able to defend myself

Please list your religious affiliation _____
Please list the activities your Mother engages in such as church groups, PTA, social clubs _____

Here is a list of things which your Mother and Father might have done, when they were trying to solve a problem. Taking all disagreements into account, not just the most serious ones, indicate how frequently each of them did the following during a conflict. Using the following code, circle the number which best describes how your Mother and Father solved the problem.

0 = Never   1 = Almost Never   2 = Sometimes   3 = Almost Always 4 = Always

		Mother	Father
A.	Tried to discuss the issue calmly.	0 1 2 3 4	0 1 2 3 4
B.	Did discuss the issue calmly.	0 1 2 3 4	0 1 2 3 4
C.	Got information to support the issue.	0 1 2 3 4	0 1 2 3 4
D.	Brought in someone else to try and help settle things.	0 1 2 3 4	0 1 2 3 4
E.	Argued a lot but did not yell or scream.	0 1 2 3 4	0 1 2 3 4
F.	Yelled, screamed or insulted each other.	0 1 2 3 4	0 1 2 3 4
G.	Sulked and refused to talk about it.	0 1 2 3 4	0 1 2 3 4
H.	Threw something (but not at the other) or smashed something.	0 1 2 3 4	0 1 2 3 4
I.	Threw something *at the other*.	0 1 2 3 4	0 1 2 3 4
J.	Stomped out of room.	0 1 2 3 4	0 1 2 3 4
K.	Pushed, grabbed, or shoved the other.	0 1 2 3 4	0 1 2 3 4
L.	Hit (or tried to hit) the other person with something hard.	0 1 2 3 4	0 1 2 3 4
M.	Threatened to hit or throw something at the other.	0 1 2 3 4	0 1 2 3 4
N.	Hit (or tried to hit) the other person but *not* with anything.	0 1 2 3 4	0 1 2 3 4

How would you describe your parent's marriage? Check one, please.

_____ very unhappy

_____ unhappy

_____ not too happy

_____ just about average

_____ a little happier than average

_____ very happy

_____ extremely happy

How long have your parents been married? _____

Here is a list of things which you and your mother and father might have done when you had a conflict. Taking all disagreements into account, not just the most serious ones, indicate how frequently each of you did the following during the problem.

Using the following code, circle the number which best describes problem solving between you and your Mother and Father.

0 = Never   1 = Almost Never   2 = Sometimes   3 = Almost Always   4 = Always

Father	Me		Mother	Me
0 1 2 3 4	0 1 2 3 4	A. Tried to discuss issue calmly.	0 1 2 3 4	0 1 2 3 4
0 1 2 3 4	0 1 2 3 4	B. *Did* discuss the issue calmly.	0 1 2 3 4	0 1 2 3 4
0 1 2 3 4	0 1 2 3 4	C. Got information to support his side	0 1 2 3 4	0 1 2 3 4
0 1 2 3 4	0 1 2 3 4	D. Brought in someone else to try and help settle things.	0 1 2 3 4	0 1 2 3 4
0 1 2 3 4	0 1 2 3 4	E. Argued a little but did not yell or scream.	0 1 2 3 4	0 1 2 3 4
0 1 2 3 4	0 1 2 3 4	F. Yelled, screamed or insulted each other.	0 1 2 3 4	0 1 2 3 4
0 1 2 3 4	0 1 2 3 4	G. Sulked and refused to talk about it.	0 1 2 3 4	0 1 2 3 4
0 1 2 3 4	0 1 2 3 4	H. Stomped out of the room.	0 1 2 3 4	0 1 2 3 4
0 1 2 3 4	0 1 2 3 4	I. Threw something (but not at the other) or smashed something.	0 1 2 3 4	0 1 2 3 4
0 1 2 3 4	0 1 2 3 4	J. Threatened to hit or throw something at the other.	0 1 2 3 4	0 1 2 3 4
0 1 2 3 4	0 1 2 3 4	K. Threw something *at the other.*	0 1 2 3 4	0 1 2 3 4
0 1 2 3 4	0 1 2 3 4	L. Pushed, grabbed or shoved the other.	0 1 2 3 4	0 1 2 3 4
0 1 2 3 4	0 1 2 3 4	M. Hit (or tried to hit) the other person but not with anything.	0 1 2 3 4	0 1 2 3 4
0 1 2 3 4	0 1 2 3 4	N. Hit or tried to hit the other person with something hard.	0 1 2 3 4	0 1 2 3 4

Please list your brothers and sisters by age and sex. Also give their highest level in school. (If you have more than three brothers and sisters select the three closest in age to you.)

Brother or Sister	Age	Sex	Highest level in school
#1	___	___	_____
#2	___	___	_____
#3	___	___	_____

Here is a list of things which you and your brothers and sisters listed above might have done when you were trying to solve a problem. Taking all disagreements into account not just the most serious ones, indicate how frequently each of you did the following during a conflict. Using the following code, circle the number which best describes how you resolved the problem.

0 = never   1 = almost never   2 = sometimes   3 = almost always   4 = always

	Me	#1	Me	#2	Me	#3
A. Tried to discuss issue calmly.	01234	01234	01234	01234	01234	01234
B. Did discuss the issue calmly.	01234	01234	01234	01234	01234	01234
C. Got information to support his side.	01234	01234	01234	01234	01234	01234
D. Brought in someone else to try and help settle things.	01234	01234	01234	01234	01234	01234
E. Argued a little but did not yell or scream.	01234	01234	01234	01234	01234	01234
F. Yelled, screamed or insulted each other.	01234	01234	01234	01234	01234	01234
G. Sulked and refused to talk about it.	01234	01234	01234	01234	01234	01234
H. Stomped out of the room.	01234	01234	01234	01234	01234	01234
I. Threw something but not at the other or smashed something.	01234	01234	01234	01234	01234	01234
J. Threatened to hit or throw something at the other.	01234	01234	01234	01234	01234	01234

K. Threw something
    at the other.   01234   01234   01234   01234   01234   01234
L. Pushed, grabbed,
    or shoved the
    other.   01234   01234   01234   01234   01234   01234
M. Hit (or tried to
    hit) the other
    person but not
    with something.   01234   01234   01234   01234   01234   01234
N. Hit or tried to
    hit the other
    person with some-
    thing hard.   01234   - 01234   01234   01234   01234   01234

FAMILY PROBLEM-SOLVING QUESTIONNAIRE— LONG FORM*

The following questionnaire is designed to find out how different family members resolve conflict. Please answer all questions carefully. Feel free to add comments and any other information which you feel is important and may not have been covered in the questionnaire. All information will be confidential.

1. Age _____   2. Sex _____   3. Marital Status _____
4. Present or highest level of schooling _____
5. Have either of your parents ever been divorced? (Check one)
    _____ mother has (before she married your father)
    _____ father has
    _____ both have (this would be their second marriage each)
    _____ neither has
6. Now check one of the following below which best describes your family situation at home and the people you will refer to in this questionnaire:
    _____ If you were living with both of your own parents, answer information based on them.
    _____ If you have lived most of your childhood with a parent or stepparent, answer the information based on them.
    _____ If you have lived for about the same time with both your natural parents and a stepparent, answer all questions about your parents based on the parent who lived with you during most of your grade school years.
    _____ If one of your parents is deceased or divorced, and there is no stepparent, answer the questions about that parent based on the time when this parent was living at home. Indicate *your* age when the death, or divorce took place _____ .   Other (please explain)

_____

*Questions not used in study have been deleted.

Education—Indicate the highest level of education attained by each of your
         parents.

	7. Mother	8. Father
Less than 7th grade	_____	_____
Between 7th and 9th grade	_____	_____
Some high school	_____	_____
High school graduate	_____	_____
Vocational training beyond high school	_____	_____
Some college	_____	_____
College graduate	_____	_____
Graduate degree MS, MA, or equivalent	_____	_____
Ph.D. or equivalent	_____	_____
Professional degree (law, medicine)	_____	_____

Answer each of these questions for both of your parents: Give a brief name or
title of their job. Please explain what each does in their job, their responsibilities,
tasks, special duties, services or skills they perform.

9.   Mother _____

10. Father _____

	11. Mother	12. Father
What type of work did each of your parents	_____	_____
do while you were in grade school?	_____	_____
(About 6-12 years old)	_____	_____

Check the category which best fits each of your parent's occupation:

	13. Mother	14. Father
Semi-skilled or unskilled workman (truck driver, factory worker, hospital aide)	_____	_____
Skilled workman or foreman (machinists, hair stylists, cook, carpenter)	_____	_____
Farmer (owner-operator or renter)	_____	_____
Clerical or sales position	_____	_____
Proprietor, except farm (i.e., owner of a business)	_____	_____
Professional (architect, chemist, doctor) etc., or managerial position (department head, store manager, postmaster, police chief)	_____	_____
Don't know	_____	_____

For whom did each of your parents work?	15. Mother	16. Father
Self-employed	_____	_____
Private business or industry	_____	_____
Government or school	_____	_____
Non-profit organization	_____	_____

Do your parents supervise others as part of their job? 17. Mother   18. Father

	17. Mother	18. Father
No	_____	_____
One or two people	_____	_____
Three or four	_____	_____
Five or nine	_____	_____
Ten to 19	_____	_____
Twenty to 29	_____	_____
Thirty to 49	_____	_____
Fifty to 99	_____	_____
one hundred or more	_____	_____

About how many people are employed in the place where each of your parents work?

	19. Mother	20. Father
1-4	_____	_____
5-9	_____	_____
10-19	_____	_____
20-49	_____	_____
50-99	_____	_____
100-199	_____	_____
200-499	_____	_____
500-999	_____	_____
1,000 or more	_____	_____

Which of the following groups comes closest to your parents' annual income *before* taxes?

	21. Mother	22. Father
Less than $4,000	_____	_____
$4,000 to $5,000	_____	_____
$6,000 to $7,999	_____	_____
$8,000 to $9,999	_____	_____
$10,000 to $11,999	_____	_____
$12,000 to 14,999	_____	_____
$15,000 to $19,999	_____	_____
$20,000 to $29,000	_____	_____
$30,000 to over	_____	_____

How satisfied would you say each of your parents were with this level of income?

	23. Mother	24. Father
Not at all satisfied	_____	_____
Slightly satisfied	_____	_____
Moderately satisfied	_____	_____
Almost completely satisfied	_____	_____
Completely satisfied	_____	_____

25. At what periods in your life was your mother employed FULL TIME for wages for one year or more (check all the answers that apply)?

_____ Never   _____ Junior high school age
_____ Preschool age   _____ Senior high school age
_____ Elementary school age

26. At what periods in your life was your mother employed PART TIME for wages for one year or more (check all the answers that apply)?

_____ Never   _____ Junior high school age

_____ Preschool age   _____ Senior high school age

_____ Elementary school age

27. How much would you say your mother likes being a homemaker (please answer even if your mother was also employed outside the home)?

_____ Dislikes homemaking a great deal

_____ Dislikes homemaking considerably

_____ Dislikes homemaking somewhat

_____ Dislikes homemaking a little

_____ Likes homemaking a little

_____ Likes homemaking somewhat

_____ Likes homemaking considerably

_____ Likes homemaking extremely well

28. If your mother is not currently employed, please list some of her activities, interests, hobbies (political committee women, civic interest, educational activities such as PTA or attending school or volunteer teacher's aide, taking part in fund raising drives, gardening, sewing, etc.). Please list any offices in these activities which your mother has held, for example, president of the women's church guild or secretary of the PTA.

How much does each parent like his or her job?	29. Mother	30. Father
Not employed	_____	_____
Dislikes his work a great deal	_____	_____
Dislikes his work considerably	_____	_____
Dislikes his work somewhat	_____	_____
Dislikes his work a little	_____	_____
Likes his work a great deal	_____	_____
Likes his work considerably	_____	_____
Likes his work somewhat	_____	_____
Likes his work extremely well	_____	_____

Which of the following comes the closest to the political preference of:

	31. Mother	32. Father	33. Self
Conservative Republican	_____	_____	_____
Liberal Republican	_____	_____	_____
Conservative Democrat	_____	_____	_____
Liberal Democrat	_____	_____	_____
Socialists	_____	_____	_____
Other (explain)	_____	_____	_____

34. Was there anyone besides you, your parents, and your brothers and sisters living in your house during your high school years?

Relation to you   Age

A. _____   _____

B. _____   _____

C. _____   _____

How much was this person dependent on your family for support?

A. Not _____   Part _____   All _____

B. Not _____   Part _____   All _____

C. Not _____   Part _____   All _____

Were your parents pleased to have this person living at home?

A. No _____   Partly _____   Yes _____

B. No _____   Partly _____   Yes _____

C. No _____   Partly _____   Yes _____

35. Rank the eight items below according to how important it would be for you to have each trait from your MOTHER'S point of view (give a rank of 1 to the most important trait, 2 to the second most important trait, etc.)

_____ That I work hard

_____ That I think for myself

_____ That I be considerate of others

_____ That I obey my parents well

_____ That I have self control

_____ That I be dependable

_____ That I be popular with other children

_____ That I be able to defend myself

36. Rank the following eight items from your father's point of view

_____ That I work hard

_____ That I think for myself

_____ That I be considerate of others

_____ That I be dependable

_____ That I be popular with other children

_____ That I have self control

_____ That I be able to defend myself

Here is a list of things that you and your father and mother might have done when you had a conflict. Now taking into account all disagreements (not just the most serious one), we would like you to say how often you had done the things listed at any time during your last year in high school. Answer by circling one of these numbers for each person.

0 = Never   1 = Almost never 2 = Sometime   3 = Almost Always 4 = Always

43. Father	44. Me		45. Mother	46. Me
01234	01234	A. Tried to discuss the issue calmly	01234	01234
01234	01234	B. Did discuss the issue calmly	01234	01234

01234	01234	C. Got information to support his side	01234	01234
01234	01234	D. Brought in someone else to try to help settle things	01234	01234
01234	01234	E. Argued a lot but did not yell or scream	01234	01234
01234	01234	F. Yelled, screamed or insulted each other	01234	01234
01234	01234	G. Sulked and refused to talk about it	01234	01234
01234	01234	H. Stomped out of the room	01234	01234
01234	01234	I. Threw something (but not at the other) or smashed something	01234	01234
01234	01234	J. Threatened to hit or throw something at the other	01234	01234
01234	01234	K. Threw something at the other	01234	01234
01234	01234	L. Pushed, grabbed, or shoved the other	01234	01234
01234	01234	M. Hit (or tried to hit) the other person but not with something	01234	01234
01234	01234	N. Hit or tried to hit the other person with something hard	01234	01234
01234	01234	O. Other. Please describe	01234	01234

47. Please list your brothers and sisters (also include stepbrothers and sisters if they live in your home).

Sibling	Age	Sex	Highest Level of Schooling
Number 1	_____	_____	_____
Number 2	_____	_____	_____
Number 3	_____	_____	_____

48. What is the area of the greatest conflict between you and this brother or sister

Number 1 _____

Number 2 _____

Number 3 _____

Here is a list of things which you and your brothers and sisters listed above might have done when you were trying to solve a problem. Taking all disagreements into account, not just the most serious ones, indicate how frequently each of you did the following during a conflict. Using the following code, circle the number which best describes how you resolve the problem.

0 = Never   1 = Almost never   2 = Sometimes   3 = Almost always   4 = Always

		49. Me	50. #1	51. Me	52. #2	53. Me	54. #3
A.	Tried to discuss issue calmly	01234	01234	01234	01234	01234	01234
B.	Did discuss the issue calmly	01234	01234	01234	01234	01234	01234
C.	Got information to support his side	01234	01234	01234	01234	01234	01234
D.	Brought in someone else to try and help settle things	01234	01234	01234	01234	01234	01234
E.	Argued a little but did not yell or scream	01234	01234	01234	01234	01234	01234
F.	Yelled, screamed or insulted each other	01234	01234	01234	01234	01234	01234
G.	Sulked and refused to talk about it	01234	01234	01234	01234	01234	01234
H.	Stomped out of the room	01234	01234	01234	01234	01234	01234
I.	Threw something but not at the other or smashed something	01234	01234	01234	01234	01234	01234
J.	Threatened to hit or throw something at the other	01234	01234	01234	01234	01234	01234
K.	Threw something at the other	01234	01234	01234	01234	01234	01234
L.	Pushed, grabbed, or shoved the other	01234	01234	01234	01234	01234	01234

M. Hit (or tried to
    hit) the other
    person but not
    with something   01234   01234   01234   01234   01234   01234
N. Hit or tried to
    hit the other
    person with some-
    thing hard   01234   01234   01234   01234   01234   01234

Here is a list of things which your Mother and Father might have done when
they were trying to solve a problem. Taking all disagreements into account,
not just the most serious ones, indicate how frequently each of them did the
following during a conflict. Using the following code, circle the number which
best describes how your Mother and Father solved the problem.

0 = Never   1 = Almost Never   2 = Sometimes   3 = Almost always   4 = Always
                                          55 = Mother   56 = Father

A. Tried to discuss the issue calmly   01234   01234
B. Did discuss the issue calmly   01234   01234
C. Got information to support his side   01234   01234
D. Brought in someone else to try and   01234   01234
    help settle things
E. Argued a lot but did not yell or scream   01234   01234
F. Yelled, screamed or insulted each other   01234   01234
G. Sulked and refused to talk about it   01234   01234
H. Stomped out of the room   01234   01234
I. Threw something (but not at the other)   01234   01234
    or smashed something
J. Threatened to hit or throw something   01234   01234
    at the other
K. Threw something *at the other*   01234   01234
L. Pushed, grabbed or shoved the other   01234   01234
M. Hit (or tried to hit) the other person   01234   01234
    with something hard.
O. Threatened to break up the marriage by   01234   01234
    separation or divorce
P. Other. Please describe   01234   01234

57. What are the three areas of greatest conflict between your parents? (1st =
    greatest; 2nd = next)
1st. _____
2nd. _____
3rd. _____

58. How would you describe your parent's marriage? Check one.

_____ very unhappy   _____ a little happier than average

_____ unhappy   _____ very happy

_____ not too happy   _____ extremely happy

_____ just about average

59. How long have your parents been married? _____

Please list your children by name, age and sex.

Child	Age	Sex
#1 _____	_____	_____
#2 _____	_____	_____
#3 _____	_____	_____

Here is a list of things which you and your children listed above might have done when you were trying to solve a problem. Taking all disagreements into account, not just the most serious ones, indicate how frequently each of you did the following during a conflict. Using the following code, circle the number which best describes how you and your children solved the problem.

0 = Never   1 = Almost never   2 = Sometimes   3 = Almost always   4 = Always

	62. Parent	63. #1	64. Parent	65. #2	66. Parent	67. #3
A. Tried to discuss issue calmly.	01234	01234	01234	01234	01234	01234
B. Did discuss the issue calmly.	01234	01234	01234	01234	01234	01234
C. Got information to support his side.	01234	01234	01234	01234	01234	01234
D. Brought in someone else to try and help settle things.	01234	01234	01234	01234	01234	01234
E. Argued a little but did not yell or scream.	01234	01234	01234	01234	01234	01234
F. Yelled, screamed or insulted each other.	01234	01234	01234	01234	01234	01234
G. Sulked and refused to talk about it.	01234	01234	01234	01234	01234	01234

H. Stomped out of
    the room.   01234   01234   01234   01234   01234   01234
I. Threw something
    but not at the
    other or smashed
    something.   01234   01234   01234   01234   01234   01234
J. Threatened to
    hit or throw
    something at
    the other.   01234   01234   01234   01234   01234   01234
K. Threw something
    at the other.   01234   01234   01234   01234   01234   01234
L. Pushed, grabbed,
    or shoved the
    other.   01234   01234   01234   01234   01234   01234
M. Hit (or tried to
    hit) the other
    person but *not*
    with anything.   01234   01234   01234   01234   01234   01234
N. Hit or tried to
    hit the other
    person with some-
    thing hard.   01234   01234   01234   01234   01234   01234
O. Other (Explain).   01234   01234   01234   01234   01234   01234

Here is a list of things which you and your husband (wife) might have done when you were trying to solve a problem. Taking all disagreements into account, not just the most serious ones, indicate how frequently you and your husband (wife) did the following during a conflict. Using the following code, circle the number which best describes how you and your husband (wife) solved the problem.

0 = Never   1 = Almost never   2 = Sometimes   3 = Almost always   4 = Always

		68. You	69. Husband (wife)
A.	Tried to discuss issue calmly.	01234	01234
B.	Did discuss the issue calmly.	01234	01234
C.	Got information to support his side.	01234	01234
D.	Brought in someone else to try and help settle things.	01234	01234
E.	Argued a lot but did not yell or scream.	01234	01234
F.	Yelled, screamed or insulted each other.	01234	01234

G.	Sulked and refused to talk about it.	01234	01234
H.	Stomped out of the room.	01234	01234
I.	Threw something (but not at the other) or smashed something.	01234	01234
J.	Threatened to hit or throw something at the other.	01234	01234
K.	Threw something *at the other*.	01234	01234
L.	Pushed, grabbed, or shoved the other.	01234	01234
M.	Hit (or tried to hit) the the other person but *not* with anything.	01234	01234
N.	Hit or tried to hit the other person with something hard.	01234	01234
O.	Other (explain).	01234	01234

DIARIES

Instructions for Recording Data

Be sure to note the date on the top of each sheet.

Try to record each conflict as it occurs (or shortly after) and record as many details as possible. The success of this research depends on the completeness of data gathered by participating families. The interviewer will be calling you daily and these sheets will be helpful in reporting data to her. It will also provide further data for the research and will be collected at the end of the phone data gathering period.

In this study YOU are the researcher. It will be up to you to note problems between family members and provide interpretations as to why family members acted this way. This is a big responsibility. But hopefully it will make participants in this research truly a part of the research team rather than passive respondents who only answer questions.

Use as many sheets as needed for each day.

Start each NEW day on a new sheet. For example, if you use 1½ sheets the first day DO NOT start the second day on the half sheet remaining, but instead start a new one.

Your participation and cooperation is greatly appreciated.

DAILY RECORD OF CONFLICT RESOLUTION

Date _____

Conflict	Family Members Involved	How Conflict Was Resolved: What Did Family Members Do	Outcomes—Success or Failure

New Castle County has an estimated (1973) population of 400,000. The population density for the state of Deleware is 291 persons per mile, making Delaware the eighth most populated state. Seventy-two percent of that population resides in New Castle County. Although once the state with the highest per capita income, it now ranks eighth. Residents of New Castle County also have a higher-than-average level of education. For the United States the mean level of education is 10 years. For Delaware it is 13.1 years. Although mean level of education is not available for New Castle County, it is likely that New Castle County is above the level for the state, especially since a large number of universities and colleges and research divisions of several large chemical and textile companies are located in New Castle County.

A comparison below of income levels for the United States and New Castle County for 1970 indicates that there is a higher percentage of New Castle, Delaware residents in higher income levels.

Income Level	Percent of U.S. Residents in Each Level	Percent of New Castle County Residents in Each Level
$1,000-2,999	10.3	6.1
3,000-5,999	15.7	10.5
6,000-9,999	26.7	26.1
10,000-14,999	26.7	31.0
15,000-24,999	16.0	19.8
25,000-49,999	3.9	5.5
50,000 and over	0.8	1.0

An occupational profile of New Castle County also suggests a well-educated population with somewhat higher-than-average U.S. incomes. Again, this reflects the presence of several large chemical and textile industries that have major facilities in New Castle County, a large state university (University of Delaware), a smaller four-year college, and numerous junior colleges.

New Castle County—Occupational Profile

Occupation	Percent of Total Labor Force Employed—16 and Over
Professional technical	20.9
Managers and administrators except farm	8.2
Sales workers	7.0
Clerical	19.2
Craftsmen	14.3
Nontransport operatives	10.8
Transport operatives	3.0
Laborers except farm	3.4
Farmers	0.7
Service workers	10.7
Private household workers	1.8
Total labor force employed—16 and over	151,125

Source: Delaware Statistical Abstract, 1974.

REFERENCES

Archer, D., and R. Gartner. 1976. "Violent Acts and Violent Times; A Comparative Approach to Postwar Homicide Rates." *American Sociological Review* 41 (December): 937-63.

Aries, P. 1965. *Centuries of Childhood: A Social History of Family Life.* New York: Random House.

Bandura, A. 1973. *Aggression—A Social Learning Analysis.* Englewood Cliffs, N.J.: Prentice Hall.

Bard, Morton. 1971. "The Study and Modification of Intra-familial Violence." In *The Control of Aggression and Violence*, ed. Jerome L. Singer, pp. 149-64. New York: Academic Press.

Bayne-Powell, R. 1939. *The English Child in the Eighteenth Century.* London.

Beatles, The. 1967. "Getting Better," *Sergeant Pepper's Lonely Hearts Club Band.* Capitol Records.

Bell, Robert R. 1971. *Social Deviance.* Homewood, Ill.: The Dorsey Press.

Bellak, L. 1970. *The Porcupine Dilemma.* New York: Citadel Press.

Bellak, L., and M. Antell. 1974. "An Intercultural Study of Aggressive Behavior on Children's Playgrounds." *American Journal of Orthopsychiatry* 44: 503-11.

Bender, L. 1959. "Children and Adolescents Who Have Killed." *American Journal of Psychiatry* 116: 510-13.

Bender, L., and F. J. Curran. 1940. "Children and Adolescents Who Kill." *Criminal Psychopathology* 3, no. 4: 297-322.

Besharov, J. D. 1975. "Building A Community Response to Child Abuse and Maltreatment." *Children Today* 4, no. 5: 2.

Bettelheim, B. 1967. "Children Should Learn About Violence." *Saturday Evening Post*, March 12, p. 10.

Bieber, Irving et al. 1962. *Homosexuality, A Psychoanalytic Study.* New York: Basic Books.

Black, D. J., and A. J. Reiss. 1967. "Studies in Crime and Law Enforcement in Major Metropolitan Areas." *Patterns of Behavior in Police and Citizen Transaction* 2, U.S. Government Printing Office.

Blood, R. O., Jr., and D. M. Wolfe. 1960. *Husbands and Wives, The Dynamics of Married Living*. New York: The Free Press.

Blumenthal, M. D., et al. 1972. *Justifying Violence: Attitudes of American Men*. Ann Arbor: University of Michigan Press.

Bourne, P. G. 1971. "From Boot Camp to My Lai." In *Crimes of War*, ed. Richard A. Falk, Gabriel Kolko, and Robert Jay Lifton. New York: Vintage Books.

Brenner, R. H., et al. 1970. *Children and Youth in America: A Documentary History*. Cambridge: Harvard University Press.

Brownmiller, Susan. 1975. *Against Our Will: Men, Women and Rape*. New York: Simon and Schuster.

Bryant, H. D. 1963. "Physical Abuse of Children: An Agency Study." *Child Welfare* 42: 125-30.

Calvert, Robert. 1974. "Criminal and Civil Liability in Husband-Wife Assaults." In *Violence in the Family*, ed. Suzanne K. Steinmertz and Murray A. Straus. New York: Dodd, Mead.

Campbell, D., and D. Fiske. 1959. "Convergence and Discriminate Validation by Multitrait Multimethod Matrix." *Psychological Bulletin* 56: 81-105.

Chicago Tribune, November 4, 1973.

Christensen, H. T. 1964. *Handbook of Marriage and the Family*. Chicago: Rand McNally.

Climent, C. E., and F. R. Ervin. 1972. "Historical Data in the Evaluation of Violent Subjects." *Archives of General Psychiatry* 27: 621-24.

Cohen, A. K. 1955. *Delinquent Boys: The Culture of the Gang*. Glencoe, Ill.: The Free Press.

Cohen, M., et. al. 1968. "Family Interaction Patterns, Drug Treatment, and Change in Social Aggression." *Archives of General Psychiatry* 19 (July): 50-56.

Coser, L. A. 1963. "Violence and the Social Structure." *Science and Psychoanalysis* 6: 30-42.

------. 1966. "Some Social Functions of Violence." *Annals of the American Academy of Political and Social Science* 364 (March): 8-18.

Craft, M. 1969. "The Natural History of Psychopathic Disorder." *British Journal of Psychiatry* 115: 39-44.

Curtis, G. C. 1963. "Violence Breeds Violence—Perhaps?" *American Journal of Psychiatry* 120: 386-87.

Dahrendorf, R. 1959. *Class and Class Conflict in Industrial Society*. Stanford, Calif.: Stanford University Press, 166.

Davis, Kingsley. 1940. "Extreme Social Isolation of a Child." *American Journal of Sociology* 45 (January): 554-65.

———. 1947. "A Final Note on a Case of Extreme Isolation." *American Journal of Sociology* 52: 432-37.

DeCourcy, P., and J. DeCourcy. 1973. *The Silent Tragedy*. New York: Alfred Publishing.

deMause, L. 1974. *The History of Childhood*. New York: The Psychohistory Press.

Donovan, R. J. 1955. *The Assassins*. New York: Harper and Row.

Duncan, J. W., and G. M. Duncan. 1971. "Murder in the Family: A Study of Some Homicidal Adolescents." *American Journal of Psychiatry* 127 (May): 1498-1502.

Duncan, G. M., et. al. 1958. "Etiological Factors in First Degree Murder." *Journal of American Medical Association* 168: 1755-58.

Easson, W. M., and R. N. Steinhilber. 1961. "Murderous Aggression by Children and Adolescents." *Archives of General Psychiatry* 4 (January): 1-9.

Eron, L. D., L. O. Walder, and M. M. Lefkowitz. 1971. *Learning of Aggression in Children*. Boston: Little, Brown.

Family Weekly The. 1977. *Sunday News Journal*. January 16, p. 22.

Fithian, P. V. 1945. *Journal and Letters of Philip Vickers Fithian, 1773-1774*. Princeton, N.J.: Princeton University Press.

Fontana, V. J. 1964. *The Maltreated Child*. Springfield, Ill.: Charles C. Thomas.

Frost, J. William. 1973. *The Quaker Family in Colonial America*. New York: St. Martin's Press.

Gallagher, J. J. 1972. "Dangerous Children." Philadelphia *Sunday Bulletin Parade* magazine, October 2, p. 11.

Gayford, J. J. 1975. "Wife Battering: A Preliminary Survey of 100 Cases." *British Medical Journal* 1: 194-97.

Geddes, David. 1975. "Run Joey Run." Big Tree Records.

Gelles, R. J. 1973. "Child Abuse as Psychopathology: A Sociological Critique and Reformulation." *American Journal of Orthopsychiatry* 43 (July): 611-21.

———. 1974. *The Violent Home: A Study of Physical Aggression Between Husbands and Wives*. Beverly Hills: Sage Publications.

———. 1976. "Abused Wives: Why Do They Stay?" *Journal of Marriage and the Family* 38, no. 4: 659-68.

Gil, D. 1970. *Violence Against Children*. Cambridge: Harvard University Press.

———. 1971. "Violence Against Children." *Journal of Marriage and The Family* 33: 637-48.

Glueck, E., and S. Glueck. 1956. *Physique and Delinquency*. New York: Harper and Row.

Goode, W. G. 1971. "Force and Violence in the Family." *Journal of Marriage and the Family* 33: 624-36.

Gove, Walter B. 1972. "The Relationship Between Sex Roles, Marital Status, and Mental Illness." *Social Forces* 51 (September): 34-44.

Hammer, R. 1971. *The Court Martial of Lieutenant Calley*. New York: Coward, McCann and Geoghegan.

Hartogs, Renatus. 1951. "Discipline in the Early Life of Sex-delinquent and Sex Criminals." *Nervous Child* 9 (March): 167-73.

Hastings. D. W. 1965. "The Psychiatry of Presidential Assassinations." *Journal Lancet* (March): 93-100, (April): 157-62, (May): 189-92, (July): 194-301.

Havernick, W. 1964. *Schlage als Strafe*. Hamburg.

Helfer, R. E., and C. H. Kempe. 1968. *The Battered Child*. Chicago: University of Chicago Press.

Hoffman, M. L. 1960. "Power Assertion by the Parent and Its Impact on the Child." *Child Development* 31: 129-43.

———. 1963. "Parent Discipline and the Child's Consideration for Others." *Child Development* 34: 573-88.

Hofstaater, R., and M. Wallace. 1970. *American Violence*. New York: Alfred A. Knopf.

Hollingshead, A., and F. Redlich. 1958. *Social Class and Mental Illness*. New York: John Wiley and Sons.

Hostetler, John A. 1968. *Amish Society*. Baltimore: John Hopkins Press.

Howard, John R. 1966. "The Making of a Black Muslim." *Transactions* (December): 15-21.

Huggins, M. D., and M. A. Straus. 1974. "Violence and the Social Structure as Reflected in Children's Books from 1850-1970." Mimeographed. Durham: University of New Hampshire.

Ingraham vs. Wright. 1977. *U.S. Law Week* 45: 4364.

Kanowitz, L. 1969. *Women and the Law: The Unfinished Revolution*. Albuquerque: University of New Mexico Press.

Kohn, Melvin. 1969. *Class and Conformity*. Homewood, Ill.: The Dorsey Press.

Kohn, M., and C. Schooler. 1973. "Occupational Experience and Psychological Functioning: An Assessment of Reciprocal Effects." *American Sociological Review* 38 (February): 97-118.

Kunzle, M., ed. 1972. "Italian Prison Horrors." *New Statesman*, August 4, pp. 149-50.

Levinger, G. 1966. "Sources of Marital Dissatisfaction Among Applicants for Divorce." *American Journal of Orthopsychiatry* 36 (October): 803-07. Reprinted in *Violence in the Family*, ed. S. K. Steinmetz and M. A. Straus. New York: Dodd, Mead, 1974.

Lifton, R. J. 1971. "Victims and Executioners." In *Crimes of War*, ed. Richard A. Falk, Gabriel Kolko, and Robert Jay Lifton. New York: Random House.

MacDonald, J. M. 1967. "Homicidal Threats." *American Journal of Psychiatry* 124: 475-82.

MacNamara, D. E., and E. Sagarin. 1971. *Perspectives on Correction*. New York: Crowell.

Manchester, W. 1970. *Arms of Krupp: 1587-1968*. New York: Bantam Books.

Mantell, D. M. 1974. "Doves vs. Hawks: Guess Who Had The Authoritarian Parents?" *Psychology Today* (September): 56-62.

Matthews et al. 1975. "Two Faces of Sara Jane Moore." *Newsweek*, September 22, pp. 22-24.

Michener, J. A. 1971. "Kent State: What Happened and Why." *Reader's Digest*, April, pp. 218, 263-76. Reprinted as "The Kent State Four/Should Have Studied More." In *Violence in the Family*, ed. S. K. Steinmetz and M. A. Straus. New York: Dodd, Mead, 1974.

Milgram, S. 1974. *Obedience to Authority: An Experimental View*. New York: Harper and Row.

Miller, Brent C. 1976. "A Multivariate Development Model of Marital Satisfaction." *Journal of Marriage and the Family* 38, no. 4: 643-57.

Miller, D. R., and G. Swanson. 1958. *The Changing American Parent*. New York: Wiley.

Milowe, I. D., and R. S. Lourie. 1964. "The Child's Role in the Battered Child Syndrome." *Journal of Pediatrics* 65, no. 6: 1079-81.

Newsweek. March 8, 1971, pp. 51-52.

Newsweek. June 5, 1972, pp. 38-39. "Bremer: Have Gun, Will Travel."

New York *Times*. February 1, 1970, Section 4, p. 3; July 22, 1972; November 4, 1973, p. 10; October 10, 1971, p. 20; "Milwaukee Man Held as Suspect." May 16, pp. 1 and 34.

Niederhoffer, A. 1967. *Behind the Shield: The Police in Urban Society*. Garden City, N.Y.: Doubleday.

Niemi, R. G. 1974. *How Family Members Perceive Each Other*. New Haven: Yale University Press.

O'Brien, J. E. 1971. "Violence in Divorce-Prone Families." *Journal of Marriage and the Family* 33: 692-98.

Oliver, J. E., and Audrey Taylor. 1971. "Five Generations of Ill-Treated Children in One Family Pedigree." *British Journal of Psychiatry* 119, no. 552: 473-80.

Osgood, C. E., and G. I. Suci. 1952. "A Measure of Relation Determined by Both Mean Difference and Profile Information." *Psychological Bulletin* 49 (May): 251-62.

Oswald, R. L., M. Land, and B. Land. 1967. *Lee, A Portrait of Lee Harvey Oswald by His Brother*. New York: Coward, McCann and Geoghegan.

Owens, D. J., and M. A. Straus. 1975. "Childhood Violence and Adult Approval of Violence." *Aggressive Behavior* 1, no. 2: 193-211.

Palmer, Stuart. 1962. *The Psychology of Murder*. New York: Thomas Y. Crowell.

Parnas, Raymond. 1964. "The Police Response to Domestic Disturbances." *Wisconsin Law Review* (Fall): 914-60.

Philadelphia Inquirer. April 18, 1975, p. 10A.

Pittman, D. J. 1964. "Patterns in Criminal Aggravated Assault." *Journal of Criminal Law, Criminology and Police Science* 55: 462-70.

Pokorney, A. 1956. "Human Violence: A Comparison of Homicide, Aggravated Assault, Suicide and Attempted Suicide." *Journal of Criminal Law, Criminology and Police Science* 56: 488-97.

Prescott, James. 1975. "Body Pleasure and the Origins of Violence." *The Futurists* (April): 64-74.

"Prison Debate—Where Does Abuse End and Coddling Begin." 1969. *Senior Scholastic*, November, pp. 5-10.

Reiss, Ira L. 1967. *The Social Context of Premarital Sexual Permissiveness*. New York: Holt, Reinhart and Winston.

Rogers, Carl A. 1965. "The Phenomenological Theory of Personality." In *Psychology of Personality: Readings in Theory*, ed. William S. Sahakian, pp. 473-93. Chicago: Rand McNally.

Rosenzweig, Saul. 1974. "Definition and Classification of Aggressive Phenomena." Paper presented at First International Conference on Aggression, Toronto.

Sadoff, R. L. 1971. "Clinical Observations on Parricide." *Psychiatric Quarterly* 45, no. 1: 65-69.

Safilios-Rothschild, C. 1969. "Family Sociology of Wives' Family Sociology? A Cross-cultural Examination of Decision-Making." *Journal of Marriage and the Family* 31: 290-301.

Sanford, N., and C. Comstock, eds. 1971. *Sanctions for Evil*. San Francisco: Jossey Bass.

Sargent, D. 1962. "Children Who Kill—A Family Conspiracy?" *Social Work* 7: 35-42.

Satten, J. K., et al. 1960. "Murder Without Apparent Motive: A Study in Personality Disorganization." *American Journal of Psychiatry* 117: 48-53.

Schreiber, Flora Rheta. 1973. *Sybil*. New York: Warner Books, p. 211.

Sears, R. R. 1961. "The Relation of Early Socialization Experiences to Aggression in Middle
Childhood." *Journal of Abnormal Social Psychology* 63: 466-92.

Sears, R. R., E. F. Maccoby, and H. Levin. 1957. *Patterns of Child Rearing*. New York:
Row, Peterson.

Seltman. 1956. *Women in Antiquity*. London:

Sellitiz, C., et al. 1959. *Research Methods in Social Relations*. New York: Holt, Rinehart,
and Winston.

Sendi, Ismail, and P. G. Blomgren. 1975. "A Comparative Study of Predictive Criteria in the
Predisposition of Homicidal Adolescents." *American Journal of Psychiatry* 132, no.
4: 423-27.

Sennett, Richard. 1973. "The Brutality of Modern Families." In *Marriage and Families*, ed.
Helena Z. Lopata, pp. 81-90. New York: D. Van Nostrand.

Shanas, E., et al. 1968. *Old People in Three Industrial Societies*. New York: Atherton Press.

Shanas, E. and G. Streib. 1963. Proceedings of symposium, "Family Intergeneration Relations and Social Structure." London: Tavistock. Reprinted as *Social Structure and
the Family: Generational Relations*, Englewood Cliffs, N.J.: Prentice Hall, 1965.

Sidel, R. 1972. *Women and Child Care in China*. New York: Hill and Wang.

Silver, L. B., C. C. Dublin, and R. S. Lourie. 1969. "Does Violence Breed Violence? Con-
tributions from a Study of the Child Abuse Syndrome." *American Journal of Psychiatry* 126, no. 3 (September): 404-07.

Skolnick, J. H. 1969. *Justice Without Trial: Law Enforcement in Democratic Society*. New
York: Wiley.

Smith, Terrence. 1968. "Early Life Termed Bitter." New York *Times*, June 6, pp. 1, 22.

Spitz, Rene A. 1964. "Hospitalism." In *The Family, Its Structure and Function*, ed. Rose L.
Coser, pp. 399-425. New York: St. Martin's Press.

Sprey, Jetse. 1969. "The Family as a System in Conflict." *Journal of Marriage and the Family* 31 (November): 699-706.

———. 1971. "On the Management of Conflict in Families." *Journal of Marriage and the
Family* 33 (November): 722-32.

Stark, R. 1972. *Police Riots: Collective Violence and Law Enforcement*. Belmont, Calif.:
Wadsworth Publishing.

Stark, R. and James McEvoy, IV. 1970. "Middle Class Violence." *Psychology Today*, November 4, pp. 52-65.

Steel, B. F., and C. B. Pollack. 1968. "A Psychiatric Study of Parents Who Abuse Infants and Small Children." In *The Battered Child*, ed. R. E. Helfer and C. H. Kempe. Chicago: University of Chicago Press.

Steel, R., et al. 1975. "The Story of Squeaky." *Newsweek*, September 15, pp. 18-19.

Steinmetz, S. K. 1971. "Occupation and Physical Punishment: A Response to Straus." *Journal of Marriage and the Family* 33 (November): 664-66.

———. 1973. "Family Backgrounds of Political Assassins." Paper presented at the American Orthopsychiatric Association annual meeting.

———. 1974a. "Occupational Environment in Relation to Physical Punishment and Dogmatism." In *Violence in the Family*, ed. S. K. Steinmetz and M. A. Straus, pp. 166-72. New York: Dodd, Mead.

———. 1974b. "Intra-Familial Patterns of Conflict Resolution: United States and Canadian Comparisons." Paper presented at Society for the Study of Social Problems, annual meeting.

———. 1974c. "The Sexual Context of Social Research." *The American Sociologist* 9 (August): 111-16.

———. 1977a. "The Use of Force for Resolving Family Conflict: The Training Ground for Abuse." *Family Coordinator* 26, no. 1: 19-26.

———. 1977b. "The Relationship Between Disciplinary Techniques and the Development of Aggressiveness, Dependency and Conscience." In *Contemporary Theories on the Family*, ed. Wesley Burr, et al. New York: The Free Press.

———. 1977c. "Wife Beating, Husband Beating—A Comparison of the Use of Physical Violence Between Spouses to Resolve Marital Fights." In *Abused and Battered Wife*, ed. Maria Roy. New York: Van Nostrand Reinhold.

Steinmetz, S. K., and M. A. Straus. 1973. "Family as Cradle of Violence." *Society*, September/October, pp. 50-56.

———, eds. 1974. *Violence in the Family*. New York: Dodd, Mead.

Straus, Murray A. 1971. "Some Social Antecedents of Physical Punishment: A Linkage Theory Interpretation." *Journal of Marriage and The Family* (November): 658-63.

———. 1973. "Leveling Civility and Violence in the Family." *Journal of Marriage and The Family* 36 (February): 13-29.

Straus, M. A., R. A. Gelles, and S. K. Steinmetz. 1973. "Theories, Methods and Controversies in the Study of Violence Between Family Members." Seminar presented to the annual meetings of the American Sociological Association, New York.

Sunday Bulletin. October 13, 1974, p. 24.

Sunday Bulletin (Philadelphia). February 1, 1975.

Sussman, M. B. 1959. "The Isolated Nuclear Family: Fact or Fiction." *Social Problems* 6: 333-40.

Tanay, E. 1969. "Psychiatric Study of Homicide." *American Journal of Psychiatry* 125: 1252-58.

——. 1975. "Reactive Parricide." *Journal of Forensic Sciences*, pp. 76-82.

Time. March 17, 1975, p. 88; January 14, 1977, p. 14; February 7, 1977, pp. 58-59.

Toby, Jackson. 1966. "Violence and the Masculine Ideal: Some Qualitative Data." In *Patterns of Violence*, ed. Marvin E. Wolfgang, vol. 34, pp. 20-27. Philadelphia: The Annals of the American Academy of Political and Social Science.

Torgeson, D. 1973. New York *Daily Times*, February 20, pp. 4.

U.S. Documents. 1969. *Crimes of Violence*. National Commission on Violence, vol. 11.

Valentine, A. 1963. *Fathers to Sons: Advice Without Consent*. Norman: University of Oklahoma Press.

Vital Statistics Report (Annual Summary for the United States). 1976. Vol. 24, No. 13. Washington, D.C.: National Center for Health Statistics.

Wasserman, S. 1967. "The Abused Parent of the Abused Child." *Children* 14 (September-October): 175-79.

Weber, Max. 1947. *Wirtschaft and Gesellschaft*. 4th ed. Tubingen, Germany.

——. 1947a. *The Theory of Social and Economic Organization*. Translated by A. M. Henderson and Talcott Parsons. New York 1950.

Westley, W. A. 1970. *Violence and the Police: A Sociological Study of Laws, Customs and Morality*. Cambridge: MIT Press.

Whitehurst, R. 1974. "Alternative Family Structures and Violence Reduction." In *Violence in the Family*, ed. S. K. Steinmetz and M. A. Straus, pp. 315-20. New York: Dodd, Mead.

Whyte, W. F. 1943. *Street Corner Society*. Chicago: University of Chicago Press.

Whyte, W. H., Jr. 1956. *Organization Man*. New York: Simon and Schuster.

Wickersham, George W. 1931. "Enforcement of Prohibition Laws." In *Official Record of the National Commission on Law Observance and Enforcement*, 3rd. sess., Senate Document No. 307 (see vol. 5, *Reforming America with a Shot Gun*, pp. 491-515). Washington, D.C.: U.S. Government Printing Office.

Wilmington *Evening Journal.* April 21, 1976, p. 2; January 7, 1975, p. 3; June 24, 1974, p. 23.

Wolfgang, M. E. 1958. *Patterns in Criminal Homicide.* Philadelphia: University of Pennsylvania Press.

Wolfgang, M. E., and F. Ferracuti. 1967. *The Subculture of Violence: Toward an Integrated Theory of Criminology.* London: Tavistock.

Zalba, S. R. 1966. "The Abused Child: A Survey of the Problem." *Social Work* 11: 3-16.

BIBLIOGRAPHIES ON AGGRESSION AND
FAMILY VIOLENCE

Chappell, Duncan, and John Monahan, eds. *Violence and Criminal Justice*. Lexington, Mass: Lexington Books, 1975, pp. 111-41.

Children's Bureau, U.S. Department of Health, Education and Welfare. *Bibliography on the Battered Child*. Rev. ed. Washington, D.C.: Children's Bureau, 1969.

Council for Exceptional Children. *Child Abuse: A Selective Bibliography*. Exceptional Child Bibliography Series, no. 601. Reston, Va.: Council for Exceptional Children, 1975.

Freerksen, Gregory N., and Donna M. Tuke. "Young Persons in the Legal Literature: An Annotated Bibliography." *Law In American Society* 4, no. 3 (September 1975): 33-38.

Goldman, Vivian S., et al. "Research Relating to Children." *Bulletin* 25 (April-December, 1969). Washington, D.C.: Clearinghouse for Research in Child Life, EDRS.

———. "Research Relating to Children." *Bulletin* 26 (January-May, 1970). Washington, D.C.: Clearinghouse for Research in Child Life, EDRS.

Goldstein, Jeffrey H. "Social and Psychological Aspects of Child Abuse: A Bibliography." *Catalog of Selected Documents in Psychology* 5, no. 289 (1976).

Kline, Donald F., and Mark A. Hopper. *Child Abuse: An Integration of the Research Related to Education of Children Handicapped as a Result of Child Abuse. Final Report*. EDRS, 1975.

Naughton, M. James, et al. *Child Protective Services: A Bibliography with Partial Annotation and Cross-Indexing—1976*. Seattle: Health Sciences Learning Resources Center, University of Washington, EDRS, 1976.

Rosengard, Barbara, ed. *Research, Demonstration, and Evaluation Studies: Fiscal Year 1973*. Washington, D.C.: Children's Bureau, 1974.

The unpublished articles in this Bibliography are available from ERIC Document Reproduction Service (EDRS), Arlington, Va.; National Technical Information Service, Springfield, Va.; and National Auxiliary Publication Service (NAPS), American Society of Information Service, New York, N.Y.

Russell, Gordon, and Joseph Zacher. "400 Books on Aggression." Mimeographed. Lethbridge, Canada: Department of Psychology, University of Lethbridge.

Southwest Educational Development Lab. *Parenting in 1975: A Listing from PMIC*. Washington, D.C.: National Institute of Education, EDRS, 1975.

Steinmetz, Suzanne K., and Murray A. Straus. "Bibliography for Violence in the Family." New York: American Society of Information Service, NAPS, document number 02182.

Wake, Sandra Byford, et al. "Research Relating to Children." *Bulletin* 27 (June 1970-February 1971). Urbana, Ill.: Clearinghouse on Early Childhood Education, EDRS.

FAMILY VIOLENCE

Abramson, Paul R. "Familial Variables Related to the Expression of Violent Aggression in Preschool-Age Children." *Journal of Genetic Psychology* 122 (June 1973): 345-46.

Ansbacher, Heinz L. "Love and Violence in the View of Adler." *Humanitas* 2, no. 2 (1966): 109-27.

Bard, Morton and Joseph Zacher. "The Prevention of Family Violence: Dilemmas of Community Intervention." *Journal of Marriage and the Family* 33 (November 1971): 677-82.

Barnes, Geoffrey B., Robert S. Chabon, and Leonard J. Hertzbert. "Team Treatment for Abusive Families." *Social Casework* 55, no. 10 (December 1974).

Beyer, Margaret, et al. "Runaway Youths: Families in Conflict." Paper presented at the Eastern Psychological Association meeting, May 3-4, 1973, Washington, D.C. Mimeographed.

Boudouris, James. "Homicide and the Family." *Journal of Marriage and the Family* 33 (November): 667-76.

Dicks, H. V. "Conflict In the Family." *New Society*, 1963, 2, no. 60 (November): 11-12.

Dominick, Joseph R. "The Influence of Social Class, the Family and Exposure to Television Violence on the Socialization of Aggression." *Dissertation Abstracts International* 31, no. 12-A (June 1971): 6641.

Engein, Richard, et al. "Behaviour Modification Techniques Applied to a Family Unit: A Case Study." *Journal of Child Psychology and Psychiatry and Allied Disciplines* 9, no. 3/4 (1968): 245-52.

Farrington, D. P., and D. J. West. "A Comparison between Early Delinquents and Young Aggressives." *British Journal of Criminology* 2, no. 4 (October 1971): 341-58.

Forrest, Tess. "The Family Dynamics of Maternal Violence." *Journal of the American Academy of Psychoanalysis* 2, no. 3 (1974): 215-30.

Gelles, Richard J., and Murray A. Straus. "Determinants of Violence in the Family: Toward
   A Theoretical Integration." In *Contemporary Theories about the Family*, edited by
   Wesley Burr, et. al. New York: The Free Press, 1977.

———. "Family Experience and Public Support of the Death Penalty." *American Journal of
   Orthopsychiatry* 45, no. 4 (July 1975): 596-613.

Gillin, J. L. *The Wisconsin Prisoner: Studies in Crimogenesis*. Madison: University of Wisconsin Press, 1946.

Goode, William J. "Force and Violence in the Family." *Journal of Marriage and the Family*
   33, no. 4 (November 1971): 624-36.

Havens, Leston L. "Youth, Violence, and the Nature of Family Life." *Psychiatric Annals* 2,
   no. 2 (February 1972): 18-29.

Leon, C. A. "Unusual Patterns of Crime during 'la Violencia' in Columbia." *American Journal of Psychiatry* 125, no. 11 (1969): 1564-75.

Lystad, Mary Hanemann. "Violence at Home: A Review of the Literature." *American Journal of Orthopsychiatry* 45, no. 3 (April 1975): 328-45.

Oliver, J. E., and Jane Cox. "A Family Kindred with Ill-Used Children: The Burden on the
   Community." *British Journal of Psychiatry* 123, no. 572 (July): 81-90.

Olsen, Nancy J. "Family Structure and Independence Training in a Taiwanese Village."
   Journal of Marriage and the Family 35, no. 3 (August 1973): 512-19.

Reid, John B. "Reciprocity in Family Interaction." *Dissertation Abstracts International* 29,
   no. 1-B (1968): 378-79.

Schindler, Sepp. "Family Constellation and Aggressive Conduct." *Zeitschrift fur Klinische
   Psychologie und Psychotherapie* 22, no. 2 (January 1974): 180-82.

Shaw, David A. "Family Maintenance Schedules for Deviant Behavior." *Dissertation Abstracts International* 32, no. 9-13 (March 1972): 5459-60.

Straus, Murray A., et. al. *Theories, Methods, and Controversies in the Study of Violence
   Between Family Members*. EDRS, June 1974.

———, Richard J. Gelles, and Suzanne K. Steinmetz. "Violence in the Family: An Assessment of Knowledge and Research Needs." In *Child Abuse: Its Treatment and Prevention: An Interdisciplinary Approach*, edited by Mary Vanstolk. Toronto: Mc-
   Clelland and Steward, 1977.

VanStolk, Mary. "Beaten Women, Battered Children." *Children Today* 5, no. 2 (March-April
   1976): 8-12.

Ziese, P. "Broken Home, Suicide, Complicated by Suicide with Endogenous Depression."
   Social Psychiatry 3, no. 2 (1968): 70-75.

MARITAL VIOLENCE

Bard, Morton. "Police Family Crisis Intervention and Conflict Management: An Action Research Analysis." Report No. PB-230-973. Springfield, Va.: National Technical Information Service, 1972.

Barden, J. C. "Wife Beaters: Few of Them Ever Appear Before a Court of Law." *New York Times*, October 21, 1974.

"Battered Wives; Chiswick Woman's Aid." *Newsweek*, July 9, 1973.

"Battered Wives: Now They're Fighting Back." *U.S. News and World Report*, September 20, 1976.

"Battered Wives: Where to Get Help." *Ms.*, August 1976.

Belson, Richard. "You Have To Know Who Is Who." *Journal of Family Counseling* 2, no. 1 (Spring 1974): 55-59.

Cormier, Bruno M. "Psychodynamics of Homicide Committed in a Marital Relationship." *Corrective Psychiatry and Journal of Social Therapy* 8 (1962): 187-94.

Durbin, K. "Wife Beating." *Ladies' Home Journal*, June 1974.

———. "Intelligent Woman's Guide to Sex: D. Martin's Battered Wives." *Mademoiselle*, December 1976.

Edmiston, Susan. "The Wife Beaters." *Woman's Day*, March 1976, p. 110.

Eisenberg, Sue, and Patricia L. Micklow. "The Assaulted Wife: Catch 22 Revisited." Mimeographed. Ann Arbor, Mich., 1974.

Faulk, M. "Men Who Assault Their Wives." *Medicine, Science and the Law* 14, no. 3 (1974): 180-83.

Field, Martha H., and Henry F. Field. "Marital Violence and the Criminal Process: Neither Justice nor Peace." *Social Service Review* 47, no. 2 (June 1973): 221-40.

Francke, L. B. "Battered Women." *Newsweek*, February 2, 1976.

Gelles, Richard J. "Power, Sex and Violence: The Case of Marital Rape." *Family Coordinator* (Forthcoming).

———. "Violence and Pregnancy: A Note on the Extent of the Problem and Needed Services." *Family Coordinator* 24, no. 1 (January 1975): 81-86.

Geracimos, A., ed. "How I Stopped Beating My Wife." *Ms*, August 1976.

Gingold, M. J. "Wife Beaters: One of These Days—Pow, Right in the Kisser." *Ms.*, August 1976.

Hoover, Carol F. "Conflict between the Parents of Schizophrenics." *Dissertation Abstracts International* 34, no. 3-A (September 1973).

James, Jane E., and Morton Goldman. "Behavior Trends of Wives of Alcoholics." *Quarterly Journal of Studies on Alcohol* 32, no. 2 (June 1971): 373-81.

Langley, Roger, and Richard C. Levy. *Wife Beating: The Silent Crisis.* New York: E. P. Dutton, 1977.

Levine, M. J. "Wife Beaters." *McCalls*, June 1975.

Louisville Division of Police. *Police Training in Family Crisis Intervention.* Final Report. EDRS (1971).

Martin, Del. *Battered Wives.* San Francisco: Glide, 1976.

Mascone, George. *Family Violence.* San Francisco: State of California, Senate Subcommittee on Nutrition and Human Needs. July 21, 1975.

Mitchell, Howard E., James W. Bullard, and Emily H. Mudd. "Areas of Marital Conflict in Successfully and Unsuccessfully Functioning Families." *Journal of Health and Human Behavior* 3, no. 2 (Summer 1962): 88-93.

Moore, Jean G. "Yo-Yo Children—Victims of Matrimonial Violence." *Child Welfare* 54, no. 8 (September-October 1975): 557-66.

"New Hope for the Battered Wife; Haven House, Los Angeles." *Good Housekeeping*, August 1976.

Pascoe, E. J. "Shelters for Battered Wives." *McCalls*, October 1976, p. 51.

Reynolds, Rosemary, and Else Siegle. "A Study of Case Work with Sadomasochistic Marriage Partners." *Social Casework* 40, no. 10 (1959): 545-51.

Roy, Maria. *Abused and Battered Wife.* New York: Van Nostrand Reinhold, 1977.

Scheurell, Robert P., and Irwin D. Rinder. "Social Networks and Deviance: A Study of Lower Class Incest, Wife Beating, and Nonsupport Offenders." *Wisconsin Sociologist* 10 (Spring-Summer 1973): 56-73.

Schultz, Leroy G. "The Wife Assaulter." *Journal of Social Therapy* 6, no. 2 (1960): 103-12.

Scott, P. D. "Battered Wives." *British Journal of Psychiatry* 125 (1974): 333-41.

Search, G. "London: Battered Wives." *Ms.*, June 1976.

Snell, John, Richard Rosenwald, and Ames Robey. "The Wifebeater's Wife." *Archives of General Psychiatry* 11 (1964): 107-13.

Truniger, E. "Marital Violence, The Legal Solutions." *Hastings Law Journal* 23 (November 1971): 259-76.

Walter, James D. "Police in the Middle: A Study of Police Intervention in Domestic Disputes." *Dissertation Abstracts International* 34, no. 11-A (May 1974): 7361.

SIBLING VIOLENCE

Allison, Tom S., and Sharon L. Allison. "Time-out from Reinforcement: Effect on Sibling Aggression." *Psychological Record* 21, no. 1 (Winter 1971): 81-86.

Arnold, J. E., A. G. Levine, and G. R. Patterson. "Changes in Sibling Behavior Following Family Intervention." *Journal of Consulting and Clinical Psychology* 43, no. 5 (October 1975): 683-88.

Biane, Howard T., and Herbert Barry. "Sex of Siblings of Male Alcoholics." *Archives of General Psychiatry* 32, no. 11 (November 1975): 1403-05.

Bordin-Sandler, Suzanne. "If You Don't Stop Hitting Your Sister, I'm Going to Beat Your Brains In." Paper presented at the 83rd Annual Meeting of the American Psychological Association, Chicago, August 30-September 2, 1975, (EDRS).

Campbell, Jagda, and Stephen P. Hersh. "Observations on the Vicissitudes of Aggression in Two Siblings." *Journal of Autism and Childhood Schizophrenia* 1, no. 4 (October-December 1971): 398-410.

Choynowski, Mieczyslaw, and Pekka Idman. "Adolescent Aggressiveness and Its Dependence on Age, Sex, and Position among Siblings." *Educational & Psychological Interactions*, no. 38 (February 1973).

Hespel, J. "Emotional Frustration in Juvenile Delinquents Seen through the P.N." *Revue de Psychologie Appliquee* 1-8, no. 3 (1968): 147-58.

Ihinger, Marilyn. "The Referee Role and Norms of Equity: A Contribution toward a Theory of Sibling Conflict." *Journal of Marriage and the Family* 37, no. 3 (August 1975): 515-24.

Marschak, Marianne. "A Puzzling Episode." *Psychiatry* 31, no. 2 (1968): 195-98.

Oberlander, Mark I., Kenneth J. Frauenfelder, and Helen Heath. "Ordinal Position, Sex of Sibling, Sex, and Personal Preferences in a Group of Eighteen-Year-Olds." *Journal of Consulting and Clinical Psychology* 32, no. 1 (1970): 122-25.

O'Leary, K. Daniel, et al. "Modification of a Deviant Sibling Interaction Pattern in the Home." *Behavioral Research and Therapy* 5 (1967): 113-20.

Pfouts, Jane H. "The Sibling Relationship: A Forgotten Dimension." *Social Work* 21, no. 3 (May 1976): 200-04.

Shantz, David W., and Thomas Pentz. "Situational Effects on Justifiableness of Aggression at Three Age Levels." *Child Development* 43, no. 1 (March 1972): 274-81.

Taviel de Andrade, Antonio R. "Some Considerations on the Reactions of Jealousy in Children." *Revista de la Clinica de la Conducta* 2, no. 4 (February 1969): 38-44.

Whitehurse, Carol, and Edward Miller. "Behavior Modification of Aggressive Behavior on a Nursery School Bus: A Case Study." *Journal of School Psychology* 11, no. 2 (Summer 1973): 123-28.

Wohlford, Paul, et al. "Older Brothers' Influence on Sex-Typed Aggressive, and Dependent Behavior in Father-Absent Children." *Developmental Psychology* 4, no. 2 (March 1971): 124-34.

CHILD ABUSE

Adelson, L. "The Battering Child." *Journal of the American Medical Association* 222 (1972): 159-61.

Alexander, Jerry. "Protecting the Children of Life-Threatening Parents." *Journal of Clinical Child Psychology* 3, no. 2 (Summer 1974): 53-54.

Alvy, Kerby T. "On Child Abuse: Values and Analytic Approaches." *Journal of Clinical Child Psychology* 4, no. 1 (Spring 1975): 36-37.

———."Preventing Child Abuse." *American Psychologist* 30, no. 9 (September 1975): 921-28.

American Humane Association, Children's Division. *Child Protective Services: A National Survey*. Final Report. Denver: American Humane Association, 1967.

Avery, Jane C. "The Battered Child: A Shocking Problem." *Mental Hygiene* 57 (Spring 1973): pp. 40-43.

Babow, Irving, and Robin Babow. "The World of the Abused Child: A Phenomenological Report." *Life-Threatening Behavior* 4, no. 1 (Spring 1974): 32-42.

Bakan, D. *Slaughter of the Innocents: A Study of the Battered Child Phenomena*. Boston: Beacon Press, 1971.

Baldwin, J. A., and J. E. Oliver. "Epidemiology and Family Characteristics of Severely-Abused Children." *British Journal of Prevention and Social Medicine* 29, no. 4 (December 1975): 205-221.

Bennie, E. H., and A. B. Sclare. "The Battered Child Syndrome." *American Journal of Psychiatry* 125 (July): 975-78.

Besharov, Douglas J. "Building A Community Response to Child Abuse and Maltreatment." *Children Today* 4, no. 5 (September-October 1975): 2-4.

Blumberg, Marvin L. "Psychopathology of the Abusing Parent." *American Journal of Psychotherapy* 28, no. 1 (January 1974): 21-29.

Broadhurst, Diane D. "Policy Making: First Step for Schools in the Fight Against Child Abuse and Negelct." *Elementary School Guidance and Counseling* 10, no. 3 (March 1976): 222-26.

Burland, J. Alexis, et al. "Child Abuse: One Tree in the Forest." *Child Welfare* 52, no. 9 (November 1973): 585-92.

Burt, Marvin R. "The Comprehensive Emergency Services System: Expanding Services to Children and Families." *Children Today* 5, no. 2 (March-April 1976): 2-5.

Caskey, Owen L., and Ivanna Richardson. "Understanding and Helping Child Abusing Parents." *Elementary School Guidance and Counseling* 9, no. 3 (March 1975): 196-207.

Children's Bureau, U.S. Department of Health, Education and Welfare. *Child Abuse and Neglect: The Problem and Its Management. Vol. 1, An Overview of the Problem. Vol. 2, The Roles and Responsibilities of Professionals. Vol. 3, The Community Team: An Approach to Case Management and Prevention*. Washington, D.C.: U.S. Government Printing Office, 1976 (EDRS).

Children's Hospital of the District of Columbia, *National Conference on Child Abuse: A Summary Report*. Rockville, Md.: National Institute of Mental Health, 1974 (EDRS).

Cohen, Stephen J., and Alan Sussman. "The Incidence of Child Abuse in the United States." *Child Welfare* 54, no. 6 (June 1975): 432-43.

Cohn, Anne Harris, et al. "Evaluating Innovative Treatment Programs." *Children Today* 4, no. 3 (May-June 1975): 10-12.

Colman, Wendy. "Occupational Therapy and Child Abuse." *American Journal of Occupational Therapy* 29, no. 7 (August 1975): 412-17.

Corey, Eleanor J., Carol L. Miller, and Frederic W. Widlak. "Factors Contributing to Child Abuse." *Nursing Research* 24, no. 4 (July-August 1975): 293-95.

Cottle, Thomas J. "Abusing Children." *New Republic*, November 1975, p. 88.

———, and Marian W. Eddman. "Our Country's Neglected Children." *Parent's Magazine*, December 1975, p. 37.

D'Ambrosio, Richard. *No Language But A Cry*. Garden City, N.Y.: Doubleday, 1970.

David, Charles A. "The Use of the Confrontation Technique in the Battered Child Syndrome." *American Journal of Psychotherapy* 28, no. 4 (October 1974): 543-52.

Davoren, Elizabeth, et al. "Working with Abusive Parents." *Children Today* 4, no. 3 (May-June 1975): 2-6.

DeFrancis, Vincent. *Protecting the Child Victim of Sex Crimes Committed by Adults: Final Report*. Denver: American Humane Association.

deMause, Lloyd. "Our Forebears Made Childhood a Nightmare." *Psychology Today*, April 1975, pp. 85-88.

Denzin, Norman K. *Children and Their Caretakers*. New Brunswick, N.J.: Transaction Books, 1973.

Donovan, Hedley, ed. "Hard Times for Kids Too." *Time*, March 1975, p. 88.

Ebeling, Nancy B., and Deborah A. Hill. *Child Abuse: Intervention and Treatment*. Acton, Mass.: Public Science Group, 1975.

Education Commission of the States, Denver, Colo. *A Comparison of the States' Child Abuse and Neglect Reporting Statutes, Report No. 84*. Denver: Education Commission of the States, 1976 (EDRS).

Elmer, E., et al. *Children in Jeopardy: A Study of Abused Minors and their Families*. Pittsburgh: University of Pittsburgh Press, 1967.

Erlanger, Howard S. "Social Class and Corporal Punishment in Childrearing: A Reassessment." *American Sociological Review* 39, no. 1 (February 1974): 68-85.

Fenner, Mildred, ed. "The Abused Child." *Today's Education*, January-February 1974, pp. 40-43.

Feshbach, Norma Deitch, and Seymour Feshbach. "Punishment: Parent Rites vs. Children's Rights." Paper presented at the 83d Annual Meeting of the American Psychological Association, Chicago, Illinois, August 30-September 3, 1975 (EDRS).

Fontana, Vincent J. *Somewhere A Child Is Crying*. New York: Macmillan Co., 1973.

⸻. "The Diagnosis of the Maltreatment Syndrome in Children." *Pediatrics* 51, no. 4 (April 1973): 780-82.

Forrer, Stephen E. "Battered Children and Counselor Responsibility." *School Counselor* 22, no. 3 (January 1975): 161-65.

Freedman, David A. "The Battering Parent and His Child: A Study in Early Object Relations." *International Review of Psycho-Analysis* 2, no. 2 (1975): 189-98.

Friedman, Stanford B., and Carol W. Morse. "Child Abuse: A Five-Year Follow-Up of Early Case Finding in the Emergency Department." *Pediatrics* 54, no. 4 (October 1974): 404-10.

Galdston, Richard. "Violence Begins at Home: The Parents' Center Project for the Study and Prevention of Child Abuse." *Journal of the American Academy of Child Psychiatry* 10, no. 2 (April 1971): 336-50.

⸻. "Preventing the Abuse of Little Children: The Parents' Center Project for the Study and Prevention of Child Abuse." *American Journal of Orthopsychiatry* 45, no. 3 (April 1975): 372-81.

Garbarino, J. "A Preliminary Study of Some Ecological Correlates of Child Abuse: The Impact of Socioeconomic Stress on Mothers." *Child Development* 47 (March 1976): 178-85.

Gelles, Richard J. "Demythologizing Child Abuse." *Family Coordinator* 25, no. 2 (April 1976): 135-41.

Gil, David G. "Unraveling Child Abuse." *American Journal of Orthopsychiatry* 45, no. 3 (April 1975): 346-56.

Giovannoni, Jeanne M. "Parental Mistreatment: Perpetrators and Victims." *Journal of Marriage and the Family* 33, no. 4 (November 1971): 649-57.

Goldberg, Gale. "Breaking the Communication Barrier: The Initial Interview with an Abusing Parent." *Child Welfare* 54, no. 4 (April 1975): 274-82.

Green, Arthur H., Richard W. Gaines, and Alice Sandgrund. "Child Abuse: Pathological Syndrome of Family Interaction." *American Journal of Psychiatry* 131, no. 8 (August 1974): 882-86.

Gueringer, George E. "What About the 'Psychologically Abused' Children?" *Journal of the International Association of Pupil Personnel Workers* 20, no. 2 (March 1976): 95-97.

Helfer, Ray E. *The Diagnostic Process and Treatment Programs*. Washington, D.C.: U.S. Government Printing Office, 1975 (EDRS).

———. "Why Most Physicians Don't Get Involved in Child Abuse Cases." *Children Today* 4, no. 3 (May-June 1975): 28-33.

———. "A Plan for Protection: The Child-Abuse Center." *Child Welfare* 49, no. 9 (November 1970): 486-94.

———, and C. Henry Kempe. *Child Abuse and Neglect; The Family and the Community*. Cambridge, Mass: Ballinger Publishing Co., 1976.

Hentoff, Nat. "A Parent-Teacher's View of Corporal Punishment." *Today's Education* 62, (May 1973): 18-21, 56.

Holmes, Sally A., Carol Barnhart, and Lucile Reymer Cantoni. "Working with the Parent in Child-Abuse Cases." *Social Casework* 56, no. 1 (January 1975): 3-12.

Hurt, Maure, Jr. *Child Abuse and Neglect: A Report on the Status of the Research*. Washington, D.C.: U.S. Government Printing Office, 1975 (EDRS).

Intradepartmental Committee on Child Abuse and Neglect, U.S. Department of Health, Education and Welfare. *Research, Demonstration and Evaluation Studies on Child Abuse and Neglect*. Washington, D.C.: U.S. Government Printing Office, 1975 (EDRS).

James, Howard. *The Little Victims/How America Treats Its Children*. New York: David McKay, 1975.

Johnson, Clara L. "Child Abuse: Some Findings from the Analysis of 1172 Reported Cases." Paper presented at the annual meeting of the Southern Association of Agricultural Scientists, New Orleans, February 2-5, 1975 (EDRS).

Joyner, Edmund N. "Child Abuse: The Role of the Physician and The Hospital." *Pediatrics* 51, no. 4 (April 1973): 799-803.

Justice, Rita, and Blair Justice. "TA Work with Child Abuse." *Transactional Analysis Journal* 5, no. 1 (January 1975): 38-41.

Kamerman, Sheila B. "Cross-National Perspectives on Child Abuse and Neglect." *Children Today* 4, no. 3 (May-June 1975): 34-40.

Kempe, C. Henry. "A Practical Approach to the Protection of the Abused Child and Rehabilitation of the Abusing Parent." *Pediatrics* 51, no. 4 (April 1973): 804-12.

Kristal, Helen, and Ford Tucker. "Managing Child Abuse Cases." *Social Work* 20, no. 5 (September 1975): 392-95.

Langer, Marion F. "New Year's Resolution: No More Corporal Punishment." *Teacher* 90, no. 5 (January 1973): 19-21.

Lauer, Brian, et al. "Battered Child Syndrome: Review of 130 Patients with Controls." *Pediatrics* 54, no. 1 (July 1974): 67-70.

Light, Richard J. "Abused and Neglected Children in America: A Study of Alternative Policies." *Harvard Educational Review* 43, no. 4 (November 1973): 556-98.

Lindenthal, Jacob Jay, et al. "Public Knowledge of Child Abuse." *Child Welfare* 54, no. 7 (July 1975): 521-23.

Lovens, Herbert D., and Jules Rako. "A Community Approach to the Prevention of Child Abuse." *Child Welfare* 54, no. 2 (February 1975): 83-88.

Lukianowicz, N. "Battered Children." *Psychiatrica Clinica* 4 (1971): 257-89.

Lynch, Annette. "Child Abuse in the School-Age Population." *Journal of School Health* 45, no. 3 (March 1975): 141-48.

Marker, Gail, Paul R. Friedman. "Rethinking Children's Rights." *Children Today* 2, no. 6 (November-December 1973): 8-11.

Melnick, Barry, and John R. Hurley. "Distinctive Personality Attributes of Child-Abusing Mothers." *Journal of Consulting Clinical Psychologists* 33, no. 6 (December 1969): 746-49.

Mitchell, Ross G. "The Incidence and Nature of Child Abuse." *Developmental Medicine and Child Neurology* 17, no. 5 (October 1975): 641-44.

Nagi, Saad Z. "Child Abuse and Neglect Programs: A National Overview." *Children Today* 4, no. 3 (May-June 1975): 13-17.

Nazzaro, Jean. "Child Abuse and Neglect." *Exceptional Children* 40, no. 5 (February 1974): 351-54.

Newberger, Eli H., and James N. Hyde, Jr. "Child Abuse: Principles and Implications of Current Pediatric Practice." Paper presented in part at the Conference of Research in Child Abuse, Bethesda, Md., June 1974 (EDRS).

Parke, R., and C. W. Collmer. "Child Abuse: An Interdisciplinary Analysis." In *Review of Child Development Research*, edited by E. M. Hetherington, Chicago: University of Chicago Press, 1975.

Paulson, Morris J. "Child Trauma Intervention: A Community Response to Family Violence." *Journal of Clinical Child Psychology* 4, no. 3 (Fall 1975): 26-29.

———, and Anne Chaleff. "Parent Surrogate Roles: A Dynamic Concept in Understanding and Treating Abusive Parents." *Journal of Clinical Child Psychology* 2, no. 3 (Fall 1973): 38-40.

———, et al. "An MMPI Scale for Identifying 'at Risk' Abusive Parents." *Journal of Clinical Child Psychology* 4, no. 1 (Spring 1975): 22-24.

Polansky, Norman A., Carolyn Hally, and Nancy F. Polansky. *Profile of Neglect: A Survey of the State of Knowledge of Child Neglect*. Washington, D.C.: U.S. Department of Health, Education and Welfare, 1975.

Raffalli, Henri C. "The Battered Child: An Overview of a Medical, Legal, and Social Problem." *Crime and Delinquency* 16, no. 2 (April 1970): 139-50.

Reskow, Judith. "Child Abuse: What the Educator Should Know." *New Jersey Education Association Review* 47, no. 3 (November 1973): 14-15.

Resnick, P. J. "Child Murder by Parents: A Psychiatric Review of Filicide." *American Journal of Psychiatry* 126, no. 3 (1969): 325-34.

Rolston, Richard H. "The Effect of Prior Physical Abuse on the Expression of Overt and Fantasy Aggressive Behavior in Children." *Dissertation Abstracts International* 32, no. 5-B (November 1971): 3016.

Rowe, Daniel S., et al. "A Hospital Program for the Detection and Registration of Abused and Neglected Children." *New England Journal of Medicine* 282, no. 17 (April 1970): 950-52.

Sanders, Lola, et al. "Child Abuse: Detection and Prevention." *Young Children* 30, no. 5 (July 1975): 332-38.

Sattin, Dana B., and John K. Miller. "The Ecology of Child Abuse Within a Military Community." *American Journal of Orthopsychiatry* 41, no. 4 (July 1971): 675-78.

Sayre, James W., et al. "Community Committee on Child Abuse." *New York State Journal of Medicine* 73, no. 16 (August 1973): 2071-75.

Schmidt, Rebecca. "What Home Economists Should Know About Child Abuse." *Journal of Home Economics* 68, no. 3 (May 1976): 13-16.

Schmitt, Barton D. "What Teachers Need to Know About Child Abuse and Neglect." *Childhood Education* 52, no. 2 (November-December 1975): 58-62.

Shanas, Bert. "Child Abuse: A Killer Teachers Can Help Control." *Phi Delta Kappan* 56, no. 7 (March 1975): 479-82.

Sherman, Edmund A., et al. *Service to Children in Their Own Homes: Its Nature and Outcome.* New York: Child Welfare League of America, 1973 (EDRS).

Smith, Selwyn M., and Ruth Hanson. "Interpersonal Relationships and Childrearing Practices in 214 Parents of Battered Children." *British Journal of Psychiatry* 127 (December 1975): 513-25.

Solomon, Theo. "History and Demography of Child Abuse." *Pediatrics* 51, no. 4 (April 1973): 773-76.

Soman, Shirley. *Let's Stop Destroying Our Children/Society's Most Pressing Problem.* New York: Hawthorn Books, 1974.

Spinetta, J. J., and D. Rigler. "The Child-Abusing Parent: A Psychological Review." *Psychological Bulletin* 77 (April 1972): 296-304.

Steele, Brandt F. *Working with Abusive Parents from a Psychiatric Point of View.* Washington, D.C.: U.S. Government Printing Office, 1975 (EDRS).

Stephenson, P. Susan, and Nerissa Lo. "When Shall We Tell Kevin? A Battered Child Revisited." *Child Welfare* 53, no. 9 (November 1974): 576-81.

Tapp, Jack T., Virginia Ryken, and Carl Kaltwasser. "Counseling the Abusing Parent by Telephone." *Crisis Intervention* 5, no. 3 (1974): 27-37.

Tracy, James J., Carolyn M. Balard, and Elizabeth H. Clark. "Child Abuse Project: A Follow-up." *Social Work* 20, no. 5 (September 1975): 398-99.

Van Stolk, Mary. "Who Owns the Child?" *Childhood Education* 50, no. 5 (March 1974): 259-65.

Wall, Charles M. "Child Abuse: A Societal Problem with Educational Implications." *Peabody Journal of Education* 52, no. 3 (April 1975): 22-25.

Weinbach, Robert W. "Case Management of Child Abuse." *Social Work* 20, no. 5 (September 1975): 396-92.

Weinberger, Casper. "Aid to Abused and Neglected Children." *Intellect* 102 (April 1974): 415.

Whiting, Leila. "Defining Emotional Neglect." *Children Today* 5, no. 1 (January-February 1976): 2-5.

Wright, Logan. "The 'Sick but Slick' Syndrome as a Personality Component of Parents of Battered Children." *Journal of Clinical Psychology* 32, no. 1 (January 1976): 41-45.

Young, L. R. *Wednesday's Children: A Study of Child Neglect and Abuse*. New York: McGraw-Hill, 1964.

Zalba, Serapio R. "Battered Children." *Transaction* 8, no. 9/10 (July-August 1971): 58-61.

SUZANNE K. STEINMETZ, an assistant professor with a joint appointment in the College of Home Economics and College Parallel Program, University of Delaware, received a bachelors degree in education from the University of Delaware and an M.A. and Ph.D. in sociology from Case Western Reserve University. Dr. Steinmetz's research and teaching interests include family, deviance, sex roles, violence, research methods, aging, and socialization. She is coeditor (with M. Straus) of *Violence in the Family*, and is on the editorial board and the book review editor of *Journal of Marriage and the Family*.

Dr. Steinmetz has been involved in several international conferences. She was a delegate to the NATO-sponsored conference on aggression held in Monte Carlo in 1973, and a participant at the International Society for the Study of Behavioral Development in England in 1975 and the International Society for Research on Aggression in Paris in 1976.

Dr. Steinmetz is a coinvestigator, under a grant from the National Institute of Mental Health, studying violence in American families, and received a Delaware Humanities Forum grant to present a series of programs on "The Battered Partner: The Law and Family Violence," and to develop a resource booklet for helping battered spouses. A member of numerous professional and honorary societies, Dr. Steinmetz is president (1976-77) of the University of Delaware chapter of Sigma Xi, a national scientific research society.

ALIENATION IN CONTEMPORARY SOCIETY:
A Multidisciplinary Examination

edited by
Roy S. Bryce-Laporte
Claudewell S. Thomas

THE FERTILITY OF WORKING WOMEN: A
Synthesis of International Research

edited by
Stanley Kupinsky

SEX AND CLASS IN LATIN AMERICA

edited by
June Nash
Helen Icken Safa

WOMEN AND WORLD DEVELOPMENT: With
an Annotated Bibliography

edited by
Irene Tinker
Michèle Bo Bramsen
Mayra Buvinić